Consolidated
Landlord and Tenant Legislation

CLARUS
PRESS

Consolidated Landlord and Tenant Legislation

Compiled and edited by

Mark O'Riordan

BCL, LLM (NUI), Barrister-at-Law

With contributions from

Anthony McBride

MA (Cantab), Barrister-at-Law

Published by
Clarus Press Ltd,
Griffith Campus,
South Circular Road,
Dublin 8.

Typeset by
Datapage International Ltd.,
18 Docklands Innovation Park,
East Wall Road,
Dublin 3.

Printed by
MPG Books Ltd., Cornwall

ISBN
10 digit: 1-905536-07-0
13 digit: 978-1-905536-07-8

PREFACE

The legislation governing the relationship of landlord and tenant in Ireland is a particularly tricky (and sometimes old) patchwork with plenty of traps for the unwary, by virtue of numerous amendments. Pending a promised reform of the law, landlord and tenant legislation in Ireland remains as it is a collection of various statutes dating from the 1800s to recent times.

The impetus for this consolidation came from the inaccessibility (and often unavailability) of the statutes involved. In particular Deasy's Act 1860, while still the cornerstone of landlord and tenant law in Ireland, is often not accessible to the practitioner and student – Judge Deale's classic annotation of the Act no longer being in print.

It is from this background that the current consolidation sprouted. Its scope it the main legislation governing commercial and residential landlord and tenant law. Agricultural landlord and tenant law is not dealt with – hence the exclusion of the Landlord and Tenant (Ireland) Act 1870 and the Notices to Quit (Ireland) Act 1876, which apply exclusively to agricultural holdings. Likewise, housing law under the numerous Housing Acts has not been included, save for certain extracts from the Housing (Miscellaneous Provisions) Act 1992, that are required by virtue of their application to all residential tenancies. Certain arbitrary choices had to be made as to what was and was not included. As the reader will note, chapters 2, 3, 4, 5 and 16 are merely the relevant extracts from the statutes involved.

This consolidation does not pretend to be a scholarly annotation. No annotations (in the form of scholarly comment on the law) are provided at all. All that is provided is updated legislation tracking each change to a particular provision of an Act. The work is simply as stated: a consolidation of various statues concerning landlord and tenant law in Ireland from 1860 to 2005. Perhaps it might save the practitioner or student some time in locating and tracking one of the numerous amendments to the legislation; if it does so, it succeeds in its task.

The Irish landlord and tenant legislative landscape is a frequently changing one. The legislation enacted in the early years of this State (and its predecessor the Irish Free State) such as the Landlord and Tenant Act, 1931 and the Landlord and Tenant (Reversionary Leases) Act, 1958 have now been repealed. In more recent times, residential landlord and tenant law has been overhauled (not to everyone's liking) by the Residential Tenancies Act, 2004. It appears that the ground rents legislation may also be soon up for revision.

Legislative reform in the wider landlord and tenant law area is both necessary and desirable to take account of modern considerations. Indeed the Law Reform Commission must be commended for its recent recommendations and continuing work in this area. A draft Bill is awaited. It is hoped that legislative lethargy does not stymie the incorporation of the Commission's recommendations into Irish legislation in the near future.

Certain Acts could not be included, but do contain block exemptions from the application of landlord and tenant legislation. One example is contained in s 56 of the Air Navigation and Transport (Amendment) Act, 1998 which provides a block exemption for Aer Rianta cpt from all landlord and tenant legislation dating from 1967. There is a similar provision, for example, in s 211 of the Planning and Development Act, 2000 for certain leases under that section granted by a local authority.

The editor wishes to thank David McCartney of Clarus Press for this enthusiasm and, more importantly, patience in seeing this project to completion. Anthony McBride BL provided much advice (on what to leave out) and assistance in locating and tracking changes in the dusty tomes of 1800s and early 1900s legislation. No responsibility can be accepted for any errors and/or omissions, but hopefully there are none. The temptation is not to ask for any errors to be pointed out, but obviously if errors are spotted I would be obliged to hear of them.

The contents of this work are stated as at January 2007.

Mark O'Riordan
Barrister-at-Law
Law Library
Dublin

CONTENTS

A NOTE ON THIS BOOK AND HOW TO USE IT

This book is divided into nineteen chapters in chronological order. Each chapter contains a different statute dating from 1860 up to 2005.

Wherever legislation has been amended, the amendment has been inserted in the text of the original legislation and a note has been inserted thereafter called "**Amendment history**" which informs the reader of when the amendment was made and whether it has prospective (or sometimes also retrospective) effect.

To avoid repetition, the text of the amendment inserted or substituted in the amended statute is not reproduced in the amending statute. Instead, a clear indication of what the amendment has done is provided there (*ie* the fact that it repealed, amended or substituted another provision and what provision it affected in this way).

Wherever a provision has not been amended, but some other statute has a bearing on its operation, this has been brought to the reader's attention by way of a note simply headed: "**Note**".

The use of square brackets ('[......]') in the text indicates that the particular words in square brackets have been repealed from the text of the provision and the following amendment note will record the source of this repeal or amendment.

Rarely does one come across errors in the statutes as they have been promulgated. Where these errors do occur they have not been corrected. Instead they have been brought to the reader's attention by means of the insertion of an appropriate note thereafter.

Chapter 1

LANDLORD AND TENANT LAW, AMENDMENT ACT, IRELAND, 1860 (DEASY'S ACT)

(23 & 24 Vict. c. 154)

AN ACT TO CONSOLIDATE AND AMEND THE LAW OF LANDLORD AND TENANT IN IRELAND

Preamble
Omitted. Repealed by Statute Law Revision Act 1892.

Interpretation of terms.

1.—In the construction of this Act the following words and expressions shall have the force and meaning hereby assigned to them, unless there be something in the subject or context repugnant thereto: [1–01]

The word "person" or "party" shall extend to and include any body politic, corporate, or collegiate, whether aggregate or sole and any public company;

The word "lease" shall mean any instrument in writing, whether under seal or not, containing a contract of tenancy in respect of any lands, in consideration of a rent or return;

The word "lands" shall include houses, messuages, and tenements of every tenure, whether corporeal or incorporeal;

The word "acre" shall mean statute acre;

The word "landlord" shall include the person for the time being entitled in possession to the estate or interest of the original landlord, under any lease or other contract of tenancy, whether the interest of such landlord shall have been acquired by lawful assignment, devise, bequest, or act and operation of law, and whether he has a reversion or not;

The word "tenant" shall mean the person entitled to any lands under any lease or other contract of tenancy, whether the interest of such tenant shall have been acquired by original contract, lawful assignment, devise, bequest, or act and operation of law;

The expression "perpetual interest" shall comprehend, in addition to any greater interest, any lease or grant for one or more than one life, with or without a term of years, or for years, whether absolute, or determinable on one or more than one life, with a covenant or agreement by a party competent thereto, in any of such cases, whether contained in the instrument by which such lease or contract is made or in any separate instrument, for the perpetual renewal of such lease or grant;

The word "rent" shall include any sum or return in the nature of rent, payable or given by way of compensation for the holding of any lands;

The word "agreement" shall include every covenant, contract, or condition expressed or implied in any lease;

The word "county" shall extend to and include [a county of a city, a county of a town,] a city and county, and a riding of a county;

The expression "chairman" shall mean the chairman of the quarter sessions of the county, and shall extend to and include the Recorder of [the city of]Dublin and [borough of]Cork, and the recorder of any borough or town under the Act passed in the third and fourth years of Her Majesty's reign, intitled An Act for the Regulation of Municipal Corporations in Ireland, and their deputies lawfully appointed;

The expression "clerk of the peace" shall extend to and include the Registrar of the Chairman of the Quarter Sessions of the County of Dublin, so long as such Registrar shall continue in the office, and the Registrar of Civil Bills for the City of Dublin, and also the acting or deputy clerk of the peace, or registrar or other officer discharging the duties of such clerk of the peace or registrar.

Note: The parts of the definition of "county" and "chairman" in square brackets were repealed by the Statute Law Revision (No. 1) Act 1893. The short title for the Act mentioned in the definition of "chairman" is the Municipal Corporations (Ireland) Act 1840.

Under the Circuit Court Rules 2001, O.67 r.8 states that where the jurisdiction transferred to the Court under s 51 of the Courts of Justice Act 1924 (and thereafter established by s 4 of the Courts (Establishment and Constitution) Act 1961) depends upon statute, each such Statute is hereby adapted or modified so that all references therein to the Civil Bill Court, County Court, or Court of Quarter Sessions shall be construed to refer to the Court where necessary, and all references to Recorders, County Court Judges, Chairmen of Quarter Sessions, or other Judges, and to Officers of any such Courts shall be construed where necessary as references to the Judge of the Court, and, in the cases of Officers, to the County Registrar or appropriate Officer of the Court, and all references to proceedings in any of such Courts, shall, where necessary, be construed as references to proceedings in the Court.

Short title.

[1–02] 2.—In citing this Act it shall be sufficient to use the expression "The Landlord and Tenant Law Amendment Act, Ireland, 1860."

Note: This Act is commonly known as Deasy's Act.

Contract of tenancy.

[1–03] 3.—The relation of landlord and tenant shall be deemed to be founded on the express or implied contract of the parties and not upon tenure or service, and a reversion shall not be necessary to such relation, which shall be deemed to subsist in all cases in which there shall be an agreement by one party to hold land from or under another in consideration of any rent.

Contract for definite periods to be by deed or note in writing.

4.—Every lease or contract with respect to lands whereby the relation of landlord and tenant is intended to be created for any freehold estate or interest, or for any definite period of time not being from year to year or any lesser period, shall be by deed executed, or note in writing signed by the landlord or his agent thereunto lawfully authorized in writing. [1–04]

Continuance of possession after expiration of contract may be deemed a new holding.

5.—In any case any tenant or his representative, after the expiration or determination of the term agreed upon in any lease or instrument in writing, shall continue in possession for more than one month after demand of possession by the landlord or his agent, such continuance shall, at the election of the landlord, be deemed to constitute a new holding of the said lands from year to year, subject to the former rent and to such of the agreements contained in the lease or instrument as may be applicable to the new holding. [1–05]

Presumed commencement of tenancy from year to year.

6.—Every tenancy from year to year shall be presumed to have commenced on the last gale day of the calendar year on which rent has become due and payable in respect of the premises, until it shall appear to the contrary. [1–06]

Surrender to be by deed or note in writing or by operation of law.

7.—The estate or interest of any tenant under any lease or other contract of tenancy shall not be surrendered otherwise than by a deed executed, or note in writing signed by the tenant or his agent thereto lawfully authorized in writing, or by act and operation of law. [1–07]

Lease may be renewed without surrender of under-tenancies, &c.

8.—The surrender of any lease made before or after the passing of this Act for the purpose of obtaining a renewal thereof, shall be valid without the surrender of the interests of the under-tenants thereunder; and the owners of such renewed lease for the time being and their representatives shall have the same rights and remedies as against such under-tenants as he or they would have had or have been entitled to had such surrender not been executed; and the chief landlord shall have the same remedies against the premises for the rents and duties reserved in such new lease, not exceeding the rents and duties reserved by the lease out of which such under-tenancies were derived, as he would have been entitled to in case no such surrender had been executed. [1–08]

Modes of assignment of estate and interest of tenant.

9.—The estate or interest of any tenant in any lands under any lease or other contract of tenancy shall be assigned, granted, or transmitted by deed executed, or instrument in writing signed by the party assigning or granting the same, or his agent thereto lawfully authorized in writing, or by devise, bequest, or act and operation of law, and not otherwise; [and in the case of the said estate or interest shall, on the death of the tenant, remain undisposed of and without any special occupant, it shall pass to the personal representative of the tenant as part of the personal estate of such tenant.] [1–09]

> **Note:** The words in square brackets in this section were repealed by s 8 of the Succession Act 1965.

Restriction on assignment contrary to agreement.

[1–10] 10.—*Omitted. Repealed by s 35(1) of the Landlord and Tenant (Ground Rents) Act 1967, which Act commenced on 1st March 1967.*

Assignee subject to condition against assignment.

[1–11] 11.—Every assignee of the estate or interest or any part thereof of any tenant, by lawful assignment, or by devise, bequest, or act and operation of law, made after the passing of this Act, shall be subject to the observance of all agreements in respect of assignment or subletting to the same extent as the original tenant might have been.

Benefit of agreements to enure against assignee, &c. of the tenant, and in favour of heir or assignee of the landlord.

[1–12] 12.—Every landlord of any lands holden under any lease or other contract of tenancy shall have the same action and remedy against the tenant, and the assignee of his estate or interest, or their respective heirs, executors, or administrators, in respect of the agreements contained or implied in such lease or contract, as the original landlord might have had against the original tenant, or his heir or personal representative respectively; and the heir or personal representative of such landlord on whom his estate or interest under any such lease or contract shall devolve or should have devolved shall have the like action and remedy against the tenant, and the assignee of his estate or interest, and their respective heirs or personal representatives, for any damage done to the said estate or interest of such landlord by reason of the breach of any agreement contained or implied in the lease or other contract of tenancy in the lifetime of the landlord, as such landlord himself might have had.

Benefit of agreements to enure against assignee of the landlord, and in favour of heir, &c. or assignee of the tenant.

[1–13] 13.—Every tenant of any lands shall have the same action and remedy against the landlord and the assignee of his estate or interest, or their respective heirs, executors, or administrators, in respect of the agreements contained or implied in the lease or other contract concerning the lands, as the original tenant might have had against the original landlord, or his heir or personal representative respectively; and the heir or personal representative of such tenant on whom his estate or interest shall devolve or should have devolved shall have the like action and remedy against the landlord, and the assignee of his estate or interest, and their respective heirs and personal representatives, for any damage done to the said estate or interest of such tenant by reason of the breach of any agreement contained or implied in the lease or other contract of tenancy in the lifetime of the tenant, as such tenant might have had.

Benefit and liability of assignee to cease after assignment over.

[1–14] 14.—No landlord or tenant, being such by assignment, devise, bequest, or act and operation of law only, shall have the benefit or be liable in respect of the breach of any covenant or contract contained or implied in the lease or other contract of tenancy, otherwise than in respect of such rent as shall have accrued due, and such breaches as shall have occurred or continued subsequent to such assignment, and whilst he shall have continued to be such assignee: Provided, however, that no assignment made by any assignee of the estate or interest of any tenant shall discharge such assignee from his liability to the landlord, unless and until notice in writing of the particulars of such assignment shall have been given to the landlord.

Assignee liable till next gale day.

15.—Every tenant, being an assignee as aforesaid, who shall have assigned his estate or interest in the lease or other contract of tenancy in the interval between two gale days, shall, notwithstanding such assignment, be liable as assignee to the payment of the rent and the performance of the agreements contained in the lease or other contract up to and including the gale day next following the service of notice of the said assignment. **[1–15]**

Discharge of tenant from agreements, on assignment with consent of landlord.

16.—From and after any assignment hereafter to be made of the estate or interest of any original tenant in any lease, with the consent of the landlord, testified in manner specified in section ten, the landlord so consenting shall be deemed to have released and discharged the said tenant from all actions and remedies at the suit of such landlord, and all persons claiming by, through, or under him, in respect of any future breach of the agreements contained in the lease, but without prejudice to any remedy or right against the assignee of such estate or interest. **[1–16]**

Fixtures of trade or agriculture, &c., erected by the tenant may be removed.

17.—Personal chattels, engines, and machinery, and buildings accessorial thereto, erected and affixed to the freehold by the tenant at his sole expense, for any purpose of trade, manufacture, or agriculture, or for ornament, or for the domestic convenience of the tenant in his occupation of the demised premises, and so attached to the freehold that they can be removed without substantial damage to the freehold or to the fixture itself, and which shall not have been so erected or affixed in pursuance of any obligation or in violation of any agreement in that behalf, may be removed by the tenant, or his executors or administrators, during the tenancy, or, when the tenancy determines by some uncertain event, and without the act or default of the tenant, within two calendar months after such determination, except so far as may be otherwise specially provided by the contract of tenancy; provided that the landlord shall be entitled to reasonable compensation for any damage occasioned to the premises by such removal. **[1–17]**

Subletting.

18.—*Omitted. Repealed by s 35(1) of the Landlord and Tenant (Ground Rents) Act 1967, which Act commenced on 1st March 1967.* **[1–18]**

In cases of subletting with consent, payment to tenant shall free sub-tenant from liability to landlord.

19.—Where any subletting shall take place with the consent of the landlord given in manner aforesaid, except in the case of a building lease, and the sub-tenant shall have paid and satisfied the rent or any part thereof due from him to the tenant or his representatives, the receipt of such tenant or his representatives shall be a full discharge to such sub-tenant and the lands sub-let, as against the landlord so consenting, in respect of all rent issuing out of the same and theretofore due, except so much, if any, as remains due from the sub-tenant; provided the landlord shall not have previously served the notice upon the default herein-after mentioned: Provided always, that such discharge to such sub-tenant shall be without prejudice to the landlord's remedies for the balance of his rent against the tenant or his representatives and the other premises out of which such rent shall accrue due. **[1–19]**

Landlord may give notice to sub-tenant to pay rent to him.

[1–20] 20.—Where any tenant subletting shall neglect to pay his landlord the rent payable in respect of the lands comprised in the lease, it shall be lawful for the landlord, or his agent lawfully acting in that behalf, after and as often as one gale of such rent shall have accrued due and remained unpaid for the space of one month, to give notice in writing to the sub-tenant, requiring him to pay to the landlord so much of the rent payable by such sub-tenant to the tenant under whom he holds as may be sufficient to discharge the gale or gales stated in such notice to be due from the tenant to the landlord, such notice to be delivered to the sub-tenant, or left at his usual place of abode with some member of his family above the age of sixteen years; and thereupon such sub-tenant shall be liable to pay to the landlord all rent that may accrue due after receipt of such notice, or so much thereof as may be sufficient to discharge such gale or gales; and the receipt of the landlord or his agent shall be a full discharge to the sub-tenant against the tenant in respect of all rent so paid; and the said landlord and his representatives shall be entitled to all such rights and remedies for the enforcing payment of such rent as the said tenant so subletting might have had.

Sub-tenant may voluntarily pay rent to landlord.

[1–21] 21.—Where any tenant subletting shall neglect to pay his landlord the rent payable in respect of the lands comprised in the lease, it shall be lawful for the sub-tenant, after and often as any one gale of such rent shall have accrued due and remain unpaid to such landlord, and before any action brought by such tenant against the sub-tenant, voluntarily to make payment of so much of the rent due by such sub-tenant to such tenant as may be sufficient to discharge such gale or gales; and the receipt of the landlord or his agent shall be a full discharge to the sub-tenant against the tenant in respect of all rent so paid.

Sub-letting with consent not a general waiver.

[1–22] 22.—When any sub-letting shall take place with such consent as aforesaid, it shall not be deemed a general wavier of the benefit of the agreement against sub-letting.

Evidence.

Proof of contents of lease by counterpart or copy.

[1–23] 23.—In all actions, suits, and proceedings, proof by or on behalf of any landlord of the perfection of the counterpart of any lease shall be equivalent to proof of the perfection of the original lease; and in case it shall appear that no counterpart existed, or that the counterpart has been lost, destroyed, or mislaid, proof of a copy of the original lease or counterpart, as the case may be, shall be sufficient evidence of the contents of the lease, as against the lessee or any person claiming from or under him.

Proof of landlord's title when derivative.

[1–24] 24.—In all actions, suits, and proceedings brought by or against any person claiming to be landlord otherwise than by original contract, after proof of the original lease or contract, it shall be sufficient *prima facie* evidence of the title of such person as landlord, as to all parties in the said suit or proceeding, to prove that he has for one year at least, or that the person under whom immediately he derives his title has for one year at least, and within three years before the transmission of such title, received the rent of the lands in respect of which such action, suit, or proceedings shall be brought from a party in possession thereof.

Mines, &c. rights and reservation.

Tenant in fee-farm not impeachable of waste 12 & 13 Vict. c. 105

25.—No tenant of any lands entitled to any perpetual interest under any lease or grant made after the first day of January one thousand eight hundred and sixty-one shall be impeachable of any waste, other than fraudulent or malicious waste, except in so far as such tenant shall, by any agreement contained in the lease or grant, be prohibited from doing or permitting any act: Provided that no fee-farm grant made under the Renewable Leasehold Conversion Act, or any renewed lease executed after the first of January one thousand eight hundred and sixty-one, in pursuance of an agreement for renewal contained in a lease made before the passing of this Act, shall be deemed to be a perpetual interest made after the first day of January one thousand eight hundred and sixty-one within the meaning of this section. **[1–25]**

Tenant of lesser interest not to open mines or quarries to commit other waste.

26.—No tenant of any lands holden for any estate or interest less than a perpetual estate or interest, made after the first of January one thousand eight hundred and sixty-one, by virtue of any lease or contract, shall, without the previous consent in writing of the landlord, being a person competent to grant such licence, or of his agent duly authorized to act on his behalf, open, dig for any unopened mines, minerals, or quarries, or (except as herein-after provided) remove the soil or surface or subsoil of the said lands, or permit or commit any other manner of waste thereon, unless the said lands shall have been, in express terms, leased for the purpose or with the permission of being so used and enjoyed. **[1–26]**

Tenant may work mines already opened.

27.—Where any lease shall be made on or after the first day of January one thousand eight hundred and sixty-one of lands containing any mines or minerals which at the time of the making of such lease shall have been opened or worked, it shall be lawful for the tenant thereof to enter upon and follow, and to work and dig for, and remove the said mines or minerals, whether they shall have been granted by name or not in the said lease, unless by the said lease it shall be otherwise provided. **[1–27]**

Tenant may work quarries already opened, but not for profit or sale.

28.—Where any lease or demise shall be made on or after the first day of January one thousand eight hundred and sixty-one of lands containing any quarries or beds of stone, limestone, sand, marl, gravel, or clay, which at the time of the making of such lease shall have been opened or worked, its shall be lawful for such tenant, unless by the said lease otherwise provided, to work, dig for, and use such quarries or beds so far as may be necessary to useful for the purposes of agriculture and good husbandry, and the lawful erection or repair of any necessary buildings on the said lands, but not for any purpose of trade or manufacture, or for profit or sale, unless the right so to use and enjoy the same shall have been expressly granted in writing by the landlord being competent so to grant as aforesaid. **[1–28]**

Tenant may cut turf, but not for profit or sale.

[1–29] 29.—Where any lease or demise shall be made on or after the first day of January one thousand eight hundred and sixty-one of lands containing turf bog, unreclaimed and unprofitable for agriculture, or where any lease shall be so made giving a right of turbary on the premises, or conferring a right of common of turbary on premises not comprised in the lease, it shall be lawful for the tenant, unless by the said lease it be specially provided to the contrary, to cut, use, and enjoy the said turf bog, so far as shall be necessary for the *bona fide* use on the demised premises of the tenant and his lawful sub-tenants, but not for any purpose of trade or manufacture, or for profit or sale, unless the right so to use and enjoy the same shall have been expressly granted in writing by the landlord being competent so to grant as aforesaid.

Tenant shall not burn land.

[1–30] 30.—No tenant under any lease or other contract of tenancy conferring an estate or interest less than a perpetual estate or interest shall burn or permit to be burned the soil or surface of the land, or any part thereof, without the previous consent in writing of the landlord, being a person competent to grant such licence, under a penalty not exceeding twenty pounds for each statute acre or any fractional part of an acre on which such burning shall take place, to be recoverable by the immediate landlord by civil bill action in the county in which the tenant usually resides, or in the country in which the lands or any part of them are situate, at the election of the landlord.

> **Note:** The Fourth Schedule (Ref. 25) to the Courts (Supplemental Provisions) Act 1961 states that the jurisdiction under s 30 of this Act is to be exercised by the Circuit Court. The venue is at the election of the landlord either (a) the judge of the circuit where the tenant resides, or (b) the judge of the circuit where the land or any part of the land is situate.

Tenant shall not cut or lop trees.

[1–31] 31.—No tenant of any lands holden under any lease or other contract of tenancy conferring an estate or interest less than a perpetual estate or interest, and made on or after the first day of January one thousand eight hundred and sixty-one, shall cut down, top, lop or grub any tree or wood growing on the said lands, unless such tenant shall be authorized thereto by covenant or agreement in the lease under which the lands are holden, if there be a lease, or unless such tenant shall have the previous consent in writing of the landlord competent to give such consent for that purpose, or shall have been lawfully required to do so, under a penalty not exceeding five pounds for each tree cut down, topped, lopped, or grubbed, to be recoverable by the immediate landlord by civil bill action in the county in which the tenant usually resides, or in the county in which the lands or any part of them are situate, at the election of the landlord: Provided that nothing in this provision contained shall affect any right which any tenant may lawfully exercise or enjoy in respect of trees duly registered and belonging to such tenant, or in respect of willows, osiers, or sallows, under any Act in force in Ireland.

> **Note:** The Fourth Schedule (Ref. 25) to the Courts (Supplemental Provisions) Act 1961 states that the jurisdiction under s 31 of this Act is

to be exercised by the Circuit Court. The venue is at the election of the landlord either: (a) the judge of the circuit where the tenant resides, or (b) the judge of the circuit where the land or any part of the land is situate.

Where mines are reserved, landlord may work or lease the mines.

32.—Where lands shall be granted or leased for any estate or interest excepting [1–32] thereout the mines and minerals upon the demised premises, it shall be lawful for the person entitled to the rent thereof, in fee simple, fee farm, fee tail, or for life, with immediate remainder to his own issue, to open, dig for, and work all mines and minerals found in or upon the said lands, and to carry away the ore thereof, or to lease the same to any person or persons for any term within the leasing power of such person in respect of mines and minerals; and such owner or his lessee shall have full liberty to enter on the said lands, and to build and make all houses, railways, tramways, and conveniences necessary for the purpose of mining, and to employ all streams on the said land not previously occupied, making to the tenant of said lands such yearly or other compensation or allowance for the damages sustained by reason of such digging of the ore, or building the said houses, or otherwise using of the said lands or streams, as shall be agreed upon between the said parties, or in case they shall not agree, then such compensation or allowance as shall be ascertained by the chairman of the county upon a civil bill action brought for that purpose with the same incidents as in ordinary civil bill process: Provided, however, that no person shall search for, open, or work any mine or mineral, by virtue of this Act, on any spot of ground on which any church or other place of worship, graveyard, cemetery, or public school shall be situate, nor within thirty yards thereof, nor upon any spot of ground on which any house, outhouse, garden, orchard, or avenue shall be situate, without the consent of the tenant in possession thereof first had and obtained.

Note: The Fourth Schedule (Ref. 26) to the Courts (Supplemental Provisions) Act 1961 states that the jurisdiction under s 32 of this Act is to be exercised by the Circuit Court by the judge of the circuit where the land or any part of the land is situate.

Compensation to be ascertained by civil bill action.

33.—Where such parties shall not agree upon the amount of compensation to be [1–33] paid for the injury sustained by the entry on or use of lands for the purpose of mining in the manner aforesaid, it shall be lawful for the party claiming such compensation to bring a civil bill action for the amount claimed before the chairman of the county in which the lands or the greater part of them are situate, and the chairman shall, with the assistance of a jury on their oaths as aforesaid, make such decree or dismiss thereon, and subject to the like appeal as in ordinary cases of civil bill actions for injuries sustained.

Note: The Fourth Schedule (Ref. 26) to the Courts (Supplemental Provisions) Act 1961 states that the jurisdiction under s 33 of this Act is to be exercised by the Circuit Court by the judge of the circuit where the land or any part of the land is situate.

Tenant, in lieu of emblements, shall continue to hold until last gale day of current year.

[1–34] 34.—Where the lease or tenancy of any farm or lands (held at rackrent) shall determine by the death or cesser of the estate of any landlord entitled for his life or for any other uncertain interest, or by the death of the lives in the tenant's lease, or by the happening of any contingency whereby such lease or tenancy shall determine without the act or default of the tenant, the tenant in occupation, in lieu of the right to emblements, where such right shall exist, shall, if he think proper so to do, continue to hold and occupy such farm or lands until the last gale day of the current year in which such tenancy shall determine, and shall then quit upon the terms of his lease or holding, in the same manner as if such lease or tenancy were then determined by effluxion of time or other lawful means, during the continuance of his landlord's estate; and the landlord or succeeding landlord or owner shall be entitled to recover rent from the tenant in the same manner as if the tenant's interest had only determined on such gale day; and the landlord, or the succeeding landlord or owner, and the tenant respectively, shall, as between themselves and as against each other, be entitled to all the benefits and advantages, and be subject to all the terms, conditions, and restrictions, to which the landlord or preceding landlord or lessor and such tenant respectively would have been entitled and subject in case the lease or tenancy had determined in manner aforesaid at the expiration of such current year: Provided always, that no notice to quit shall be necessary or required by or from either party to determine any such holding and occupation as aforesaid.

Prevention of waste, and law of repairs.

Justice's precept to restrain waste.

[1–35] 35.—Where any person shall be in possession of lands, or of any dwelling house, outhouse, or building, as tenant thereof, or as servant or caretaker of any owner, or having obtained the possession thereof from any such tenant, servant, or caretaker, and the landlord or owner or other person interested in the preservation of the premises, or any agent acting on his behalf, shall, by affidavit, satisfy any justice of the peace of the county, not being a party interested in the said premises, (who is hereby authorized and required to take such affidavit), that there exists probable and just grounds of suspicion that such person is about to commit or to permit or suffer any unlawful waste, injury, alteration, destruction upon, or removal from any such dwelling house, outhouse, or other building, or intends unlawfully to burn or break up any part of the soil or surface or subsoil of the lands, or unlawfully to remove the soil or surface or subsoil of the said lands, or unlawfully to cut down, top, lop, or grub any trees, woods, or underwoods growing on the said lands, or otherwise use or misuse the premises or any part thereof, contrary to his agreement, or that he is in the act of doing or suffering any of the aforesaid matters, it shall be lawful for such justice of the peace to issue his precept in writing under his hand and seal, stating that information had been received that such waste or injury is intended to be or is in the act of being done or permitted, and commanding all such persons and all other persons whomsoever to desist from such waste or injury, and not to continue the same until special leave and authority for that purpose shall be first produced from the magistrate who shall have signed such precept, or until the subject matter of the said information be inquired into at the next petty sessions of the district in which the said premises are situate, or such other time as may be therein mentioned; and such precept may be according to the Form No. 1 in the Schedule (A) to this Act annexed, and shall be served on every or any person by whom it shall be suspected that such waste or injury is intended to be or is being committed, by delivering a copy thereof to such person, if he can be found, and if not, by affixing a copy thereof on the principal door or entrance to the dwelling house, outhouse, or other building, and if there be no such house or building, on some conspicuous part of the premises; and the said persons shall and may attend at the petty sessions, and such order may be made thereat by the court of petty sessions for annulling or continuing for a limited period the said precept, or otherwise as may be agreeable to justice.

Note: The jurisdiction of a Justice of the Peace is now exercised by the District Court — see s 77 of the Courts of Justice Act 1924.

Punishment of disobedience of precept.

36.—If any person shall, after the service or posting of such precept, in disobedience thereto, without such leave and authority as aforesaid, proceed with or continue to do the act prohibited by such precept, or wilfully aid, abet, or assist in so doing, he shall, on conviction thereof before two or more justices of the peace at petty sessions, be liable to be imprisoned for a period not exceeding one calendar month; and all the provisions of the Petty Sessions (Ireland) Act, respecting summary convictions before justices at petty sessions, and respecting appeals therefrom, shall be applicable to every conviction under this section. **[1–36]**

Annulling of precept, &c.

37.—It shall be lawful for any of the superior courts of law or equity in Ireland, or any judge thereof, or for the going justices of assize, or one of them, or for the chairman presiding in the county, on a summary application on behalf of any person aggrieved by any such precept, order, or conviction, of which due notice shall be given to the opposite party, to annul or vary any such precept granted by any justice of the peace, or any order or conviction made at petty sessions in relation thereto, and to award as between the parties a reasonable sum for the costs occasioned by the procuring and sustaining, or annulling or varying, the said precept, or order or conviction, and reasonable compensation for any loss or damage caused by the procuring such precept or order. **[1–37]**

Note: The Fourth Schedule (Ref. 27) to the Courts (Supplemental Provisions) Act 1961 states that the jurisdiction under s 37 of this Act is to be exercised by the Circuit Court by the judge of the circuit where the land in relation to which the precept, order or conviction was made is situate.

Landlord may enter to inspect waste.

38.—It shall be lawful for the landlord of any premises holden under lease or other contract of tenancy made on or after the first day of January one thousand eight hundred and sixty-one, upon which any waste, misuser, or destruction shall have been committed or suffered, and his agent lawfully authorized, at any reasonable time to enter upon the premises so wasted or misused, and to inspect and, if necessary, to **[1–38]** survey the same for the purpose for ascertaining the nature and extent of any waste or injury done or the quantity of land burned contrary to the provisions of this Act; and if any person shall hinder or obstruct such landlord or agent in making such entry, inspection, or survey, he shall forfeit to the said landlord a sum not exceeding ten pounds, to be recovered by civil bill action in the same manner and with the like appeal as in ordinary cases of civil bill actions.

> **Note:** The Fourth Schedule (Ref. 28) to the Courts (Supplemental Provisions) Act 1961 states that the jurisdiction under s 38 of this Act is to be exercised by the Circuit Court by the judge of the circuit where the defendant resides.

Ordinary civil remedies preserved.

[1–39] 39.—Nothing in this Act contained shall deprive any landlord or owner of any lands of any other remedy, either at law or in equity, which he might previously have had or pursued against any person for any injury sustained by such landlord or other person, or for preventing such injury.

On destruction of subject of the lease, tenant may surrender the lease.

[1–40] 40.—If any dwelling house or other building constituting the substantial matter of the demise, and holden by any tenant under any lease or other contract of tenancy not containing an express covenant or agreement binding on the tenant to repair the same, shall be destroyed, become ruinous and uninhabitable, or incapable of beneficial occupation or enjoyment, by accidental fire or other inevitable accident, and without the default or neglect of the said tenant, it shall be lawful for such tenant to surrender the said premises, and on tendering the said surrender, and on payment of all rent and arrears due or accruing due, or tendering the same, the said tenant shall be thenceforth discharged from all obligations to pay the rent or perform the covenants and conditions in the lease thenceforward.

Covenants and conditions.

Agreements implied on behalf of landlord.

[1–41] 41.—Every lease of lands or tenements made after the commencement of this Act shall (unless otherwise expressly provided by such lease) imply an agreement on the part of the landlord making such lease, his heirs, executors, administrators, and assigns, with the tenant thereof for the time being, that the said landlord has good title to make such lease, and that the tenant shall have the quiet and peaceable enjoyment of the said lands or tenements without the interruption of the landlord or any person whomsoever during the term contracted for, so long as the tenant shall pay the rent and perform the agreements contained in the lease to be observed on the part of the tenant.

Agreements implied on behalf of tenant.

[1–42] 42.—Every lease of lands or tenements made after the commencement of this Act shall (unless otherwise expressly provided by such lease) imply the following agreements on the part of the tenant for the time being, his heirs, executors, administrators, and assigns, with the landlord thereof: that is to say,

1. That the tenant shall pay, when due, the rent reserved and all taxes and impositions payable by the tenant, and shall keep the premises in good and substantial repair and condition;
2. That the tenant shall give peaceable possession of the demised premises, in good and substantial repair and condition, on the determination of the lease (accidents by fire without the tenant's default excepted), subject, however, to any right of removal (or of compensation for improvements) that may have lawfully arisen in respect of them, and to any right of surrender in case of the destruction of the subject matter of the lease as herein-before mentioned.

Note: See s 11(8) of the Rent Restrictions (Amendment) Act 1967 which states that s 42 of this Act does not apply to a letting to which s 11 of the Act of 1967 applies.

See s 193(a) of the Residential Tenancies Act 2004 which states that s 42 of this Act does not apply to a dwelling to which the Act of 2004 applies.

Waiver and dispensation of covenants.

43.—Where any lease made after the commencement of this Act shall contain or imply any condition, covenant, or agreement to be observed or performed on the part of the tenant, no act hereafter done or suffered by the landlord shall be deemed to be a dispensation with such condition, covenant, or agreement, or a waiver of the benefit of the same in respect of any breach thereof, unless such dispensation or waiver shall be signified by the landlord or his authorized agent in writing under his hand. **[1–43]**

Surrender of portion of premises not to prejudice rights of landlord.

44.—The surrender to or resumption by a landlord, or eviction of any portion of the premises demised by a lease, shall not in any manner prejudice or affect the rights of the landlord, whether by action, or entry, or ejectment, as to the residue of said premises. **[1–44]**

Actions for Rent

Action for rent in arrear.

45.—Every person entitled to any rent in arrear, whether in his own right or in right of his see, dignity, benefice, or corporation, or in right of his wife, or as executor or administrator of any party deceased, under any lease or other contract of tenancy, whether of freehold or for years or both, and whether the estate or interest in such lease or contract shall be continuing or not, shall be entitled to recover such arrear from the tenant of such lands at the time of the accruing of the said rent, or his executors or administrators, by an action in any of the superior courts of law at Dublin, or, where the amount shall not exceed the sum of one hundred pounds, by civil bill action in the court of the chairman of the county or riding in which the lands or any part of them shall be situate. **[1–45]**

Note: The Third Schedule (Ref. 11) to the Courts (Supplemental Provisions) Act 1961 (as amended by s 2 of the Courts Act, 1991, No 20 of 1991 which came into effect on 15th August 1991) states that the jurisdiction in actions for rent under s 45 of this Act where the rent in arrear exceeds £30,000 [€38,092.14] is vested in the Circuit Court in the judge of the circuit where the land in respect of which the rent arrear is payable or any part of that land is situate.

Action for use and occupation.

[1–46] 46.—Every person entitled to any lands, and who shall suffer the said lands to be holden or occupied by any person under and agreement not specifying or determining the amount of rent, shall be entitled to recover a reasonable satisfaction for the use and occupation of the said premises holden or occupied by the said person in an action in any of the superior courts of law at Dublin, or where the amount shall not exceed the sum of one hundred pounds, by civil bill action in the court of the chairman of the county in which the lands or any part of them shall be situate.

Note: The Third Schedule (Ref. 12) to the Courts (Supplemental Provisions) Act 1961 (as amended by s 2 of the Courts Act, 1991, No 20 of 1991 which came into effect on 15th August 1991) states that the jurisdiction in actions in for use and occupation under s 46 of this Act where the amount claimed exceeds £30,000 [€38,092.14] is vested in the Circuit Court in the judge of the circuit where the land or any part of the land is situate.

Receipts to specify gale, and, if not, to be deemed to apply to last gale.

[1–47] 47.—Every receipt or acknowledgement for rent or for money paid on account thereof, and given on or after the first day of January one thousand eight hundred and sixty-one, shall specify the gale for or on account of which the same was accepted and paid, and in default thereof such money shall, in any action, suit, or proceeding whatsoever, be deemed to have been paid and accepted for and on account of the gale of rent which became due upon the gale day immediately preceding the date of such payment, and shall be *prima facie* evidence that all previously accrued gales have been satisfied.

Set-off against rent.

[1–48] 48.—All claims and demands by any landlord against his tenant in respect of rent shall be subject to deduction or set-off in respect of all just debts due by the landlord to the tenant.

Apportionment of rent where lease has continuance.

[1–49] 49—*Omitted. Repealed by the Statute Law Revision Act 1893.*

Provision for cases not coming within the provisions of clause 34.

[1–50] 50.—In every case not coming within the provisions of clause thirty-four, when the tenancy determines, otherwise than by the act of the landlord, at any time before the day on which the rent would become payable, the landlord at the time of such determination (unless it is otherwise agreed) shall be entitled to a reasonable proportion of the rent according to the time that has elapsed from the commencement of the tenancy, or the last gale day, to the day of the determination of such tenancy, including such day.

No distress for more than one year's rent.

51.—From and after the commencement of this Act, it shall not be lawful for any landlord, or any one on his behalf, to take or seize any distress for rent which became due more than one year before the making of such distress. [1–51]

Ejectment for year's rent unpaid.

52.—Whenever a year's rent shall be in arrear in respect of lands held under any fee farm grant, lease, or other contract of tenancy, or from year to year, and whether by writing or otherwise, it shall be lawful for the landlord immediately thereon, and before the expiration of the time, if any, limited for re-entry thereupon in any lease or agreement, to proceed by ejectment for the recovery of the possession of the said lands in any of the superior courts of law at Dublin, or, where the rent shall not exceed one hundred pounds by the year, in the court of the chairman of the county in which the lands or any part thereof are situated; and the plaintiff's right to sue as such landlord shall not be defeated by proof merely that the legal estate in the rent or lands is vested in any other person not a party to such suit or proceedings, but who would be a trustee for the plaintiff, provided that the plaintiff was at the time of the institution of such suit or other proceedings the person substantially and beneficially entitled to the said rent. [1–52]

Note: The Third Schedule (Ref. 10) to the Courts (Supplemental Provisions) Act 1961 (as amended by s 2 of the Courts Act, 1991, No 20 of 1991 which came into effect on 15th August 1991) states that the jurisdiction in actions in ejectment under s 52 of this Act where the rateable valuation of the lands exceeds £200 [€253.95] is vested in the Circuit Court in the judge of the circuit where the land in respect of which the rent arrear is payable or any part of that land is situate.

Section 52 does not apply to dwellinghouses falling within s 27(1) of the Landlord and Tenant (Ground Rents) (No.2) Act 1978 — see s 27(2) of that Act.

Proof of demand, &c. and of legal reversion unnecessary.

53.—In any ejectment under this Act it shall not be necessary to allege or prove the making of any demand or re-entry, or the existence of any clause or condition of re-entry in the lease or other contract, or of any legal reversion expectant on the determination of the same, and subsisting in the landlord, provided a tenancy between the parties shall appear to exist whether by original contract, or by lawful assignment, devise, bequest, or act and operation of law. [1–53]

Form of civil bill for nonpayment of rent as in Sched. (A).

54.—[Every Civil Bill of ejectment for non-payment of rent under this Act may be in according to the Form No. 2 in the Schedule A to this Act annexed, and]It shall be lawful for the chairman, on proof of the service of such civil bill in the manner herein- [1–54] after directed, and that a sum equal to one full year's rent, not exceeding the rate of one hundred pounds by the year after all just and fair allowances, was due when such proceeding by civil bill was commenced, and still remains due to the landlord, to decree the said landlord to be put into possession of the said premises, and to ascertain the amount of the rent then due.

Note: The words in square brackets at the beginning of s 54 of this Act were repealed by the Statute Law Revision Act 1893.

Under the Circuit Court Rules 2001, O.67, r.8 states that where the jurisdiction transferred to the Court under s 51 of the Courts of Justice Act 1924 (and thereafter established by s 4 of the Courts (Establishment and Constitution) Act 1961) depends upon statute, each such Statute is hereby adapted or modified so that all references therein to the Civil Bill Court, County Court, or Court of Quarter Sessions shall be construed to refer to the Court where necessary, and all references to Recorders, County Court Judges, Chairmen of Quarter Sessions, or other Judges, and to Officers of any such Courts shall be construed where necessary as references to the Judge of the Court, and, in the cases of Officers, to the County Registrar or appropriate Officer of the Court, and all references to proceedings in any of such Courts, shall, where necessary, be construed as references to proceedings in the Court.

Who to be served with summons and process in ejectment.

[1–55] 55.—In any ejectment for nonpayment of rent brought by any landlord under this Act it shall not be necessary to serve [with the summons and plaint in ejectment, or] with civil bill process, any person other than the person or persons in the actual possession of the lands as tenant or under-tenant.

Note: The words in square brackets in this section were repealed by the Statute Law Revision Act 1893.

Service on persons in possession

[1–56] 56.—Service of the [summons and plaint or] civil bill process in ejectment for nonpayment of rent on any person in the actual possession as tenant or under-tenant of the premises sought to be recovered, or any part of them, shall be effected either by personal service of the [summons and plaint or] civil bill process on such tenant or under-tenant at any place in Ireland, or by leaving a copy thereof with the wife, child, father, mother, brother, or sister of the party, or with any servant or clerk of the said party, at his dwelling house or office or place of business (the person with whom such copy shall be left being of the age of sixteen years or upwards), or in such other manner as shall appear to the court [or judge thereof] to be sufficient.

Note: The words in square brackets in this section were repealed by the Statute Law Revision Act 1893.

Service where no person is in possession.

57.—In case there shall be no person in the actual possession of the premises as tenant or under-tenant on whom service of such [summons and plaint or] civil bill process in ejectment can be effected, it shall be lawful instead thereof to affix a copy of such [summons or] civil bill process on some conspicuous part of the premises, and also on the usual place for affixing notices in the nearest market town to the said lands: Provided, however, than in such case, before any decree or judgment by default shall be given, the Court [or a judge] shall be satisfied that there was no person in actual possession on whom other service might have been effected: Provided also, that in case of an ejectment for nonpayment of rent reserved upon any lease of tithes, tithe rentcharge, or other ecclesiastical dues, the Court in which the ejectment is brought may order service to be made by posting the ejectment upon the church door of the parish or union of parishes wherein such tithe, tithe rentcharge, or ecclesiastical dues are payable, and if there be no such church in the parish or union of parishes, upon some public and conspicuous place in the said parish or union. [1–57]

Note: The words in square brackets in this section were repealed by the Statute Law Revision Act 1893.

Judgment by default.

58.—In any ejectment for nonpayment of rent brought in any of the Superior Courts of Law, when the tenant shall not take defence to the ejectment, the affidavit of the landlord, his agent, receiver, or clerk, stating the amount of rent due at the time of the bringing of the ejectment, over and above all just and fair allowances, shall be sufficient evidence of the amount due, and shall when the same amounts to or exceeds one year's rent entitle the landlord to judgment for the possession of the premises, provided an affidavit of the service of the summons and plaint in such ejectment shall have been duly filed, according to the practice of such Court. [1–58]

Defence to civil bill.

59.—Every defendant in a civil bill ejectment under this Act shall be entitled to every defence at the hearing of such civil bill which he might have had at law or in equity. [1–59]

Civil bill process to state amount of rent claimed.

60.— Every [summons and plaint in ejectment in the Superior Courts, and] civil bill process in ejectment in the court of the chairman, for non-payment of rent, shall contain or have endorsed thereon a statement of the amount claimed to be due by the landlord for rent after all just and fair allowances up to the time of the bringing of such ejectment, and the times at which such rent accrued due, and that if the amount thereof, together with a sum for costs, not exceeding [in the case of such summons and plaint one pound ten shillings, and] in the case of a civil bill process ten shillings, be paid to the plaintiff or his attorney or known agent or receiver within ten days from the service of such [summons or] process, all further proceedings will be stayed; and upon payment or tender within the time so mentioned of the sum so claimed, and costs, to the plaintiff or his attorney or known agent or receiver, all further proceedings in respect of the rent then claimed shall cease and be stayed accordingly. [1–60]

Note: The words in square brackets in this section were repealed by the Statute Law Revision Act 1893.

Under the Circuit Court Rules 2001, O.67 r.8 states that where the jurisdiction transferred to the Court under s 51 of the Courts of Justice Act 1924 (and thereafter established by s 4 of the Courts (Establishment and Constitution) Act 1961) depends upon statute, each such Statute is hereby adapted or modified so that all references therein to the Civil Bill Court, County Court, or Court of Quarter Sessions shall be construed to refer to the Court where necessary, and all references to Recorders, County Court Judges, Chairmen of Quarter Sessions, or other Judges, and to Officers of any such Courts shall be construed where necessary as references to the Judge of the Court, and, in the cases of Officers, to the County Registrar or appropriate Officer of the Court, and all references to proceedings in any of such Courts, shall, where necessary, be construed as references to proceedings in the Court.

Where amount is disputed, lodgment may be made with clerk of the peace.

[1–61] 61.—It shall be lawful for any defendant in a civil bill ejectment for nonpayment of rent disputing the amount of rent claimed to be due, at any time not later than three days before the day on which he is required to appear, to deposit with the clerk of the peace of the county a sum of money for rent, together with the sum mentioned in said civil bill process for costs, for which deposit, on payment of the fee of one shilling and sixpence, the clerk of the peace shall give the defendant a certificate of the lodgment and duplicate, which duplicate shall be delivered to or left at the abode of the plaintiff, his agent receiver, or attorney in the cause, not later than the second day before the day on which the defendant is required to appear; and in case the said plaintiff, or his attorney in the cause, shall receive such deposit from the clerk of the peace (which the clerk of the peace is hereby required to pay over to the plaintiff of his attorney, on demand), such payment shall be in full discharge of the rent and costs claimed by the said civil bill; but in case the said plaintiff, after delivery of such certificate, shall not accept of the said deposit on or before the day next previous to the day on which the defendant is required to appear, exclusive of any Sunday, and it shall appear at the hearing of such civil bill that no greater sum was due for rent at the time of the service of such process than the sum so deposited as aforesaid, and that such duplicate was delivered as aforesaid, it shall be lawful for the chairman to dismiss the said civil bill, with costs of the proceedings subsequent to the delivery of the said duplicate, and the plaintiff shall be entitled to the amount so deposited, reduced by the amount of such costs; and if it shall appear that any greater sum was due than the sum deposited, it shall be lawful for the said chairman to ascertain the amount of rent actually due at the time of the service of the summons in ejectment, and the sum so deposited shall be returned to the defendant, unless the plaintiff shall elect to take the same in lieu of the possession, in which case the plaintiff shall be entitled to receive the same in payment of his rent, and to have a decree for his costs or for the balance of his rent and costs.

Note: The Fourth Schedule (Ref. 29) to the Courts (Supplemental Provisions) Act 1961 states that the jurisdiction under s 61 of this Act is to be exercised by the Circuit Court by the judge of the circuit where the land or any part of the land is situate.

Lodgment in Court of rent, and undertaking to pay costs.

62.—It shall be lawful for any defendant in any action of ejectment for nonpayment of rent in any of the Superior Courts of Law, at any time before judgment or service of a notice of trial, to pay into court a sum of money for rent, with an undertaking to pay the costs then incurred when taxed and ascertained, and in case of nonpayment to suffer final judgment to be marked, or an attachment to be issued against him; and thereupon the plaintiff, if he shall not accept of the said sum in full discharge of the action, with costs to be taxed by the proper officer, may proceed in the said action at his peril; and if upon the trial of the issue it shall appear that no greater sum was due for rent at the time of the service of the summons in ejectment than the sum paid into court, the verdict shall be entered for the defendant. [1–62]

Tender before civil bill decree executed.

63.—It shall be lawful for the defendant in any civil bill ejectment for nonpayment of rent, or any other person having a specific interest in the lease or other contract of tenancy, at any time before the decree for possession shall have been executed, to pay to the plaintiff, or his executor or administrator, or agent or attorney, in the said civil bill, all rent and arrear due at the time of the service of the ejectment, together with the costs incurred, or a sum sufficient to cover such costs, or to tender the same, and in case such tender shall be refused, to deposit the money with the clerk of the peace of the county, for which lodgment a certificate and duplicate shall be granted in manner aforesaid, and thereupon it shall be lawful for the chairman to order all further proceedings to be stayed and to cease, upon payment of such costs incurred up to the date of such tender as he shall deem reasonable, and the money so lodged with the clerk of the peace shall be paid over to the plaintiff, or his executor or administrator or attorney, on demand: Provided that the decision of the chairman shall be subject to appeal in like manner as if it were a decree or dismiss on a civil bill ejectment for nonpayment of rent. [1–63]

> **Note:** The Fourth Schedule (Ref. 29) to the Courts (Supplemental Provisions) Act 1961 states that the jurisdiction under s 63 of this Act is to be exercised by the Circuit Court by the judge of the circuit where the land or any part of the land is situate.

Tender before writ of habere executed.

64.—It shall be lawful for the defendant in any ejectment for nonpayment of rent in any one of the Superior Courts, or any other person having a specific interest in the lease or other contract of tenancy, at any time before the writ of habere facias possessionem shall be executed, to pay to the plaintiff, his executors or administrator, or his known agent or receiver, or to the attorney in the cause, all the rent and arrears due at the time of the service of the ejectment, together with the costs , or a sum sufficient to cover such costs, or to tender the same, and in case such tender shall be refused, to lodge the money in Court, and thereupon it shall be lawful for the Court, or a judge thereof, to order all further proceedings to be stayed and to cease, upon payment of such costs incurred up to the date of such tender as the Court or a judge shall deem to be reasonable; and the money so lodged in Court shall be paid to the plaintiff, or his executor or administrator or attorney, on demand; and the defendant shall, notwithstanding any such payment, be at liberty to have the costs taxed and [1–64] paid back, if disallowed, with the costs of the taxation in case more than one sixth shall be disallowed.

Amount of rent to be stated on writ, etc. Stay of execution on payment.

[1–65] 65.—Upon every writ of habere facias possessionem and warrant under a decree for possession in any ejectment for nonpayment of rent, there shall be a statement of the amount of rent then due; and if at any time before execution executed the defendant shall pay to the sheriff the sum so marked for rent and costs, such sheriff shall stay such execution, and shall endorse on such writ, as a return thereto, the receipt of such rent and costs.

Remedy for rent not to be prejudiced by recovery of possession.

[1–66] 66.—Every landlord recovering possession by such judgment or decree in any ejectment for nonpayment of rent shall have the same remedy for all arrears of rent to the time of execution of such judgment or decree as such landlord might have had if possession had not been obtained under such judgment or decree.

Writ of error no stay of execution unless bail given.

[1–67] 67.—*Omitted. Repealed by the Statute Law Revision Act 1893.*

Appeal from civil bill decree.

[1–68] 68.—Every decree or dismiss, or dismiss without prejudice, made or pronounced by any chairman in any action or proceeding under this Act, shall be subject to appeal, and under the same restrictions and regulations as other cases of civil bills, unless so far as the said regulations shall be inconsistent with the provisions of this Act.

> **Note:** Under the Circuit Court Rules 2001, O.67, r.8 states that where the jurisdiction transferred to the Court under s 51 of the Courts of Justice Act 1924 (and thereafter established by s 4 of the Courts (Establishment and Constitution) Act 1961) depends upon statute, each such Statute is hereby adapted or modified so that all references therein to the Civil Bill Court, County Court, or Court of Quarter Sessions shall be construed to refer to the Court where necessary, and all references to Recorders, County Court Judges, Chairmen of Quarter Sessions, or other Judges, and to Officers of any such Courts shall be construed where necessary as references to the Judge of the Court, and, in the cases of Officers, to the County Registrar or appropriate Officer of the Court, and all references to proceedings in any of such Courts, shall, where necessary, be construed as references to proceedings in the Court.

Appeal not to stay execution unless rent lodged.

[1–69] 69.—In any civil bill ejectment for nonpayment of rent, in case there shall be a decree for possession pronounced by the chairman therein, execution of such decree shall not be stayed by reason of any appeal, unless the defendant shall deposit with the clerk of the peace of the county the amount of the rent proved to be due on the hearing of such civil bill, and the costs thereof; and such deposit shall be in lieu of a recognizance in ordinary cases of appeal, and shall be disposed of as the Court shall direct.

> **Note:** Under the Circuit Court Rules 2001, O.67, r.8 states that where the jurisdiction transferred to the Court under s 51 of the Courts of Justice Act 1924 (and thereafter established by s 4 of the Courts (Establishment and Constitution) Act 1961) depends upon statute, each such Statute is hereby adapted or modified so that all references therein to the Civil Bill Court, County Court, or Court of Quarter Sessions shall be construed to refer to the Court where necessary, and all references to Recorders, County Court Judges, Chairmen of Quarter Sessions, or other Judges, and to Officers of any such Courts shall be construed where necessary as references to the Judge of the Court, and, in the cases of Officers, to the County Registrar or appropriate Officer of the Court, and all references to proceedings in any of such Courts, shall, where necessary, be construed as references to proceedings in the Court.

Restitution to be applied for within six months.

70.—In case the defendant in any ejectment for nonpayment of rent, and the persons interested in the lease or other contract of tenancy, shall suffer a decree of possession or writ of habere facias possessionem to be executed, putting the landlord into possession of the premises, without paying the rent and arrears thereof, with full costs, or lodging the same in the Superior Court in which the ejectment was brought, or in case of a civil bill ejectment, lodging the same with the clerk of the peace of the county within six months after the execution of the said decree or habere or writ of possession, and also making an application to be restored to the said possession to the Court out of which such decree or writ shall have been issued, or to a judge thereof, within the said period of six months, or at the earliest opportunity after on which application can be reasonably made (and of which application the landlord shall receive due notice), in every such case, or in case the said Court or judge shall, upon such application, decline to make an order for restitution thereon, the said defendant, and all other persons interested in the lease or other contract of tenancy, shall be debarred from all relief or remedy in law or in equity, other than by bringing an appeal from the said decree of the assistant barrister, or a writ of error to reverse such judgment of the Superior Court in case such decree or judgment shall be erroneous, and the said landlord shall from thenceforth hold the demised premises discharged from such lease or tenancy; provided that nothing herein contained shall affect the right of redemption now by law reserved to any existing mortgagee claiming under a duly registered mortgage. [1–70]

> **Note:** The Fifth Schedule to the Courts (Supplemental Provisions) Act 1961 states that the reference to the assistant barrister in s 70 of this Act shall be construed as a reference to a judge of the Circuit Court.
>
> Section 3(1)(a) of the Land Act 1984 provides that this section shall not apply to a lease of agricultural land made after 1st January 1985.

Court may award restitution of possession in certain cases.

[1–71] 71.—It shall be lawful for the said chairman, in case of any decree for possession for nonpayment of rent, and for the said Superior Court of Law in which any such judgment in ejectment for nonpayment of rent in favour of any landlord shall have been given and executed as aforesaid, or a judge thereof, on the application of the defendant or any other person having a specific interest in the lease or other contract of tenancy, and made within the period aforesaid, and after such payment or lodgment of the rent, arrears, and costs as aforesaid, to hear and determine in a summary manner the claim of such defendant to be restored to the possession of the premises so recovered, and to give such relief therein as a court of equity might have done, and to award a writ of restitution, or to refuse such application; provided that the order or decision of a single judge in chamber may be reversed or varied by the Court, and that it shall be lawful for any person aggrieved by any such order or decision of any chairman to appeal therefrom to the next going judge of assize for the county, on payment of the costs already incurred, and entering into security by recognizance in the sum of three pounds to abide by the order of the said judge on such appeal, and such judge of assize shall, upon such appeal, have authority to make such order touching the application as shall seem to be just.

> **Note:** The Fourth Schedule (Ref. 29) to the Courts (Supplemental Provisions) Act 1961 states that the jurisdiction under s 71 of this Act is to be exercised by the Circuit Court by the judge of the circuit where the land or any part of the land is situate.
>
> Section 3(1)(a) of the Land Act 1984 provides that this section shall not apply to a lease of agricultural land made after 1st January 1985.

Ejectment for overholding.

Civil Bill ejectment in case of overholding of tenements at rent of under one hundred pounds.

[1–72] 72.—If any tenant of any lands holden at a rent not exceeding the rate of one hundred pounds per annum shall neglect or refuse to give possession of the same after the determination of his interest, either by notice to quit or otherwise, it shall be lawful for such landlord to proceed by civil bill ejectment against such tenant and such other person, if any, as shall be in the actual possession of the said premises, [which civil bill may be according to the form No.3 in the Schedule (A) to this Act annexed] and thereupon to serve with civil bill process such tenant or other persons, and in the like manner as herein-before required in cases of ejectment for nonpayment of rent, requiring such persons to appear to answer the bill of the said landlord, praying to be put into possession thereof; and it shall be lawful for the chairman, upon such civil bill, and proof of the service or affixing of such process in manner aforesaid, and that the premises had been holden of the said landlord by the tenant, or the person under whom the party in possession derives, at a rent not exceeding the rate of one hundred pounds per annum, and that the interest to such tenant has ended or determined by efflux of time, notice to quit, or otherwise, to decree the said landlord to be put into the possession of the said premises.

Note: The words in square brackets in this section were repealed by the Statute Law Revision Act 1893.

The Third Schedule (Ref. 9) to the Courts (Supplemental Provisions) Act 1961 states that the jurisdiction in actions in ejectment where the rateable valuation of the lands exceeds €253.95 is vested in the Circuit Court in the judge of the circuit where the land or any part of the land is situate.

Defence and appeal in civil bill ejectment.

73.—Every such civil bill ejectment for overholding shall be subject to the like defence and appeal as in case of a civil bill ejectment for nonpayment of rent, and it shall not be necessary to make any affidavit verifying the contents of any civil bill ejectment, whether for nonpayment of rent of otherwise. [1–73]

Service of summonses in ejectment for overholding.

74.—*Omitted. Repealed by the Statute Law Revision Act 1893.* [1–74]

Security from overholding tenant in civil bill ejectment.

75.—In any case in which the term or interest of any tenant under any lease of any lands for any term of number of years certain, or from year to year, or at the will and pleasure of the parties, shall have expired, or shall expire or be determined by notice to quit, given by either the landlord or the tenant, and such tenant, or any one holding or claiming by or under him, shall refuse to deliver up possession accordingly, after lawful demand in writing made and signed by the landlord or his agent, and served personally upon or left at the dwelling house or usual place of abode of such tenant or person, and the landlord shall proceed by action of ejectment for the recovery of the possession of the premises, it shall be lawful for him, at foot of the summons and plaint, to address a notice to such tenant or person of an application to the Court in which the action shall be pending, that the defendant be required to find bail for such purposes as are herein-after mentioned; and upon the appearance of the party on such motion, or in default of such appearance, on making the usual affidavit of the service of the summons and notice, it shall be lawful for the landlord producing the lease or other instrument regulating the terms of the tenancy, or some counterpart or duplicate thereof, and proving the execution of the same, and that the premises have been actually enjoyed under such lease or instrument in writing, and that the interest of the tenant has expired or been determined by a regular notice to quit, and that possession has been lawfully demanded, to move the Court, or a judge thereof, that the tenant or other person shall, within six days from the date of such application, enter into a recognizance by himself and two sufficient sureties in a reasonable sum, conditioned to pay the costs and damages and mesne profits which shall be recovered by the plaintiff in the action; and it shall be lawful for the Court or a judge to make such order thereon as shall seem to it to be just; and in case the tenant or other person shall refuse or neglect to comply with such order within the period aforesaid, then, upon an affidavit of the service thereof, the plaintiff shall be at liberty, notwithstanding any defence [*or demurrer*] filed by such defendant, to enter up judgment in ejectment for the recovery of the possession of the premises and his costs of suit. [1–75]

Note: The words in square brackets in this section were deleted by the Statute Law Revision Act 1893.

Payment of double rent for overholding.

[1–76] 76.—In case any tenant of any lands, or any person who shall come into possession by or under or by collusion with such tenant, shall wilfully hold over any lands or premises, or part thereof, after the determination of the tenancy, whether by notice to quit given by the landlord or by the tenant, or otherwise, and after a demand of the possession made in writing by the landlord or his agent, such tenant or other person shall pay to the landlord for such time as he shall so hold or keep the possession double the rent or sum which he should otherwise have paid, to be recovered at the same times and in the same manner as the single rent or sum could have been recovered during the term.

Note: The Third Schedule (Ref. 13) to the Courts (Supplemental Provisions) Act 1961 (as amended by s 2 of the Courts Act 1991, No 20 of 1991 which came into effect on 15th August 1991) states that the jurisdiction in actions for double rent for overholding where the amount claimed exceeds £30,000 [€38,092.14] is vested in the Circuit Court in the judge of the circuit where the land or any part of the land is situate.

Premises and mesne profits to the day of trail may be recovered in ejectment.

[1–77] 77.—In case of any ejectment for nonpayment of rent or for overholding any premises, in any of the superior courts of law, where the summons and plaint shall include a claim for rent or mesne profits, the plaintiff, on proof of his right, may recover the possession of the whole or some part of the premises mentioned in the summons or plaint in ejectment and the rent or mesne profits claimed thereby, and also the further mesne profits thereof which might have accrued from the day to which the mesne rates claimed have been calculated, or from the day on which the rent for the nonpayment of which the ejectment shall be brought fell due, to the day of such trial, or some preceding day to be specified.

Ejectment for deserted tenements.

Civil bill Ejectment for deserted tenements.

[1–78] 78.—In case it shall happen that a half year's rent shall be in arrear of any lands or premises holden under any lease or other contract of tenancy, or from year to year, and the tenant thereof shall desert or otherwise abandon such lands or premises, leaving the same unoccupied, or the lands or greater portion of them uncultivated or unemployed, and without sufficient distress, contrary to the course of husbandry, or carry off the stock or crop thereof, it shall be lawful for the landlord thereof to proceed by civil bill ejectment before the chairman of the county in which the lands or any part of them shall be situate, to recover the possession of them [and such civil bill may be according to the form No.4 in the Schedule (A) to this Act annexed] such landlord having first obtained a certificate of desertion in the manner herein-after provided, and serving a copy of same, together with such civil bill process, on the tenant against whom such proceedings shall be had, in the manner herein-before provided in respect of ejectments for nonpayment of rent, requiring such tenant or other person to appear to answer the bill of the said landlord, praying to be put into possession thereof; and it shall be lawful for the chairman on proof of the due execution of such certificate by any person who may have witnessed the execution of the same, and that one half year's rent of the said premises was due to the landlord when such certificate was granted, and that such civil bill process and copy of such certificate were duly served in manner aforesaid, and upon hearing the tenant, in case he shall appear, and such evidence as he may offer, to decree the said landlord to be put into possession of the said premises.

Note: The Fourth Schedule (Ref. 29) to the Courts (Supplemental Provisions) Act 1961 states that the jurisdiction under s 78 of this Act is to be exercised by the Circuit Court by the judge of the circuit where the land or any part of the land is situate.

The words in square brackets in this section were repealed by the Statute Law Revision Act 1893.

Justices may view premises and give certificate of desertion.

79.—In case any lands or premises shall be deserted or abandoned by the tenant thereof, and the premises left unoccupied, or the lands or greater portion thereof suffered by the tenant to remain uncultivated or unemployed, contrary to the course of husbandry, or the stock or crop thereof removed from the said premises, it shall be lawful for any two or more justices of the peace of the county in which such lands or premises or any part thereof shall be situate, and being in no way interested in the said lands or premises, at the request of the landlord thereof, or of his agent or receiver, to go upon and view the same between the hours of ten o'clock in the morning and four o'clock in the afternoon, and having fully ascertained to their satisfaction, by examination of witnesses or by their own view, that the premises are so deserted or abandoned by the tenant, and left unoccupied or uncultivated or unemployed, contrary to the course of husbandry, or that the crops or stock have been removed, to certify to the chairman of the county, under their hands and seals, that they have together viewed the said premises, fully describing the same, and that the same appeared to them to be deserted and unoccupied or uncultivated or unemployed, contrary to the course of husbandry, or that the stock or crops have been so removed from the premises, and such certificate [may be according to the Form No.5 in the Schedule (A) to this Act annexed, and] shall be evidence of the facts stated therein, unless the same shall be disproved to the satisfaction of the chairman or the judge of assize on appeal. [1–79]

Note: The Fifth Schedule to the Courts (Supplemental Provisions) Act 1961 states that the references to the chairman of the county shall be construed as references to the judge of the circuit where the lands or premises to which the certificate of desertion relates or any part thereof are situate.

The words in square brackets in this section were repealed by the Statute Law Revision Act 1893.

Civil Bill ejectment against occupiers who have signed acknowledgment on execution of habere, &c.

[1–80] 80.—It shall be lawful for the chairman of any county and he is hereby authorized to hear and determine by way of civil bill, within his jurisdiction, all disputes relating to the possession of lands or premises holden under any acknowledgment made upon the execution of any writ of habere or civil bill decree between the plaintiff in any action of ejectment or civil bill ejectment, or any person claiming under him, and any occupier who shall have signed such acknowledgment in the manner herein-after provided, or any person claiming or deriving under him, and to make an order or decree for the delivery of the possession of the said lands to the party entitled thereto; and the civil bill process therein shall be served upon every person in the actual possession of the lands claimed by such civil bill, and if there be no person in actual possession, then the same shall be served by affixing such civil bill on some conspicuous part of the premises and also on the usual place for posting notices in the nearest market town to the premises.

> **Note:** The Fourth Schedule (Ref. 29) to the Courts (Supplemental Provisions) Act 1961 states that the jurisdiction under s 80 of this Act is to be exercised by the Circuit Court by the judge of the circuit where the land or any part of the land is situate.

What to be deemed cottier tenancies under this Act.

[1–81] 81.—Where any landlord shall by any agreement or memorandum in writing let a tenement, wherever situate, consisting of a dwelling house or cottage without land, or with any portion of land not exceeding half an acre, statute measure, at a rent not exceeding the rate of five pounds by the year, for one month, or from month to month, or in like manner for any lesser period of time, and shall thereby undertake to keep and maintain the said dwelling house or cottage in tenantable condition and repair, such tenancy shall constitute and be deemed to be a cottier tenancy within the meaning of this Act, and shall be subject to the provisions hereafter contained in respect thereof.

Where cottier tenancy is determined by landlord, compensation to be made for crop, &c.

[1–82] 82.—In case any such tenancy shall be determined by notice to quit, served by the landlord, the said landlord shall pay to the tenant a fair compensation for any crops which he may be growing on the land belonging to such tenement, or any benefit accruing from the manuring of such land, to be recovered by civil bill process before the chairman of the county or riding in which the premises may be situate, which civil bill proceedings shall be subject to the same right of appeal as ordinary civil bill actions now are or hereafter shall be.

> **Note:** The Fourth Schedule (Ref. 29) to the Courts (Supplemental Provisions) Act 1961 states that the jurisdiction under s 82 of this Act is to be exercised by the Circuit Court by the judge of the circuit where the land or any part of the land is situate.

Cottier tenements to be repaired by the landlord.

83.—The landlord of such cottier tenement shall be bound to keep and maintain the dwelling house in tenantable condition and repair; and in case it shall be proved that the said dwelling house was, by the landlord's default, unfit for occupation by reason of the want of such repairs, no rent or compensation for the occupation of the said tenement during the time it shall continue in such state and condition shall be recoverable. [1–83]

Summary recovery of possession of tenements in case of wilful injury by tenants.

84.—In case any such cottier tenant or any tenant for a shorter period of time than a month, or at will, or by sufferance, shall maliciously or wilfully injure or destroy, or permit to be injured or destroyed, any part of the premises holden by him, and which the landlord is bound to keep in repair, it shall be lawful for the landlord to make his complaint before any one or more of the justices of the peace for the county, not being interested in the said premises, at petty sessions, and such justice or justices shall summon the tenant before him or them, and hear and determine such complaint; and if it shall be proved to his or their satisfaction that such tenant committed or permitted such injury or destruction upon the said premises, the said justice or justices shall, by their warrant in writing, direct any person to be therein named as special bailiff on the part of the landlord or owner; and such warrant shall be obeyed and executed by such special bailiff, who shall have full power and authority so to do. [1–84]

> **Note:** The jurisdiction of a justice of the peace is now exercised by the District Court — see s 77 of the Courts of Justice Act 1924.

Summary recovery of possession of cottier tenements for nonpayment of rent.

85.—In case of any gale of rent or compensation reserved or payable upon any such cottier tenement shall be in arrear for the space of forty days, it shall be lawful for the landlord of the premises to exhibit his complaint in respect thereof before a justice or justices of the peace in petty sessions, and to cause the said tenant to be served with a summons in writing, signed by a justice or justices having jurisdiction in the place in which the premises shall be situate, to appear before two or more justices at the petty session or other place in which such justices usually meet for the despatch of public business, to show cause why possession of the said premises should not be delivered up to his landlord, or his agent or receiver, and such justices, or any two or more of them, shall, in the presence of such tenant, or on proof of the service of the said summons on the said tenant personally, or by leaving a copy of the same at his usual place of abode, determine the matter; and if it shall appear to the said justices that at least one gale of such rent, over and above all just credits and allowances, and any valid set-off claimed by the tenant, is in arrear for the space of forty days aforesaid, the said justices shall cause their warrant to be prepared, directing possession of the said premises to be delivered to the landlord, and to be executed by any special bailiff therein named, and such warrant shall be obeyed and executed by such bailiff, who shall have full power and authority so to do. [1–85]

Note: The jurisdiction of a justice of the peace is now exercised by the District Court — see s 77 of the Courts of Justice Act 1924.

Summary recovery of possession of tenements overholden.

[1–86] 86.—In case the term or interest of any tenant in any such cottier tenement shall have ended, or shall have been duly determined by a notice to quit, and such tenant or any person by whom the premises or any part of them shall be then actually occupied shall neglect or refuse to deliver up the possession of the same, or in case any person shall have been put or shall be put into possession of any lands or premises by permission of the owner, as servant, herdsman, or caretaker, and shall refuse or omit to quit and deliver up the possession of the premises, on demand made by the owner thereof, or his known agent or receiver, it shall be lawful for the landlord or owner of the said premises, or his heirs, executors, or administrators, or his known agent or receiver, to cause the person so neglecting or refusing to quit or deliver up the possession to be served with a summons in writing, signed by a justice or justices not interested in the said premises, but having jurisdiction in the place in which the premises shall be situate, to appear before two or more justices at the petty sessions, town hall, or divisional justice room, or other place in which such justices usually meet for the despatch of public business of such city, town, district, or other place, to show cause why possession of the said premises should not be delivered up to such landlord or owner, or his agent or receiver as aforesaid; and if the said tenant or occupier shall not appear at the time and place appointed, or if such tenant or occupier shall appear and shall not show to the satisfaction of such justices reasonable cause why possession should not be given, and shall still neglect or refuse to deliver up possession of the said premises, or such part of them as was in his actual occupation at the time of the service of such summons, to the said landlord or owner, or his agent or receiver, it shall be lawful for such justices or any two or more of them, not interested as aforesaid, on proof being made before them of the holding or permissive possessions, as the case may be, and of its end or determination, and the time and manner thereof, and where the title of the landlord shall have accrued since the letting of the premises, the right by which he claims the possession, to issue a warrant under their hands and seals, to any person as a special bailiff in that behalf, on the part of the landlord or owner, requiring and authorizing him, within a period to be therein named, and not less than seven or more than fourteen clear days from the date of such warrant, to give the possession of the said premises to the said landlord, or his agent or receiver, and such warrant shall be a sufficient authority to the said bailiff to enter upon the said premises, with such assistants as he shall deem to be necessary, and to give possession accordingly: Provided that no entry shall be made under such warrant on any Sunday, Good Friday, or Christmas Day, or at any time except between the hours of nine in the morning and four in the afternoon: Provided also, that nothing herein contained shall prejudice or affect the right of any owner of property intrusted to the care of any servant or caretaker peaceably to resume the possession thereof without process of law, if he shall so think fit.

Note: The jurisdiction of a justice of the peace is now exercised by the District Court — see s 77 of the Courts of Justice Act 1924.

Service of the summons.

87.—Such summons as last aforesaid may be served either personally or by leaving the same with some person being in occupation of such house or part of a house or tenement, and where the tenant of such house or part of a house or tenement shall not reside therein, by serving the same personally or by leaving the same at the place of abode of the tenant so holding over as aforesaid four clear days before the day appointed for the hearing of the matter of the said summons: Provided that if the person so holding over cannot be found, and admission into the premises so overholden cannot be obtained, and the place of abode of such person shall not be known, the posting of such summons on some conspicuous part of the premises so holden over shall be deemed to be good service of such person. **[1–87]**

Stay of execution of warrant on undertaking to give possession in fourteen days, and pay rent, &c.

88.—If any tenant so summoned to give up possession shall appear before the said justices and give an undertaking (to be deemed in writing by the clerk of the court) quietly and peaceably to deliver up, within fourteen days from the date thereof, the possession of the premises of which he is such tenant or occupier, in good order and repair to the landlord, or his agent or receiver, and in the meantime to pay all rent and arrears claimed by such landlord in respect of such tenement, in such case the said justices shall not issue their warrant for giving up the possession until after the expiration of such period of fourteen days; and if the tenant shall at the expiration of such period continue in possession otherwise than by permission of the landlord, or his agent or receiver, it shall be lawful for such justices to issue their warrant for giving possession of the same forthwith, and such warrant shall be executed accordingly, without further notice to such tenant. **[1–88]**

> **Note:** The jurisdiction of a justice of the peace is now exercised by the District Court — see s 77 of the Courts of Justice Act 1924.

Irregularity in proceeding not to make landlord, &c., a trespasser.

89.—Where the landlord applying for such warrant has at the time of the granting of it some lawful right to the possession of the premises or of the part so holden over, the said landlord, or his agent or receiver, or other person acting on his behalf, shall not be deemed to be a trespasser by reason merely of any irregularity or informality in the mode of proceeding for obtaining possession under the authority of this Act, but the party aggrieved may bring an action for such irregularity or informality, in which the damages alleged to be sustained shall be specially laid and may, unless such party shall have tendered sufficient amends before the commencement of such action, recover therein full satisfaction for such special damage, with costs of suit; but in case such special damage laid as aforesaid be not proved, the defendant shall be entitled to a verdict, and in case the said plaintiff shall recover no greater sum than five shillings for such special damage, he shall be entitled to no greater sum for costs than the amount of the damages so recovered, unless the judge before whom the cause is tried shall certify on the back of the record that in his opinion full costs ought to be allowed. **[1–89]**

General provisions.

Costs may be awarded against one defendant in civil bill ejectment.

[1–90] 90.—The chairman, upon the hearing of any civil bill ejectment where there is more than one defendant, may, upon pronouncing his decree, order the costs of such proceedings to be paid by and recovered against any one or more of the defendants by name, and not against the other or others of them.

> **Note:** Under the Circuit Court Rules 2001, O 67, r 8 states that where the jurisdiction transferred to the Court under s 51 of the Courts of Justice Act 1924 (and thereafter established by s 4 of the Courts (Establishment and Constitution) Act 1961) depends upon statute, each such Statute is hereby adapted or modified so that all references therein to the Civil Bill Court, County Court, or Court of Quarter Sessions shall be construed to refer to the Court where necessary, and all references to Recorders, County Court Judges, Chairmen of Quarter Sessions, or other Judges, and to Officers of any such Courts shall be construed where necessary as references to the Judge of the Court, and, in the cases of Officers, to the County Registrar or appropriate Officer of the Court, and all references to proceedings in any of such Courts, shall, where necessary, be construed as references to proceedings in the Court.

Taxation of costs in civil bill ejectment.

[1–91] 91.—The chairman shall in all cases of civil bill ejectment under this Act, upon request of either party or his attorney, tax the costs between party and party, and include the same in his decree or dismiss, and shall, at the like request, tax the costs between attorney and client; and no costs shall be recovered in respect of any proceedings in ejectment in the court of the chairman, or preparatory thereto, unless the same shall have been taxed as aforesaid; and the said chairman may examine upon oath, which oath he is hereby authorized to administer, any attorney seeking to establish a charge against his client as to all matters necessary to ascertain the right to such costs.

> **Note:** Under the Circuit Court Rules 2001, O 67, r 8 states that where the jurisdiction transferred to the Court under s 51 of the Courts of Justice Act 1924 (and thereafter established by s 4 of the Courts (Establishment and Constitution) Act 1961) depends upon statute, each such Statute is hereby adapted or modified so that all references therein to the Civil Bill Court, County Court, or Court of Quarter Sessions shall be construed to refer to the Court where necessary, and all references to Recorders, County Court Judges, Chairmen of Quarter Sessions, or other Judges, and to Officers of any such Courts shall be construed where necessary as references to the Judge of the Court, and, in the cases of Officers, to the County Registrar or appropriate Officer of the Court, and all references to proceedings in any of such Courts, shall, where necessary, be construed as references to proceedings in the Court.

Sheriff to execute civil bill decree in ejectment.

[1–92] 92.—*Omitted. Repealed by the Civil Bill Courts (Ireland) Act 1864 (27 & 28 Vict. c. 99).*

Sheriff to appoint special bailiff, if required.

93.—*Omitted. Repealed by the Civil Bill Courts (Ireland) Act 1864 (27 & 28 Vict. c. 99).* [1–93]

Habere and decree may be executed without disturbing possession of under-tenants.

94.—The sheriff or his officer or bailiff may with the consent in writing of the plaintiff or his attorney, execute any writ of habere facias possessionem or civil bill decree for possession in ejectment, without removing from the possession of the lands or premises any under-tenant or occupier who shall at the time of such execution sign with his name or mark an attornment or acknowledgment, in or substantially according to the Forms No. 6 or No. 7 in the Schedule (A) to this Act annexed, attested by such sheriff, officer, or bailiff, which attornment or acknowledgment shall be annexed to such writ or decree, and a copy thereof given to the plaintiff or his attorney, and such execution shall be as valid as if such persons were not in occupation, or as if such writ or decree had been executed in common form of law. [1–94]

Renewal of writ after such partial execution.

95.—It shall be lawful for any plaintiff who shall have executed any such writ or decree as aforesaid without disturbing the possession of any under-tenant or occupier who shall have made such acknowledgment in the Form No. 7 aforesaid, and shall not have attorned as tenant in manner aforesaid, and for the heirs, executors, administrators, or assigns of such plaintiff, at any time within six calendar months after such execution of the writ or decree, on application to the chairman or court from which such writ or decree shall have issued, to obtain a renewal of the same, to be again executed at the cost of such plaintiff or his representative or assignee in common form of law, as to the whole or any part of the said lands, and such renewal shall be without prejudice to any right or interest vested in the said party by virtue of the first execution of the said writ or decree: Provided, however, that in case of an ejectment for nonpayment of rent no such renewal shall take place in case the tenant's interest in the lease or other contract of tenancy shall have been redeemed in the meantime. [1–95]

Note: The Fourth Schedule (Ref. 29) to the Courts (Supplemental Provisions) Act 1961 states that the jurisdiction under s 95 of this Act is to be exercised by the Circuit Court by the judge of the circuit where the land or any part of the land is situate.

Fresh execution of writ on justice's certificate.

96.—In any case in which any such writ or decree shall have been executed as last aforesaid, and any such former tenant or occupier shall, within the said period of six months from the date of such execution, without lawful authority, re-enter into or resume the possession of the said premises or any part of them, upon an application made to any justice of the peace of the county at petty sessions, and upon proof made before him to his satisfaction of the due service of a summons or notice of such intended application, and of the facts of such execution and unlawful re-entry, upon affidavit or on oath (which affidavit or oath such justice is hereby authorized to take or administer), it shall be lawful for such justice and he is hereby required to certify in writing under his hand that in his opinion in such case a sufficient cause had been shown for having the said writ or decree executed anew as to the part or parts of the premises of which the possession shall have been resumed as aforesaid, and upon the [1–96] production of such certificate on the part of the plaintiff in such action or civil bill, or his heir, executor, administrator, or assignee, the writ or decree shall be executed anew by the sheriff or his special bailiff as to the part or parts of which the possession shall have been resumed as aforesaid.

> **Note:** The jurisdiction of a justice of the peace is now exercised by the District Court — see s 77 of the Courts of Justice Act 1924.

Registry of decree in ejectment or order for restitution &c.

[1–97] 97.—The clerk of peace of the county in which any civil bill decree shall be made under this Act shall, on the application of any person interested, and on payment of a fee of two shillings and sixpence, enter in a book to be kept in his office for that purpose a memorandum of any judgment or decree in ejectment or order for restitution which shall be made under this Act, and also of any summary order for delivery of the possession of any lands or premises made by any justice or justices of the peace under this Act, and of the return of any sheriff of the execution of any habere, decree, or order, which entry shall specify the names of the plaintiff and defendant, and of the lands recovered, and the nature and date of the decree or order, and the date of the execution thereof.

> **Note:** The jurisdiction of a justice of the peace is now exercised by the District Court — see s 77 of the Courts of Justice Act 1924.

Where lands are situate in two or more counties, proceedings made be taken in either.

[1–98] 98.—In case any lands or premises respecting which any proceeding by way of civil bill shall be brought under this Act shall be situate partly in two or more counties, such proceeding by way of civil bill may be brought in any or either of them, and the sheriffs of the respective counties in which any part of such lands or premises shall be situate shall, so far as relates to the portion of the premises within their respective jurisdictions, execute such decree as may be made on delivery to each of them a copy of such decree, signed by the chairman who shall have made the same: Provided that where any lands shall be situate partly or wholly within a place which is a county of a city or county of a town of itself (except the County of the City of Dublin), the assistant barrister of the county at large and the justices of the peace of the said county at large shall have the same jurisdiction and exercise the like powers respecting such premises as if the same had been situate in the county at large.

> **Note:** Under the Circuit Court Rules 2001, O 67, r 8 states that where the jurisdiction transferred to the Court under s 51 of the Courts of Justice Act 1924 (and thereafter established by s 4 of the Courts (Establishment and Constitution) Act 1961) depends upon statute, each such Statute is hereby adapted or modified so that all references therein to the Civil Bill Court, County Court, or Court of Quarter Sessions shall be construed to refer to the Court where necessary, and all references to Recorders, County Court Judges, Chairmen of Quarter Sessions, or other Judges, and to Officers of any such Courts shall be construed where necessary as references to the Judge of the Court, and, in the cases of Officers, to the County Registrar or appropriate Officer of the Court, and all references to proceedings in any of such Courts, shall, where necessary, be construed as references to proceedings in the Court.

In s 70 of this Act the reference to assistant barrister is modified by the Fifth Schedule to the Courts (Supplemental Provisions) Act 1961. No such modification is expressly made in respect of s 98 of this Act.

The jurisdiction of a justice of the peace is now exercised by the District Court — see s 77 of the Courts of Justice Act 1924.

Where chairman interested, proceedings may be taken in an adjoining County.

99.—In any case in which the chairman of the county shall happen to be the landlord or tenant, or claim to be entitled to the possession of any lands or premises situate in any one or more than one county, and the same or any part thereof shall be situate within his own jurisdiction, and he or any other person shall be desirous to institute proceedings in respect of the said lands or premises under this Act on behalf of or against such chairman, such proceedings may be had in some adjacent county without the jurisdiction of the said chairman, or in the county in which the other part of the lands are situate; and the chairman of such adjacent county shall the like jurisdiction therein as if the said lands or the entire of them were situate in the said adjacent county, and an appeal shall lie therefrom in the like manner, and any decree or dismiss shall be executed by the sheriff of the county in which the lands are situate, as if it were a decree of the chairman of such county. **[1–99]**

Note: Under the Circuit Court Rules 2001, O.67, r.8 states that where the jurisdiction transferred to the Court under s 51 of the Courts of Justice Act 1924 (and thereafter established by s 4 of the Courts (Establishment and Constitution) Act 1961) depends upon statute, each such Statute is hereby adapted or modified so that all references therein to the Civil Bill Court, County Court, or Court of Quarter Sessions shall be construed to refer to the Court where necessary, and all references to Recorders, County Court Judges, Chairmen of Quarter Sessions, or other Judges, and to Officers of any such Courts shall be construed where necessary as references to the Judge of the Court, and, in the cases of Officers, to the County Registrar or appropriate Officer of the Court, and all references to proceedings in any of such Courts, shall, where necessary, be construed as references to proceedings in the Court.

No action against justice for granting warrant, &c.

100.—No action shall be brought or prosecuted against any justice or other person hereby authorized, by whom any precept or warrant shall be issued or certificate shall be granted, nor against any constable or bailiff by whom such precept or warrant may be executed under and by virtue of this Act, by reason that the person on whose application the same shall be granted had not lawful right to recover the rent or the possession of the premises therein mentioned, or to prohibit the act therein prohibited. **[1–100]**

Note: The jurisdiction of a justice of the peace is now exercised by the District Court — see s 77 of the Courts of Justice Act 1924.

Title to lands not to be drawn into question.

[1–101] 101.—The title to any lands or premises shall not be drawn into question in any proceeding by way of civil bill under this Act.

Technical errors not to defeat proceedings.

[1–102] 102.—No civil bill proceeding under this Act shall be defeated by reason of any technical objection whatsoever, or of any mistake, variance, or omission which is not manifestly calculated to mislead and injuriously prejudice the opposite party in the merits of his case.

Schedules to be part of the Act.

[1–103] 103.—The Schedules to this Act annexed shall be deemed and taken to be a part of this Act, and the forms therein contained, or any other forms to the like effect, may be used in the respective cases to which they are applicable.

Repeals of Acts and parts of Acts as in Schedule (B).

[1–104] 104.—From and after the commencement of this Act, the several Acts and parts of Acts set forth in the Schedule (B) to this Act annexed, so far as the same refer to the relation of landlord and tenant in Ireland, but not otherwise, and to the extent to which such Acts or parts of Acts are by such schedule expressed to be repealed, and not further or otherwise, shall be and are hereby repealed, except so far as may be necessary to support or enforce any lease made or contract entered into, or as to anything heretofore done, or any right acquired or liability incurred, and except so far as any of the said Acts or parts of Acts repeal any former Act or part of an Act [, and except so far as may be necessary for the purpose of supporting and continuing and proceedings heretofore taken or to be taken after the commencement of this Act upon any proceeding commenced before the commencement of this Act, and except as to the recovery and application of any penalty for any offence which shall have been committed before the commencement of this Act.]

Note: This section was amended by Statute Law Revision Act 1875 (38 & 39 Vict c.66), whereby the words in square brackets were deleted.

Commencement.

[1–105] 105.—This Act shall come into operation on the first day of January one thousand eight hundred and sixty-one.

Schedule A *Omitted.*

Schedule B *Omitted*.

Chapter 2

CONVEYANCING ACT, 1881

[Extracts]

(44 & 45 Vict. c.41)

AN ACT FOR SIMPLIFYING AND IMPROVING THE PRACTICE OF CONVEYANCING; AND FOR VESTING IN TRUSTEES, MORTGAGEES, AND OTHERS VARIOUS POWERS COMMONLY CONFERRED BY PROVISIONS INSERTED IN SETTLEMENTS, MORTGAGES, WILLS, AND OTHER INSTRUMENTS; AND FOR AMENDING IN VARIOUS PARTICULARS THE LAW OF PROPERTY; AND FOR OTHER PURPOSES.

[22ND AUGUST 1881]

BE IT ENACTED BY THE QUEEN'S MOST EXCELLENT MAJESTY, BY AND WITH THE ADVICE AND CONSENT OF THE LORDS SPIRITUAL AND TEMPORAL, AND COMMONS, IN THIS PRESENT PARLIAMENT ASSEMBLED, AND BY THE AUTHORITY OF THE SAME, AS FOLLOWS:

PART I – PRELIMINARY

Short title; commencement; extent.

1.—(1) This Act may be cited as the Conveyancing and Law of Property Act, 1881. **[2–01]**

(2) This Act shall commence and take effect from and immediately after the thirty-first day of December one thousand eight hundred and eighty-one.

(3) This Act does not extend to Scotland.

> **Note:** The short title of this Act may be further shortened to the Conveyancing Act 1881 — see s 16(4) of the Conveyancing Act 1911.

Interpretation of property, land, &c.

2.—In this Act— **[2–02]**

(i) Property, unless a contrary intention appears, includes real and personal property, and any estate or interest in any property, real or personal, and any debt, and any thing in action, and any other right or interest:

(ii) Land, unless a contrary intention appears, includes land of any tenure, and tenements and hereditaments, corporeal or incorporeal, and houses and other buildings, also an undivided share in land:

(iii) In relation to land, income includes rents and profits, and possession includes receipt of income:

(iv) Manor includes lordship, and reputed manor or lordship:

(v) Conveyance, unless a contrary intention appears, includes assignment, apportionment, lease, settlement, and other assurance, and covenant to surrender, made by deed, on a sale, mortgage, demise, or settlement of any property, or on any other dealing with or for any property; and convey, unless a contrary intention appears, has a meaning corresponding with that of conveyance:

(vi) Mortgage includes any charge on any property for securing money or money's worth; and mortgage money means money, or money's worth secured by a mortgage; and mortgagor includes any person from time to time deriving title under the original mortgagor, or entitled to redeem a mortgage, according to his estate, interest, or right, in the mortgaged property; and mortgagee includes any person from time to time deriving title under the original mortgage; and mortgagee in possession is, for the purposes of this Act, a mortgagee who, in right of the mortgage, has entered into and is in possession of the mortgaged property:

(vii) Incumbrance includes a mortgage in fee, or for a less estate, and a trust for securing money, and a lien, and a charge of a portion, annuity, or other capital or annual sum; and incumbrancer has a meaning corresponding with that of incumbrance, and includes every person entitled to the benefit of an incumbrance, or to require payment or discharge thereof:

(viii) Purchaser, unless a contrary intention appears, includes a lessee or mortgagee, and an intending purchaser, lessee, or mortgagee, or other person, who, for valuable consideration, takes or deals for any property; and purchase unless a contrary intention appears, has a meaning corresponding with that of purchaser; but sale means only a sale properly so called:

(ix) Rent includes yearly or other rent, toll, duty, royalty, or other reservation, by the acre, the ton, or otherwise; and fine includes premium or fore-gift, and any payment, consideration, or benefit in the nature of a fine, premium, or fore-gift:

(x) Building purposes include the erecting and the improving of, and the adding to, and the repairing of buildings; and a building lease is a lease for building purposes or purposes connected therewith:

(xi) A mining lease is a lease for mining purposes, that is, the searching for, winning, working, getting, making merchantable, carrying away, or disposing of mines and minerals, or purposes connected therewith, and includes a grant or licence for mining purposes:

(xii) Will includes codicil:

(xiii) Instrument includes deed, will, inclosure award, and Act of Parliament:

(xiv) Securities includes stocks, funds, and shares:

(xv) Bankruptcy includes liquidation by arrangement, and any other act or proceeding in law having, under any Act for the time being in force, effects or results similar to those of bankruptcy; and bankrupt has a meaning corresponding with that of bankruptcy:

(xvi) Writing includes print; and words referring to any instrument, copy, extract, abstract, or other document being in writing or in print, or partly in writing and partly in print:

(xvii) Person includes a corporation:

(xviii) Her Majesty's High Court [of Justice] is referred to as the Court.

Note: The expression "mortgagor" in para (vi) does not include an incumbrancer deriving title under the original mortgagor for the purposes of s 18(1) of this Act or s 3 of the Conveyancing Act 1911 — see s 3(10) of the 1911 Act.

The words "of Justice" in square brackets were originally contained in s 2(xviii) in parenthesis to High Court, but were repealed by the Statute Law Revision Act 1898. However, note s 72 of this Act provides for certain modifications in the application of this Act to Ireland; by virtue of s 72(2) the "High Court [of Justice]" in Ireland shall mean the High Court [of Justice] in Ireland. Presumably the words "of justice" also fall in the modification made by s 72(2) by reason of the amendment made by the Statute Law Revision Act 1898.

PART II – SALES AND OTHER TRANSACTIONS

Omitted.

PART III – LEASES

Rent and benefit of lessee's covenants to run with reversion.

10.—(1) Rent reserved by a lease, and the benefit of every covenant or provision therein contained, having reference to the subject-matter thereof, and on the lessee's part to be observed or performed, and every condition of re-entry and other condition therein contained, shall be annexed and incident to and shall go with the reversionary estate in the land, or in any part thereof, immediately expectant on the term granted by the lease, notwithstanding severance of that reversionary estate, and shall be capable of being recovered, received, enforced, and taken advantage of by the person from time to time entitled, subject to the term, to the income of the whole or any part, as the case may require, of the land leased. [2–03]

(2) This section applies only to leases made after the commencement of this Act.

Note: This Act commenced on 31st December 1881 — see s 1(2) of this Act. The application of this section was extended by s 2(1) of the Conveyancing Act 1911.

Obligation of lessor's covenants to run with reversion.

11.—(1) The obligation of a covenant entered into by a lessor with reference to the subject-matter of the lease shall, if and as far as the lessor has power to bind the reversionary estate immediately expectant on the term granted by the lease, be annexed and incident to and shall go with that reversionary estate, or the several parts thereof, notwithstanding severance of that reversionary estate, and may be taken advantage of and enforced by the person in whom the term is from time to time vested by conveyance, devolution in law, or otherwise; and, if and as far as the lessor has power to bind the person from time to time entitled to that reversionary estate, the obligation aforesaid may be taken advantage of and enforced against any person so entitled. [2–04]

(2) This section applies only to leases made after the commencement of this Act.

> **Note:** This Act commenced on 31st December 1881 — see s 1(2) of this Act.

Apportionment of conditions on severance, &c.

[2–05] 12.—(1) Notwithstanding the severance by conveyance, surrender, or otherwise, of the reversionary estate in any land comprised in a lease, and notwithstanding the avoidance or cesser in any other manner of the term granted by a lease as to part only of the land comprised therein, every condition or right of re-entry, and every other condition, contained in the lease, shall be apportioned, and shall remain annexed to the severed parts of the reversionary estate as severed, and shall be in force with respect to the term whereon each severed part is reversionary, or the term in any land which has not been surrendered, or as to which the term has not been avoided or has not otherwise ceased, in like manner as if the land comprised in each severed part, or the land as to which the term remains subsisting, as the case may be, had alone originally been comprised in the lease.

(2) This section only applies to leases made after the commencement of this Act.

> **Note:** This Act commenced on 31st December 1881 — see s 1(2) of this Act.

On sub-demise, title to leasehold reversion not to be required.

[2–06] 13.—(1) On a contract to grant a lease for a term of years to be derived out of a leasehold interest, with a leasehold reversion, the intended lessee shall not have the right to call for the title to that reversion.

(2) This section applies only if and as far as a contrary intention is not expressed in the contract, and shall have effect subject to the terms of the contract and to the provisions therein contained.

(3) This section applies only to contracts made after the commencement of this Act.

> **Note:** This Act commenced on 31st December 1881—see s 1(2) of this Act.

Forfeiture

Restrictions on and relief against forfeiture of leases.

[2–07] 14.—(1) A right of re-entry or forfeiture under any proviso or stipulation in a lease, for breach of any covenant or condition in the lease, shall not be enforceable, by action or otherwise, unless and until the lessor serves on the lessee a notice specifying the particular breach complained of and, if the breach is capable of remedy, requiring the lessee to remedy the breach, and, in any case, requiring the lessee to make compensation in money for the breach, and the lessee fails, within a reasonable time thereafter, to remedy the breach, if it is capable of remedy, and to make reasonable compensation in money, to the satisfaction of the lessor, for the breach.

(2) Where a lessor is proceeding, by action or otherwise, to enforce such a right of re-entry or forfeiture, the lessee may, in the lessor's action, if any, or in any action brought by himself, apply to the Court for relief; and the Court may grant or refuse relief, as the Court, having regard to the proceedings and conduct of the parties under the foregoing provisions of this section, and to all the other circumstances, thinks fit; and in case of relief may grant it on such terms, if any, as to costs, expenses, damages, compensation, penalty, or otherwise, including the granting of an injunction to restrain any like breach in the future, as the Court, in the circumstances of each case, thinks fit.

(3) For the purposes of this section a lease includes an original or derivative under-lease, also a grant at a fee farm rent, or securing a rent by condition; and a lessee includes an original or derivative under-lessee, and the heirs, executors, administrators, and assigns of a lessee, also a grantee under such a grant as aforesaid, his heirs and assigns; and a lessor includes an original or derivative under-lessor, and the heirs, executors, administrators, and assigns of a lessor, also a grantor as aforesaid, and his heirs and assigns.

(4) This section applies although the proviso or stipulation under which the right of re-entry or forfeiture accrues is inserted in the lease in pursuance of the directions of any Act of Parliament.

(5) For the purposes of this section a lease limited to continue as long only as the lessee abstains from committing a breach of covenant shall be and take effect as a lease to continue for any longer term for which it could subsist, but determinable by a proviso for re-entry on such a breach.

(6) This section does not extend—

(i) [To a covenant or condition against the assigning, under-letting, parting with possession, or disposing of the land leased; or] to a condition for forteiture on the bankruptcy of the lessee, or on the taking in execution of the lessee's interest; or

Note: The words in square brackets in s 14(6)(i) were repealed by s 35(1) of the Landlord and Tenant (Ground Rents) Act, 1967 which Act came into force on 1st March 1967.

(ii) In case of a mining lease, to a covenant or condition for allowing the lessor to have access to or inspect books, accounts, records, weighing machines or other things, or to enter or inspect the mine or workings thereof.

Note: Section 2(2) of the Conveyancing and Law of Property Act, 1892 states that s 14(6) of this Act applies to a condition for forfeiture on bankruptcy of the lessee, or on taking in execution of the lessee's interest only after the expiration of one year from the date of the bankruptcy, or taking in execution, and provided the lessee's interest be sold within such one year, but in case the lessee's interest be sold within such one year, s14(6) of this Act shall cease to be applicable thereto. Certain qualifications to this application appear in s 2(3) of the 1892 Act.

(7) *Omitted. Repealed by the Statute Law Revision Act 1894.*

(8) This section shall not affect the law relating to re-entry or forfeiture or relief in case of non-payment of rent.

(9) This section applies to leases made either before or after the commencement of this Act, and shall have effect notwithstanding any stipulation to the contrary.

Note: Section 5 of the Conveyancing and Law of Property Act 1892 extends the definition of "lease" in this section as including an agreement for a lease where the lessee has become entitled to have his lease granted, and the definition of "under-lease" is also extended to include an agreement for an under-lease where the under-lessee has become entitled to have his under-lease granted.

Section 14 of this Act does not apply to a dwelling to which the Residential Tenancies Act 2004 applies — see s 193(b) of the 2004 Act.

PART IV – MORTGAGES

Ss. 15 to 17 Omitted.

Leases

Leasing powers of mortgagor and of mortgagee in possession.

[2–08] 18.—(1) A mortgagor of land while in possession shall, as against every incumbrancer, have, by virtue of this Act, power to make from time to time any such lease of the mortgaged land, or any part thereof, as is in this section described and authorized.

(2) A mortgagee of land while in possession shall, as against all prior incumbrancers, if any, and as against the mortgagor, have by virtue of this Act, power to make from time to time any such lease as aforesaid.

(3) The leases which this section authorizes are—

(i) An agricultural or occupation lease for any term not exceeding twenty-one years; and

(ii) A building lease for any term not exceeding ninety-nine years.

(4) Every person making a lease under this section may execute and do all assurances and things necessary or proper in that behalf.

(5) Every such lease shall be made to take effect in possession not later than twelve months after its date.

(6) Every such lease shall reserve the best rent that can reasonably be obtained, regard being had to the circumstances of the case, but without any fine being taken.

(7) Every such lease shall contain a covenant by the lessee for payment of the rent, and a condition of re-entry on the rent not being paid within a time therein specified not exceeding thirty days.

(8) A counterpart of every such lease shall be executed by the lessee and delivered to the lessor, of which execution and delivery the execution of the lease by the lessor shall, in favour of the lessee and all persons deriving title under him, be sufficient evidence.

(9) Every such building lease shall be made in consideration of the lessee, or some person by whose direction the lease is granted, having erected, or agreeing to erect within not more than five years from the date of the lease, buildings, new or additional, or having improved or repaired buildings, or agreeing to improve or repair

buildings within that time, or having executed, or agreeing to execute, within that time, on the land leased, an improvement for or in connexion with building purposes.

(10) In any such building lease a peppercorn rent, or a nominal or other rent less than the rent ultimately payable, may be made payable for the first five years, or any less part of the term.

(11) In case of a lease by the mortgagor, he shall, within one month after making the lease, deliver to the mortgagee, or, where there are more than one, to the mortgagee first in priority, a counterpart of the lease duly executed by the lessee; but the lessee shall not be concerned to see that this provision is complied with.

(12) A contract to make or accept a lease under this section may be enforced by or against every person on whom the lease if granted would be binding.

(13) This section applies only if and as far as a contrary intention is not expressed by the mortgagor and mortgagee in the mortgage deed, or otherwise in writing, and shall have effect subject to the terms of the mortgage deed or of any such writing and to the provisions therein contained.

(14) Nothing in this Act shall prevent the mortgage deed from reserving to or conferring on the mortgagor or the mortgagee, or both, any further or other powers of leasing or having reference to leasing; and any further or other powers so reserved or conferred shall be exerciseable, as far as may be, as if they were conferred by this Act, and with all the like incidents, effects, and consequences, unless a contrary intention is expressed in the mortgage deed.

(15) Nothing in this Act shall be construed to enable a mortgagor or mortgagee to make a lease for any longer term or on any other conditions than such as could have been granted or imposed by the mortgagor, with the concurrence of all the incumbrancers, if this Act had not been passed.

(16) This section applies only in case of a mortgage made after the commencement of this Act; but the provisions thereof, or any of them, may by agreement in writing made after the commencement of this Act, between mortgagor and mortgagee, be applied to a mortgage made before the commencement of this Act, so, nevertheless, that any such agreement shall not prejudicially affect any right or interest of any mortgagee not joining in or adopting the agreement.

(17) The provisions of this section referring to a lease shall be construed to extend and apply, as far as circumstances admit, to any letting, and to an agreement, whether in writing or not, for leasing or letting.

Ss. 19 to 26 Omitted.

PART V – STATUTORY MORTGAGE

Omitted.

PART VI – TRUST AND MORTGAGE ESTATES ON DEATH

Omitted.

PART VII – TRUSTEES AND EXECUTORS

Omitted. Repealed by Trustee Act 1893.

PART VIII – MARRIED WOMEN

Omitted.

PART IX – INFANTS

Omitted.

PART X – RENTCHARGES AND OTHER ANNUAL SUMS

Omitted.

PART XI – POWERS OF ATTORNEY

Omitted.

PART XII – CONSTRUCTION AND EFFECT OF DEEDS AND OTHER INSTRUMENTS

Omitted.

PART XIII – LONG TERMS

Enlargement of residue of long term into fee simple.

[2–09] 65.—(1) Where a residue unexpired of not less than two hundred years of a term which, as originally created, was for not less than three hundred years, is subsisting in land, whether being the whole land originally comprised in the term, or part only thereof, without any trust or right of redemption affecting the term in favour of the freeholder, or other person entitled in reversion expectant on the term, and without any rent, or with merely a peppercorn rent or other rent having no money value, incident to the reversion, or having had a rent, not being merely a peppercorn rent or other rent having no money value, originally so incident, which subsequently has been released, or has become barred by lapse of time, or has in any other way ceased to be payable, then the term may be enlarged into a fee simple in the manner, and subject to the restrictions, in this section provided.

(2) Each of the following persons (namely):

(i) Any person beneficially entitled in right of the term whether subject to any incumbrance or not, to possession of any land comprised in the term; [but, in case of a married woman, with the concurrence of her husband, unless she is entitled for her separate use, whether with restraint on anticipation or not, and then without his concurrence;]

(ii) Any person being in receipt of income as trustee, in right of the term, or having the term vested in him in trust for sale, whether subject to any incumbrance or not;

(iii) Any person in whom, as personal representative of any deceased person, the term is vested, whether subject to any incumbrance or not;

shall as far as regards the land to which he is entitled, or in which he in interested, in right of the term, in any such character as aforesaid, have power by deed to declare to the effect that, from and after the execution of the deed, the term shall be enlarged into a fee simple.

> **Amendment history:** The words in square brackets in subs 2 were repealed by the Married Women's Status Act 1957.

(3) Thereupon, by virtue of the deed and of this Act, the term shall become and be enlarged accordingly, and the person in whom the term was previously vested shall acquire and have in the land a fee simple instead of the term.

(4) The estate in fee simple so acquired by enlargement shall be subject to the same trusts, powers, executory limitations over, rights, and equities, and to all the same covenants and provisions relating to user and enjoyment, and to all the same obligations of every kind, as the term would have been subject to if it had not been so enlarged.

(5) But where any land so held for the residue of a term has been settled in trust by reference to other land, being freehold land, so as to go along with that other land as far as the law permits, and, at the time of enlargement, the ultimate beneficial interest in the term, whether subject to any subsisting particular estate or not, has become absolutely and indefeasibly vested in any person, then the estate in fee simple acquired as aforesaid shall, without prejudice to any conveyance for value previously made by a person having a contingent or defeasible interest in the term, be liable to be, and shall be, conveyed and settled in like manner as the other land, being freehold land, aforesaid, and until so conveyed and settled shall devolve beneficially as if it had been so conveyed and settled.

(6) The estate in fee simple so acquired shall, whether the term was originally created without impeachment of waste or not, include the fee simple in all mines and minerals which at the time of enlargement have not been severed in right, or in fact, or have not been severed or reserved by inclosure Act or award.

(7) This section applies to every such term as aforesaid subsisting at or after the commencement of this Act.

> **Note:** This Act commenced on 31st December 1881 — see s 1(2) of this Act.

> **Amendment history:** s 11 of the Conveyancing Act 1882 extends s 65 of this Act to apply to and include, and to have always applied to and included, every such term as mentioned in that section, whether having as the immediate reversion thereon the freehold or not; but not—
>
> (i) Any term liable to be determined by re-entry for condition broken; or
>
> (ii) Any term created by sub-demise out of a superior term, itself incapable of being enlarged into a fee simple.

PART XIV – ADOPTION OF ACT

Omitted.

PART XV – MISCELLANEOUS

Regulations respecting notice.

[2–10] 67.—(1) Any notice required or authorized by this Act to be served shall be in writing.

(2) Any notice required or authorized by this Act to be served on a lessee or mortgagor shall be sufficient, although only addressed to the lessee or mortgagor by that designation, without his name, or generally to the persons interested, without any name, and notwithstanding that any person to be affected by the notice is absent, under disability, unborn, or unascertained.

(3) Any notice required or authorized by this Act to be served shall be sufficiently served if it is left at the last-known place of abode or business in the United Kingdom of the lessee, lessor, mortgagee, mortgagor, or other person to be served, or, in case of a notice required or authorized to be served on a lessee or mortgagor, is affixed or left for him on the land or any house or building comprised in the lease or mortgage, or, in the case of a mining lease, is left for the lessee at the office or counting-house of the mine.

(4) Any notice required or authorized by this Act to be served shall also be sufficiently served, if it is sent by post in a registered letter addressed to the lessee, lessor, mortgagee, mortgagor, or other person to be served, by name, at the aforesaid place of abode or business, office, or counting-house, and if that letter is not returned through the post office as undelivered; and that service shall be deemed to be made at the time at which the registered letter would in the ordinary course be delivered.

(5) This section does not apply to notices served in proceedings in the Court.

Short title of 5 & 6 Will. 4 c.62.

68.—*Omitted. Repealed by the Statute Law Revision Act 1894.*

PART XVI – COURT; PROCEDURE; ORDERS

Omitted.

PART XVII – REPEALS

Omitted. Repealed by Statute Law Revision Act 1894.

PART XVIII – IRELAND

Modifications respecting Ireland.

[2–11] 72.—(1) In the application of this Act to Ireland the foregoing provisions shall be modified as in this section provided.

(2) The Court shall be Her Majesty's High Court [of Justice] in Ireland.

> **Note:** The words "of Justice" were originally contained in s 72(2) in parenthesis to "High Court" but were repealed by the Statute Law Revision Act 1898.

(3) All matters within the jurisdiction of the Court shall, subject to the Acts regulating that Court, be assigned to the Chancery Division of that Court; but

General Rules under this Act may direct that any of those matters be assigned to the Land Judges of that Division.

(4) The proper office of the Supreme Court [of Judicature] in Ireland shall be substituted for the central office of the Supreme Court [of Judicature].

Note: The words "of Judicature" were originally contained in s 72(4) in parenthesis to "Supreme Court" but were repealed by the Statute Law Revision Act 1894.

Under s 17 of the Courts of Justice Act 1924 the jurisdiction of the High Court of the Supreme Court of Judicature in Ireland or any division or judge thereof was transferred to the High Court.

(5) General rules for purposes of this Act for Ireland shall be deemed Rules of Court within the Supreme Court of Judicature Act (Ireland), 1877, and may be made accordingly at any time [after the passing of this Act, to take effect on or after the commencement of this Act].

Note: The words in square brackets s 72(5) were repealed by the Statute Law Revision Act 1898.

Death of bare trustee intestate, &c.

73.—*Omitted. Repeals sections 5 and 7 of the Vendor and Purchaser 1874.*

SCHEDULES

Omitted.

Chapter 3

CONVEYANCING ACT, 1882

[Extracts]

(45 & 46 Vict. c.39)

AN ACT FOR FURTHER IMPROVING THE PRACTICE OF CONVEYANCING AND FOR OTHER PURPOSES.

[10TH AUGUST 1882]

BE IT ENACTED BY THE QUEEN'S MOST EXCELLENT MAJESTY, BY AND WITH THE ADVICE AND CONSENT OF THE LORDS SPIRITUAL AND TEMPORAL, AND COMMONS, IN THIS PRESENT PARLIAMENT ASSEMBLED, AND BY THE AUTHORITY OF THE SAME, AS FOLLOWS:

PRELIMINARY

Short titles; commencement; extent; interpretation.

1.—(1) This Act may be cited as the Conveyancing Act, 1882; and the Conveyancing and Law of Property Act, 1881 (in this Act referred to as the Conveyancing Act of 1881) and this Act may be cited together as the Conveyancing Acts, 1881, 1882. **[3–01]**

(2) This Act, except where it is otherwise expressed, shall commence and take effect from and immediately after the thirty-first day of December one thousand eight hundred and eighty-two, which time is in this Act referred to as the commencement of this Act.

(3) This Act does not extend to Scotland.

(4) In this Act and in the Schedule thereto—

(i) Property includes real and personal property, and any debt, and any thing in action, and any other right or interest in the nature of property, whether in possession or not;

(ii) Purchaser includes a lessee or mortgagee, or an intending purchaser, lessee, or mortgagee, or other person, who, for valuable consideration, takes or deals for property, and purchase has a meaning corresponding with that of purchaser.

(iii) *Omitted. Amends the short title of the Fines and Recoveries Act 1833 and the Fines and Recoveries (Ireland) Act 1834.*

SEARCHES

Omitted.

NOTICE

Omitted.

LEASES

Contract for lease not part of title to lease.

[3–02] 4.—(1) Where a lease is made under a power contained in a settlement, will, Act of Parliament, or other instrument, any preliminary contract for or relating to the lease shall not, for the purpose of the deduction of title to an intended assign, form part of the title, or evidence of the title, to the lease.

(2) This section applies to leases made either before or after the commencement of this Act.

POWERS

Omitted.

MARRIED WOMEN

Omitted.

POWERS OF ATTORNEY

Omitted.

EXECUTORY LIMITATIONS

Omitted.

LONG TERMS

Amendment of enactment respecting long terms.

[3–03] 11.—Section sixty five of the Conveyancing Act of 1881 shall apply to and include, and shall be deemed to have always applied to and included, every such term as in that section mentioned, whether having as the immediate reversion thereon the freehold or not; but not—

(i) Any term liable to be determined by re-entry for condition broken; or

(ii) Any term created by sub-demise out of a superior term, itself incapable of being enlarged into a fee simple.

MORTGAGES

Omitted.

Chapter 4

CONVEYANCING AND LAW OF PROPERTY ACT, 1892

[Extracts]

(55 & 56 Vict. c.13)

AN ACT TO AMEND THE CONVEYANCING AND LAW OF PROPERTY ACT, 1881.

[20TH JUNE 1892]

BE IT ENACTED BY THE QUEEN'S MOST EXCELLENT MAJESTY, AND BY AND WITH THE ADVICE AND CONSENT OF THE LORDS SPIRITUAL AND TEMPORAL, AND COMMONS, IN THIS PRESENT PARLIAMENT ASSEMBLED, AND BY AUTHORITY OF THE SAME, AS FOLLOWS:

PRELIMINARY

Short title and extent.

1.—(1) This Act may be cited as the Conveyancing and Law of Property Act, 1892 and the Conveyancing and Law of Property Act, 1881, and the Conveyancing Act, 1882, and this Act shall be read together and may be cited together as the Conveyancing Acts, 1881, 1882, and 1892. [4–01]

(2) This Act does not extend to Scotland.

> **Note:** The Acts of 1881, 1882, 1892 and 1911 may together be cited as the Conveyancing Acts, 1881 to 1911 — see s 16(3) of the Conveyancing Act 1911.

LEASES, UNDER-LEASES, FORFEITURE

Costs of waiver, and forfeiture in case of bankruptcy or execution.

2.—(1) A lessor shall be entitled to recover as a debt due to him from a lessee, and in addition to damages (if any) all reasonable costs and expenses properly incurred by the lessor in the employment of a solicitor and surveyor or valuer, or otherwise, in reference to any breach giving rise to a right of re-entry of forfeiture which, at the request of the lessee, is waived by the lessor by writing under his hand or from which the lessee is relieved, under the provisions of the Conveyancing and Law of Property Act, 1881, or of this Act. [4–02]

(2) Sub-section six of section fourteen of the Conveyancing and Law of Property Act, 1881, is to apply to a condition for forfeiture on bankruptcy of the lessee, or on taking in execution of the lessee's interest only after the expiration of one year from

the date of the bankruptcy, or taking in execution, and provided the lessee's interest be not sold within such one year, but in case the lessee's interest be sold within such one year, sub-section six shall cease to be applicable thereto.

(3) Sub-section two of this section is not to apply to any lease of—

(a) Agricultural or pastoral land:

(b) Mines or minerals:

(c) A house intended to be used as a public-house or beershop:

(d) A house let as a dwelling-house, with the use of any furniture, books, works of art, or other chattels not being in the nature of fixtures:

(e) Any property with respect to which the personal qualifications of the tenant are of importance for the preservation of the value or character of the property, or on the ground of neighbourhood of the lessor, or to any person holding under him.

Note: This section does not apply to a dwelling to which the Residential Tenancies Act 2004 applies — see s 193(c) of the 2004 Act.

No fine to be exacted for licence to assign.

[4–03] 3.—In all leases containing a covenant, condition, or agreement against assigning, underletting, or parting with the possession, or disposing of the land or property leased without licence or consent, such covenant, condition, or agreement shall, unless the lease contains an expressed provision to the contrary, be deemed to be subject to a proviso to the effect that no fine or sum of money in the nature of a fine shall be payable for or in respect of such licence or consent; but this proviso shall not preclude the right to require the payment of a reasonable sum in respect of any legal or other expense incurred in relation to such licence or consent.

Note: This section does not apply to a dwelling to which the Residential Tenancies Act 2004 applies — see s 193(c) of the 2004 Act.

Power of Court to protect under-lessees on forfeiture of superior leases.

[4–04] 4.—Where a lessor is proceeding by action or otherwise to enforce a right of re-entry or forfeiture under any covenant, proviso, or stipulation in a lease, the Court may, on application by any person claiming as under-lessee any estate or interest in the property comprised in the lease or any part thereof either in the lessor's action (if any) or in any action brought by such person for that purpose, make an order vesting for the whole term of the lease or any less term the property comprised in the lease or any part thereof in any person entitled as under-lessee to any estate or interest in such property upon such conditions, as to execution of any deed or other document, payment of rent, costs, expenses, damages, compensation, giving security, or otherwise, as the Court in the circumstances of each case shall think fit, but in no case shall any such under-lessee be entitled to require a lease to be granted to him for any longer term than he had under his original sub-lease.

Note: This section does not apply to a dwelling to which the Residential Tenancies Act 2004 applies — see s 193(c) of the 2004 Act.

Extension of definitions of "lease", "under-lease", and "under-lessee".

5.— In section fourteen of the Conveyancing and Law of Property Act, 1881, as amended by this Act, and in this Act, "lease" shall also include an agreement for a lease where the lessee has become entitled to have his lease granted, and "under-lease" shall also include an agreement for an under-lease where the under-lessee has become entitled to have his under-lease granted, and in this Act "under-lessee" shall include any person deriving title under or from an under-lessee. **[4–05]**

TRUSTEES

Omitted.

Chapter 5

CONVEYANCING ACT, 1911

[Extracts]

(1 & 2 Geo. 5, c.37)

AN ACT TO AMEND THE CONVEYANCING AND LAW OF PROPERTY ACT, 1881.

[16TH DECEMBER 1911]

BE IT ENACTED BY THE KING'S MOST EXCELLENT MAJESTY, BY AND WITH THE ADVICE AND CONSENT OF THE LORDS SPIRITUAL AND TEMPORAL, AND COMMONS, IN THIS PRESENT PARLIAMENT ASSEMBLED, AND BY THE AUTHORITY OF THE SAME, AS FOLLOWS:

Discharge of incumbrances by the court.

1.—*Omitted.* **[5–01]**

Benefit of condition already broken to run with reversion.

2.—(1) Section ten of the Act of 1881 shall apply to the benefit of every condition of re-entry or forfeiture for a breach of any covenant or condition contained in a lease, so as to enable the same to be enforced and taken advantage of by the person from time to time entitled, subject to the term, to the income of the whole or any part, as the case may require, of the land leased, although that person became, by conveyance or otherwise, so entitled after the condition of re-entry or forfeiture had become enforceable, provided that he became so entitled as aforesaid after the commencement of this Act. **[5–02]**

(2) This section shall not render enforceable any condition of re-entry or other condition waived or released before the person became entitled as aforesaid.

Powers (with a view to the grant of an authorised lease) for mortgagor and mortgagee in possession to accept surrenders of leases.

3.—(1) For the purpose only of enabling a lease, authorised under section eighteen of the Act of 1881, as varied by this section, or under any agreement made pursuant to section eighteen aforesaid, or by the mortgage deed (in this section referred to as an authorised lease) to be granted, a mortgagor of land while in possession shall, in like manner as if the legal estate were vested in him and as against every incumbrancer, have, by virtue of this Act, power to accept from time to time a surrender of any lease of the mortgaged land or any part thereof comprised in the lease, with or without an exception of all or any of the mines and minerals, or any of them, and, on a surrender of part only of the land or mines and minerals leased, the rent may be apportioned. **[5–03]**

(2) For the same purpose, a mortgagee of land while in possession shall, in like manner, and as against all prior or other incumbrancers, if any, and as against the mortgagor, have, by virtue of this Act, power to accept from time to time any such surrender as aforesaid.

(3) On a surrender of part only of the land or mines and minerals leased, the original lease may be varied, provided that the lease when varied would have been valid as an authorised lease if granted by the person accepting the surrender; and, on a surrender and the making of a new or other lease, whether for the same or for any extended or other term, and whether subject or not to the same or to any other covenants, provisions, or conditions, the value of the lessee's interest in the lease surrendered may, subject to the provisions of this section, be taken into account in the determination of the amount of the rent to be reserved, and of the nature of the covenants, provisions, and conditions to be inserted in the new or other lease.

(4) Nothing in this section shall, where any consideration (except an agreement to accept an authorised lease) for the surrender is given by or on behalf of the lessee or on behalf of the person accepting the surrender, authorise a surrender to a mortgagor without the consent of the incumbrancers, or authorise a surrender to a second or subsequent incumbrancer without the consent of any prior incumbrancer.

(5) No surrender shall, by virtue of this section, be rendered valid unless:—

(a) An authorised lease is granted of the whole of the land or mines and minerals comprised in the surrender to take effect in possession immediately or within one month after the date of the surrender; and

(b) The term certain or interest granted by the new lease is not less in duration than the unexpired term or interest which would have been subsisting under the original lease if that lease had not been surrendered; and

(c) Where the whole of the land, mines and minerals originally leased has been surrendered, the rent reserved by the new lease is not less than the rent which would have been payable under the original lease if it had not been surrendered; or where part only of the land or mines and minerals has been surrendered, the aggregate rents respectively remaining payable or reserved under the original lease and the new lease are not less than the rent which would have been payable under the original lease if no partial surrender had been accepted.

(6) A contract to make or accept a surrender under this section may be enforced by or against every person on whom the surrender, if completed, would be binding.

(7) Subsections (13) (16) and (17) of section eighteen of the Act of 1881 shall have effect as if they were re-enacted in this section and references to the commencement of that Act shall, for the purposes of this section, be read as references to the commencement of this Act.

(8) Nothing in this section shall prevent the mortgage deed from reserving to or conferring on the mortgagor or mortgagee, or both, any further or other powers relating to the surrender of leases; and any further or other powers so conferred or reserved shall be exerciseable, as far as may be, as if they were conferred by this Act, and with the like results, unless a contrary intention is expressed in the mortgage deed.

(9) Nothing in this section shall operate to enable a mortgagor or mortgagee to accept a surrender which could not have been accepted by the mortgagor, with the concurrence of all the incumbrancers, if this Act had not been passed.

(10) For the purposes of this section, and of subsection (1) of section eighteen of the Act of 1881, the expression "mortgagor" does not include an incumbrancer deriving title under the original mortgagor.

(11) The powers of leasing and of accepting surrenders respectively conferred by section eighteen of the Act of 1881, and this section, shall, after a receiver of the

income of the mortgaged property or any part thereof has been appointed by a mortgagee, under that Act, and so long as the receiver acts, be exerciseable by such mortgagee instead of by the mortgagor, as respects any land affected by the receivership, in like manner as if such mortgagee were in possession of the land.

Ss. 4 to 15. Omitted.

Short title, commencement, and construction.

16.—(1) This Act may be cited as the Conveyancing Act, 1911. [5–05]

(2) This Act shall come into operation on the first day of January one thousand nine hundred and twelve.

(3) This Act and the Conveyancing Acts, 1881 to 1892, shall be construed together, and may be cited together as the Conveyancing Acts, 1881 to 1911.

(4) In this Act the Conveyancing and Law of Property Act, 1881, is referred to as the Act of 1881 and that Act may be cited as the Conveyancing Act, 1881.

Chapter 6

LANDLORD AND TENANT (GROUND RENTS) ACT, 1967

(1967, No. 3)

AN ACT TO PROVIDE FOR THE EXTINGUISHING OF CERTAIN RENTS BY ENABLING LESSEES AND TENANTS LIABLE TO PAY SUCH RENTS IN RESPECT OF LAND TO PURCHASE THE FEE SIMPLE IN THE LAND, TO PROVIDE FOR THE APPORTIONMENT OF CERTAIN RENTS, TO MAKE PROVISION IN RELATION TO THE WAIVER AND RELAXATION OF CERTAIN RESTRICTIVE COVENANTS IN LEASES, TO AMEND IN OTHER RESPECTS THE LAW OF LANDLORD AND TENANT AND TO PROVIDE FOR OTHER MATTERS CONNECTED WITH THE MATTERS AFORESAID.
[22ND FEBRUARY 1967]

BE IT ENACTED BY THE OIREACHTAS AS FOLLOWS:—

Commencement.

1.—This Act shall come into operation on such day as may be appointed by order of the Minister. [6–01]

> **Note:** This Act commenced on 1st March 1967 — see Landlord and Tenant (Ground Rents) Act, 1967 Commencement Order, 1967 (SI No 42 of 1967).

Interpretation.

2.—(1) In this Act— [6–02]

"the Act of 1931" means the Landlord and Tenant Act, 1931;

"the Act of 1958" means the Landlord and Tenant (Reversionary Leases) Act, 1958;

"building lease" has the meaning assigned to it by section 4 of the Act of 1958;

"business" means any trade, profession or business, whether carried on for gain or reward or not, and the public service and

"used for the purposes of business" means used wholly or in part for the purposes of business;

"the Court" means the Circuit Court;

"development" has the meaning assigned to it by the Local Government (Planning and Development) Act, 1963;

"fee simple" does not include the interest in land of a person holding the land under a fee farm grant;

"immediate lessor", in relation to a lessee or yearly tenant, means the person for the time being entitled to the next superior interest in the land held by the lessee or tenant, as the case may be;

"lessee" shall, where the context so admits, be construed as including the personal representatives and successors in title of the lessee;

"lessor" shall, where the context so admits, be construed as including the personal representatives and successors in title of the lessor;

"the Minister" means the Minister for Justice;

"planning authority" has the meaning assigned to it by the Local Government (Planning and Development) Act, 1963;

"prescribed" means prescribed by regulations made by the Minister under this Act and cognate words shall be construed accordingly;

"proprietary lease" has the meaning assigned to it by section 7 of the Act of 1958;

"superior lessor", in relation to a lessee or yearly tenant, means any person entitled to an interest in the land held by the lessee or tenant superior to the interest of the person from whom the lessee or tenant holds the land.

(2) References in this Act to a covenant, condition or agreement in a lease include references to a reservation, stipulation or proviso or to any other similar provision in the lease.

(3) References in this Act to the county registrar for the area in which any land is situate shall, where the land is situate in the areas of two or more county registrars, be construed as references to the county registrar for the area in which the larger or largest portion of the land is situate.

(4) References in this Act to any enactment shall be construed as references to that enactment as amended by any subsequent enactment.

General right to acquire fee simple.

[6–03] 3.—(1)–(4) *Omitted. Repealed by s 7(1) of the Landlord and Tenant (Ground Rents) (No. 2) Act 1978.*

(5) (a) The inclusion in the certificate signed by or on behalf of the Commissioner of Valuation on an extract from the Valuation List issued pursuant to section 9 of the Annual Revision of Rateable Property (Ireland) Amendment Act, 1860, of a statement that a valuation shown in the extract is the rateable valuation obtaining on a date specified in the certificate shall be prima facie evidence, for the purposes of [paragraph (d) of subsection (2) of this section] Part II of the Landlord and Tenant (Ground Rents) (No. 2) Act, 1978, of that fact.

(b) Where land demised by a lease or held on a yearly tenancy does not on a particular date bear a separate rateable valuation, the Commissioner of Valuation shall have power for the purposes of this subsection to apportion the rateable valuation or valuations of the properties in which the land was comprised on that date and to charge a fee for the apportionment. Every such fee shall be determined, accounted for and applied in the same manner as the fees charged by the Commissioner pursuant to the said section 9.

Amendment history: Section 7(2) of the No. 2 Act of 1978 substitutes reference to Part II of that Act into what remains of this section. Subsection (5) was itself amended by s 7(2) of that Act, the words in square brackets were replaced by the reference to Part II of the No. 2 Act of 1978.

(6) *Omitted. Repealed by s 7(1) of the Landlord and Tenant (Ground Rents) (No. 2) Act 1978.*

Notice of intention to acquire fee simple.

4.—A person who proposes to acquire the fee simple in land by virtue of this Act shall serve a notice in the prescribed form upon each of the following persons who can be found and ascertained, that is to say, the person who is for the time being entitled to the next superior interest in the land, every (if any) person who is, in relation to the land, the superior lessor of the person so proposing and every (if any) person who is the owner of an incumbrance thereon. [6–04]

Procedure in relation to acquisition of fee simple.

5.—(1)–(2) *Omitted. Repealed by s 7(1) of the Landlord and Tenant (Ground Rents) (No. 2) Act 1978.* [6–05]

(3) A person who is entitled to acquire under this Act the fee simple in land held by him under a lease shall be entitled to have the rent payable by him in respect of the land and any other land held under the same lease apportioned under this Act between the land the fee simple in which he is acquiring and the other land.

Conveyance of fee simple.

6.—(1) Where, in relation to land the fee simple in which is proposed to be acquired by a person under this Act, a notice under section 4 of this Act is served, the person by whom it is served and the person upon whom it is served shall, without unreasonable delay, take all necessary steps to effect a conveyance free from incumbrances of the fee simple and any intermediate interests in the land to the person proposing to acquire the fee simple. [6–06]

(2) In subsection (1) of this section "incumbrances" does not include a mortgage or charge on the interest of the person proposing to acquire the fee simple, and, upon conveyance of the fee simple in land to a person who is acquiring the fee simple therein under this Act and whose previous interest in the land was subject to such a mortgage or charge, the mortgage or charge shall, if it has not been extinguished, be deemed to be a mortgage or charge on the fee simple in the land.

Notice requiring information.

7.—(1) For the purpose of securing the joinder of all necessary parties in the conveyance of the fee simple in land to a person entitled to acquire it under this Act, the person may— [6–07]

(a) serve a notice in the prescribed form upon his immediate lessor in relation to the land requiring information as to the nature and duration of his reversion in the land and the existence and nature of any incumbrance thereon, the name and address of the person for the time being entitled to the next superior interest in the land and of the owner of any such incumbrance and any other information reasonably necessary for the purpose aforesaid, and

(b) serve a similar notice upon each other person having a superior interest in the land.

(2) Where a person upon whom a notice may be served under subsection (1) of this section in relation to land cannot be found or ascertained, a notice in the prescribed form may be served upon the person receiving the rent in respect of the land requiring the name and address of the person to whom the rent is paid by the person upon whom the notice is served and any other information reasonably necessary for the purpose specified in subsection (1) of this section.

(3) A person upon whom a notice is served under this section shall, within one month of such service, give so much of the information required by the notice as is within his possession or procurement to the person by whom the notice is served.

(4) Where a person on whom a notice is served under this section refuses or fails to provide the information as required by this section, the person who served the notice may apply to the Court which may make such order as justice may require to compel the person on whom the notice was served to provide the information.

Amendment history: Subsection (4) added by s 10 of the Landlord and Tenant (Amendment) Act 1984.

Provisions in relation to parties to conveyance of fee simple.

[6–08] 8.—(1) Where a person who is required by this Act to convey or join in the conveyance of the fee simple in land is, by reason of having a fiduciary capacity or a limited estate or by reason of restrictive covenants in the lease under which he holds, incapable in law of conveying or joining in (as the case may be) the conveyance of the fee simple, the county registrar for the area in which the land is situate may, on the application of any person concerned, empower the person so required to convey or join in conveying (as the case may be) the fee simple.

(2) Where a person who is required by this Act to convey or join in conveying the fee simple in land is an infant or a person of unsound mind, or cannot be found or refuses or fails to execute such conveyance, the county registrar for the area in which the land is situate may, on the application of any person concerned, appoint an officer of the Court to execute such conveyance for and in the name of the person so required and thereupon the execution of such conveyance by such officer for and in the name of such person shall for all purposes be as effectual as the execution thereof by such person.

(3) Where any person who is required by this Act to convey or join in conveying the fee simple in land is unknown or unascertained, the county registrar for the area in which the land is situate may, on the application of the person entitled under this Act to acquire the fee simple, appoint any person who is receiving the rent in respect of the interest in the land of the person so entitled, or such other person as the county registrar may think fit to appoint, to represent such unknown or unascertained person in all proceedings in connection with the conveyance of the fee simple in the land, and may, at the same time or subsequently, appoint an officer of the Court to execute such conveyance for and on behalf of the person so required and unknown or unascertained and thereupon the execution of such conveyance by such officer for and on behalf of such person shall for all purposes he as effectual as the execution thereof by such unknown or unascertained person.

(4) Where under subsection (2) or (3) of this section, a county registrar appoints a person to execute, or join in the execution of, a conveyance of the fee simple in land for and in the name of or for and on behalf of any person, the county registrar may order that the purchase money payable to that person in consideration of the conveyance of his interest in the land the paid into Court before the execution of the conveyance and, upon such payment, any estate, right or interest in or claim against the land of that person existing at the time of such payment shall be transferred and shall attach to the money and the Court may make such order, or give such direction,

for the disbursement and distribution of the money and any interest or dividends thereon, as it may deem proper.

(5) Where a person upon whom a notice under section 4 of this Act in relation to land is required to be served cannot be found or ascertained, the person shall be deemed, for the purposes of this section, to be a person who is required by this Act to convey or join in conveying the fee simple in the land.

(6) A power conferred on a county registrar by this section or by section 14 of this Act shall be exercised in relation to an infant or a person of unsound mind who is a ward of court only by leave of the court of which he is a ward, and the power conferred on the Court by subsection (4) of this section shall be exercised in relation to any such ward who is a ward of the High Court in accordance with the directions of the High Court.

Liability for cost in relation to acquisition of fee simple.

9.—A person (in this section referred to as the applicant) who proposes to acquire the fee simple in land by virtue of this Act shall be liable for the payment of the reasonable costs and expenses actually and necessarily incurred in complying with the provisions of this Act by a person upon whom a notice under section 4 of this Act in relation to the land has been served but, if a notice under section 10 of this Act in relation to the land is served on the person, the applicant shall not be liable for the payment of any such costs or expenses incurred by the person after the service of the latter notice. **[6–09]**

Note: This section does not apply where the applicant is in occupation of the dwellinghouse. See s 23(6) of the Landlord and Tenant (Ground Rents) (No.2) Act of 1978.

Power to discontinue acquisition of fee simple.

10.—Where a notice under section 4 of this Act in relation to land is served by a person, the person may, at any time before conveyance to him of the fee simple in the land, discontinue the acquisition of the fee simple by serving a notice in the prescribed form upon each person upon whom a notice under the said section 4 was served stating that he is withdrawing the said notice and does not intend to acquire the fee simple in the land. **[6–10]**

General right to appointment of rent.

11.—(1) Where land demised by a lease (being either a building lease or a proprietary lease) is held by more than one person each of whom is a lessee under a building lease or a proprietary lease, an assignee from any such lessee of part of such land or a successor in title of any such assignee and the rent reserved by the first-mentioned lease is being paid to the lessor by one only of the persons, that person shall be entitled to have the rent apportioned between the part of the land held by him and the part of the land held by each such other person who is liable for the payment of part of the rent to the person so entitled **[6–11]**

(2) Where a rent reserved by a lease is apportioned under this Act between different parts of the land demised by the lease—

(a) any such part shall be subject to the payment to the lessor only of the portion of the rent apportioned in respect thereof and shall not be subject to the payment to any other person of any portion of the rent, and

(b) any such part shall be subject only to the performance and observance of the covenants and conditions contained in the lease in so far as they are applicable to that part, in the same manner as if that part only were demised by the lease subject to the apportioned rent and subject to the performance and observance of the covenants and conditions aforesaid.

(3) Where a rent reserved by a lease is apportioned under this Act—

(a) a fine, or payment in the nature of a fine, shall not be charged or payable for or in respect of the apportionment,

(b) the total of the rents payable as a result of the apportionment shall not exceed the amount of the rent reserved by the lease together with the estimated additional cost (if any), attributable to the apportionment, of collecting the apportioned rents,

(c) the estimated additional cost (if any), attributable to the apportionment, of collecting the apportioned rents shall be determined at the time of the apportionment and shall be included in the apportioned rent payable by the person by whom the notice under section 12 of this Act relating to the lease was served.

Notice of intention to have rent apportioned.

[6–12] 12.—A person who proposes to have a rent reserved by a lease apportioned under this Act shall serve a notice in the prescribed form upon each of the following persons who can be found and ascertained, that is to say, the person to whom the rent is payable and any other person who holds any of the land demised by the lease as lessee under a building lease or a proprietary lease, as assignee from any such lessee or as successor in title of any such assignee.

Apportionment of rent.

[6–13] 13.—Where, in relation to a rent which is proposed to be apportioned under this Act, notices under section 12 of this Act are served, the person by whom they are served and the persons upon whom they are served shall, without unreasonable delay, take all necessary steps to effect an apportionment of the rent to which the notices relate.

Provisions in relation to parties to apportionment of rent.

[6–14] 14.—(1) Where a person who is required by this Act to join in the apportionment of a rent is, by reason of having a fiduciary capacity or a limited estate or by reason of restrictive covenants in the lease under which he holds, incapable in law of joining in the apportionment, the county registrar for the area in which the land as respects which the rent is payable is situate may, on the application of any person concerned, empower the person so required to join in the apportionment.

(2) Where a person who is required by this Act to join in the apportionment of a rent is an infant or a person of unsound mind, or cannot be found or refuses or fails to execute any relevant document, the county registrar for the area in which the land as

respects which the rent is payable is situate may, on the application of any person concerned, appoint an officer of the Court to execute such document for and in the name of the person so required and thereupon the execution of such document by such officer for and in the name of such person shall for all purposes be as effectual as the execution thereof by such person.

(3) Where any person who is required by this Act to join in the apportionment of a rent is unknown or unascertained, the county registrar for the area in which the land as respects which the rent is payable is situate may, on the application of the person seeking the apportionment, appoint any person who is receiving the rent in respect of the interest in the land of the person making the application, or such other person as the county registrar may think fit to appoint, to represent such unknown or unascertained person in all proceedings in connection with the apportionment, and may, at the same time or subsequently, appoint an officer of the Court to execute any relevant document for and on behalf of the person so required and unknown or unascertained, and thereupon the execution of such document by such officer for and on behalf of such person shall for all purposes be as effectual as the execution thereof by such unknown or unascertained person.

(4) Where a person upon whom a notice under section 12 of this Act in relation to rent is required to be served cannot be found or ascertained, the person shall be deemed, for the purposes of this section, to be a person who is required by this Act to join in the apportionment of the rent.

Liability for costs in relation to apportionment of rent.

15.—A person (in this section referred to as the applicant) who proposes to have a **[6–15]**
rent apportioned under this Act shall be liable for the payment of the reasonable costs and expenses actually and necessarily incurred in complying with the provisions of this Act by a person upon whom a notice under section 12 of this Act in relation to the rent has been served, but if a notice under section 16 of this Act in relation to the rent is served upon the person, the applicant shall not be liable for any such costs or expenses incurred by the person after the service of the latter notice.

Power to discontinue apportionment of rent.

16.—Where a notice under section 12 of this Act in relation to a rent is served by a **[6–16]**
person, the person may, at any time before the apportionment of the rent, discontinue the apportionment by serving a notice in the prescribed form upon each person upon whom a notice under the said section 12 was served stating that he is withdrawing the said notice and does not intend to have the rent apportioned.

Determination of certain matters by arbitration.

17.—(1) If any dispute, question or difficulty arises in regard to the acquisition of **[6–17]**
the fee simple or any other interest in land under this Act, the purchase price thereof, the apportionment of such purchase money payable in respect of such acquisition or of a rent under or for the purposes of this Act, costs or expenses incurred under this Act, compliance by a person with a provision of this Act or any other matter arising under this Act (other than sections 25 to 30 of this Act), any person concerned may apply to the county registrar for the area in which the land to which the application relates is situate to have the matter determined by his arbitration and the county registrar shall make such award as justice shall require.

(2) Without prejudice to the generality of subsection (1) of this section, a county registrar may, in an arbitration under this Act, make an award in relation to land—

(a) determining the person (if any) entitled to acquire the fee simple therein under this Act,

(b) determining the purchase price to be paid in respect of the acquisition,

(c) determining the person or persons entitled to receive the purchase money in respect of the acquisition and the amount which each person is entitled to receive,

(d) determining if a person is entitled to have a rent apportioned under section 5 or 11 of this Act, and

(e) apportioning (whether under the said section 5 or 11 or otherwise for the purposes of this Act) any rent payable in respect of land part of which is land the fee simple in which is being acquired under this Act.

(3) A county registrar shall have, for the purpose of and in relation to an arbitration under this Act, the same power of making orders in respect of—

(a) security for costs,

(b) discovery and inspection of documents and interrogatories,

(c) the giving of evidence by affidavit,

(d) examination on oath of any witness,

as the Court has for the purpose of and in relation to any action or matter in that court.

(4) Whenever it appears to a county registrar for any county that he cannot properly deal with a matter falling to be determined by his arbitration under this Act by reason of the fact that he has a personal interest therein or such personal knowledge of the facts or of the parties as might prejudice his determination of the matter, he shall nominate the county registrar for an adjoining county to hear and determine the matter and, upon such nomination, the matter may be heard and determined accordingly.

(5) Sections 29, 35, 36, 37 and 41 of the Arbitration Act, 1954, shall not apply in relation to an arbitration under this Act.

> **Note:** Section 17 applies to disputes as to the apportionment of rent under s 2(7)(c)(ii) of the Landlord and Tenant (Ground Rents) Act 1978 — see s 2(8) of the Act of 1978.

Provisions in relation to determination of purchase price of fee simple by arbitration.

18.—*Omitted. Repealed by s 7(1) of the Landlord and Tenant (Ground Rents) (No. 2) Act 1978.*

Provisions in relation to costs of arbitration.

[6–18] 19.—(1) Where an award or order is made in an arbitration under this Act, the county registrar conducting the arbitration shall direct to and by whom and in what manner the costs of the arbitration shall be paid and shall tax or settle the amount of costs to be so paid.

Note: This subsection does not apply where the applicant is in occupation of the dwellinghouse. See s 23(6) of the Landlord and Tenant (Ground Rents) (No. 2) Act 1978.

(2) Notwithstanding any other provision of this Act, where, in the opinion of a county registrar, a party to an arbitration under this Act conducted by him has behaved (whether by act or omission) unreasonably or has, without reasonable cause—

(a) refused or failed to comply with a provision of this Act or delayed in so complying, or

(b) refused or failed to reach agreement or delayed in reaching agreement in relation to the acquisition of the fee simple in land under this Act or the apportionment of a rent under this Act or the costs of such acquisition or apportionment,

and such behaviour, refusal, failure or delay occasioned the incurring of the whole or part of the costs of the arbitration, the county registrar may direct that, as he may consider reasonable, the whole, or such part as he may specify, of the costs of the arbitration shall be paid by the party aforesaid.

(3) A county registrar shall not direct fees of counsel retained on behalf of a party to an arbitration under this Act to be paid by another party to the arbitration unless a question of law was involved in the arbitration of such kind as, in the opinion of the county registrar, rendered it necessary to retain counsel.

(4) References in this section to the costs of an arbitration are references to party and party costs.

Assistance of Commissioner of Valuation in relation to arbitrations.

20.—(1) A county registrar conducting an arbitration under this Act may and, if so requested by any party concerned, shall cause to be sent to the Commissioner of Valuation a request for a valuation, estimate or statement in respect of any particular matter relevant to the determination of the purchase price of the fee simple in land being acquired under this Act or to the apportionment of a rent under this Act and may for the purpose adjourn the arbitration. [6–19]

(2) Upon receipt of a request under this section, the Commissioner of Valuation shall cause such valuation, estimate or statement as is mentioned in the request to be prepared and sent to the county registrar concerned together with a statement of the fee, calculated in accordance with regulations made by the Minister for Finance, payable therefor.

(3) Any party concerned shall be entitled to obtain from the county registrar concerned a copy of a valuation, estimate or statement furnished by the Commissioner of Valuation to him in pursuance of this section, subject to payment therefor at the rate for the time being chargeable by law for copies of documents obtained from a Circuit Court Office.

(4) The fee payable under this section for a valuation, estimate or statement sent by the Commissioner of Valuation to a county registrar in pursuance of this section shall be borne and paid to the county registrar by such party or parties and in such proportion as he shall direct and shall be paid by the county registrar into, or disposed of by him for the benefit of, the Exchequer in such manner as the Minister for Finance shall direct.

(5) Where a request is sent under this section in relation to land to the Commissioner of Valuation at the request of a party, the county registrar concerned shall, in determining the purchase price of the fee simple in the land or in apportioning a rent payable in respect thereof, as the case may be, have regard to the valuation, estimate or statement furnished by the said Commissioner.

Registers of arbitration awards.

[6–20] 21.—(1) A county registrar shall keep—

(a) a register in the prescribed form of all awards made by him in arbitrations under this Act in relation to the price of the fee simple in land being acquired under this Act, and

(b) a register in the prescribed form of all other awards made by him in arbitrations under this Act.

(2) Registers kept under this section shall be made available for public inspection and copies of entries in the registers shall be made available to the public and the Minister may prescribe the places at which and the times during which the registers shall be so made available and, with the concurrence of the Minister for Finance, the fees to be charged for such inspection and for such copies.

(3) A copy of an entry in a register kept under this section by a county registrar purporting to be signed by the county registrar shall, without proof of the signature of the person purporting to sign the copy or that he was the county registrar, be evidence until the contrary is proved of the matters stated in the entry.

Powers of Court in relation to arbitrations.

[6–21] 22.—(1) An appeal shall lie to the Court against an award, order or other decision of a county registrar in an arbitration under this Act.

(2) The Court may remit, before giving its decision, any matter the subject of an appeal to it under this section to the reconsideration of the county registrar who conducted the arbitration in question or remit the matter to the rehearing of another county registrar.

(3) An award or order of a county registrar in an arbitration under this Act may, by leave of the Court, be enforced as a judgement or order to the same effect and, where leave is so given, judgement may be entered in terms of the award.

Note: S 21(5) of the Landlord and Tenant (Ground Rents) (No. 2) Act 1978 provides that an appeal to the Court under this section shall be heard and determined by a judge of the Court for the time being assigned to the Circuit in which are situate the premises or any part thereof in relation to which the appeal is taken.

Service of notices.

[6–22] 23.—(1) Service of a notice under this Act may be effected by post and, if so effected, shall be by registered post.

(2) Service of a notice under this Act on behalf of a person shall be deemed, for the purposes of this Act, to be service of the notice by the person.

Provision in relation to mortgages.

24.—(1) For the purposes of the application of section 3 or 11 of this Act or section 11 or 12 of the Act of 1958 to a person in relation to any land, the existence of a mortgage on the interest of the person in that land shall be disregarded. [6–23]

(2) Where—

(a) either before or after the commencement of this Act, a lessee executes a mortgage by subdemise of the whole or part of the land comprised in his lease, retaining a nominal reversion therein, and

(b) either before or after such commencement, the land comprised in the subdemise is sold for the enforcement of the mortgage,

the purchaser shall, for the purposes of this Act, be deemed to have acquired the interest of the lessee in the demised land for the entire of the unexpired term of the lease, including the period of the nominal reversion.

Amendment of sections 11 and 12 of Act of 1958.

25.—*Omitted. Amends ss 11 and 12 of the Landlord and Tenant (Reversionary Leases) Act 1958.*

> **Note:** The Act of 1958 was repealed in full by s 11 of the Landlord and Tenant (Amendment) Act 1980, which Act came into force on 8th September 1980.

Amendment of section 18 of Act of 1958.

26.—*Omitted. Amends s 18 of the Landlord and Tenant (Reversionary Leases) Act 1958*

> **Note:** The Act of 1958 was repealed in full by s 11 of the Landlord and Tenant (Amendment) Act 1980, which Act came into force on 8th September 1980.

Amendment of section 57 of Act of 1931.

27.—*Omitted. Amends s 57 of the Landlord and Tenant Act 1931.*

> **Note:** The Act of 1931 was repealed in full by s 11 of the Landlord and Tenant (Amendment) Act 1980, which Act came into force on 8th September 1980.

Amendment of section 58 of Act of 1931.

28.—*Omitted. Amends s 58 of the Landlord and Tenant Act 1931.*

> **Note:** The Act of 1931 was repealed in full by s 11 of the Landlord and Tenant (Amendment) Act 1980, which Act came into force on 8th September 1980.

Relaxation of certain restrictive covenants.

[6–24] 29.—(1) Where a person who holds land under a lease (whether granted before or after the commencement of this Act) which is a building lease or a proprietary lease proposes to do, in relation to the land, anything—

(a) which is development and as respects which permission has been granted under Part IV of the Local Government (Planning and Development) Act, 1963,

(b) which is exempted development for the purposes of that Act, or

(c) as respects which consultation is required by section 84 of that Act and has taken place to the extent required by that section,

and which, if done, would, apart from this section, be a breach of any covenant, condition or agreement in the lease prohibiting the alteration of the user of the land or the making of an improvement (within the meaning of the Act of 1958) thereon, the covenant, condition or agreement shall not, in so far as it prohibits such alteration or the making of such an improvement, apply or have effect in relation to that thing.

(2) Subsection (1) of this section does not apply in relation to a covenant, condition or agreement—

(a) to which section 31 of this Act applies, or

(b) which is contained in a lease made by a harbour authority, within the meaning of the Harbours Act, 1946, as lessor, whether before or after the passing of this Act,

(c) which has the effect of prohibiting the erection, provision or reconstruction (not being an improvement within the meaning of the Act of 1958) of any building or structure, in so far as the covenant, condition or agreement has such effect, or

(d) prohibiting any alteration of the user of the land demised by the lease which would impose a liability or an increased liability on the lessor for the payment of rates, in so far as the covenant, condition or agreement prohibits such alteration.

Note: References in this section to an "improvement" are construed as references to an improvement within the meaning of s 67(3) of the Landlord and Tenant (Amendment) Act 1980 — see s 67(4) of the 1980 Act.

Variation of certain covenants to insure with particular insurer.

[6–25] 30.—Where a lessee under a building or proprietary lease is, by virtue of a covenant, condition or agreement (whether contained in the lease or in an ancillary or collateral agreement, not being a mortgage), required to effect a contract of insurance in relation to a building or buildings on the land demised by the lease with a specified insurer or an insurer selected or approved of either by the lessor under the lease or another person or through a specified agent, or an agent selected or approved of either by the said lessor or another person, the covenant, condition or agreement shall be construed and have effect as if it were a covenant, condition or agreement requiring the lessee to effect such contract of insurance, either directly or through any agent, as the case may be, with any insurer who is for the time being the holder of an assurance licence granted under the Insurance Act, 1936.

Continuance of certain covenants affecting fee simple acquired under this Act.

31.—*Omitted. Repealed by s 7(1) of the Landlord and Tenant (Ground Rents) (No. 2) Act 1978.*

Costs of leases.

32.—(1) Notwithstanding any rule of law, a party to a lease shall not be under an obligation to pay the solicitor's costs of the lease of any other party to the lease and so much of any contract made after the commencement of this Act as provides for the payment of all or any of the solicitor's costs of the lease of any party to the lease by any other party thereto shall be void. [6–26]

(2) In this section "lease" includes an agreement for a lease or for a tenancy but does not include a mortgage by subdemise.

Certain contracts to be void.

33.—(1) Subject to subsection (2) of this section, so much of any contract made after the commencement of this Act as provides that any provision of this Act shall not apply in relation to a person or that the application of any such provision shall be varied, modified or restricted in any way in relation to a person shall be void. [6–27]

(2) Nothing in this Act shall prevent a person from giving or accepting, for the purpose of the acquisition of the fee simple or other interest in land under this Act, or the apportionment of a rent under this Act, a shorter title to a fee simple or any other interest in land than the title which a purchaser is, in the absence of special contract, entitled to require.

Regulations.

34.—(1) The Minister may make regulations in relation to any matter referred to in this Act as prescribed. [6–28]

(2) Every regulation made by the Minister under this Act shall be laid before each House of the Oireachtas as soon as may be after it is made and if a resolution annulling the regulation is passed by either such House within the next subsequent twenty-one days on which that House has sat after the regulation is laid before it, the regulation shall be annulled accordingly, but without prejudice to the validity of anything previously done under the regulation.

Repeals.

35.—(1) *Omitted. Repeals s 10 and s 18 of Deasy's Act and deletes part of s 14 of the Conveyancing Act 1881.* [6–29]

(2) Where a breach of an agreement which, but for this section, would have been a contravention of the said section 10 or 18 took place before the commencement of this Act and a right of re-entry or forfeiture for the breach was not enforce and proceedings to enforce such right were not instituted before such commencement, this section shall, in relation to the breach, be deemed to have come into operation immediately before the occurrence of the breach.

Short title, construction and collective citation.

36.—(1) This Act may be cited as the Landlord and Tenant (Ground Rents) Act, 1967. [6–30]

(2) The Landlord and Tenant Acts, 1931 and 1958, and this Act shall be construed together as one Act and may be cited together as the Landlord and Tenant Acts, 1931 to 1967.

Chapter 7

LANDLORD AND TENANT (AMENDMENT) ACT, 1971

(1971, No. 30)

AN ACT TO AMEND THE LAW RELATING TO REVERSIONARY LEASES AND, IN PARTICULAR, TO EXTEND, WITH EFFECT IN CERTAIN CIRCUMSTANCES FROM THE 3RD DAY OF MARCH, 1970, RIGHTS UNDER THAT LAW TO A CLUB OR ORGANISATION USING LAND FOR OUTDOOR RECREATIONAL PURPOSES, TO AMEND IN OTHER RESPECTS THE LAW OF LANDLORD AND TENANT AND TO PROVIDE FOR OTHER MATTERS CONNECTED WITH THE MATTERS AFORESAID.

[7TH DECEMBER 1971]

BE IT ENACTED BY THE OIREACHTAS AS FOLLOWS:—

Definition.

1.—In this Act— [7–01]

"the Act of 1958" means the Landlord and Tenant (Reversionary Leases) Act, 1958;

"the Court" means the Circuit Court;

"sporting lease" has the meaning assigned to it in section 2;

"sports club" has the meaning assigned to it in section 2 and shall, where the context so admits, be construed as including predecessors in title of the sports club.

Note: Throughout this Act references to the provisions of the Act of 1958 have effect as if they were references to the corresponding provisions of the Landlord and Tenant (Amendment) Act 1980 — see s 11(2) of the Landlord and Tenant (Amendment) Act 1980. The Landlord and Tenant (Reversionary Leases) Act 1958 was repealed in full by s 11(1) of the Act of 1980.

Sporting leases.

2.—(1) A club or organisation (in this Act referred to as a sports club) carrying on some outdoor sport, game or recreation (in this section referred to as the sport) and holding land in accordance with the conditions specified in this section shall, subject to the provisions of this Act, be entitled to obtain a lease (in this Act referred to as a sporting lease) of the land. [7–02]

(2) The following are the conditions to be complied with:

(a) that—

(i) the land is held for the purpose of carrying on the sport under a lease for a term of not less than twenty-one years,

(ii) the land has been continuously occupied by the sports club for that purpose for the period of not less than twenty-one years immediately preceding the date of the application for a sporting lease, or

(iii) the land has been continuously in the possession of the sports club for that purpose for the period of not less than twenty-one years immediately preceding the date of the application for a sporting lease,

(b) that the sports club has spent money—

(i) on erecting permanent buildings or structures on the land which are used in connection with the land for that purpose,

(ii) on reconstructing, altering, renovating or adapting any permanent buildings or structures on the land which are so used so as to render them more suitable for that purpose, or

(iii) on developing, improving or adapting the land so as to render it more suitable for that purpose, and

(c) that the total amount so spent was not less than the greater of the following, namely, one thousand pounds or fifteen times the average yearly amount of any rent or other sum paid or payable in respect of the land in the five years immediately preceding the date of the application for a sporting lease, disregarding any penal rent or other sum payable for any breach of a covenant, condition or agreement and any exceptional rent or sum in respect of a specified period not exceeding five years.

(3) Where—

(a) land (in this section referred to as the qualifying land) is held by a sports club for a freehold estate or in accordance with subsection (2)(a) and is so held in compliance with the conditions specified in subsection (2)(b) and (2)(c) in conjunction with other land primarily used for the same purpose.

(b) that other land does not comply with those conditions, and

(c) that other land—

(i) is held under a lease for a term of not less than twelve years,

(ii) has been continuously occupied by the sports club for a period of not less than twelve years, or

(iii) has been continuously in the possession of the sports club for a period of not less than twelve years,

the sports club shall be entitled to obtain a sporting lease of that other land if the area of the other land is not more than one-fourth of the total area of the qualifying land and the other land.

(4) If the qualifying land ceases to be primarily used for the purpose of carrying on the sport, the lessor of the sporting lease granted under subsection (3) shall be entitled to terminate the lease on giving three months' notice to the lessee.

(5) Any money spent—

(a) on the maintenance of buildings, structures or land, or

(b) on the erection, reconstruction, alteration, renovation or adaptation of buildings or structures, or the development, improvement or adaptation of land, in contravention of any covenant, condition or agreement,

shall be disregarded for the purposes of subsection (2).

(6) Where land which complies with the conditions specified in subsection (2) is used both for the purpose of carrying on the sport and for some other purpose, the sports club shall not be entitled to obtain a lease of that land under this section unless the Court is satisfied that the land is primarily used for the purposes of the sport.

(7) Where, on the 3rd day of March, 1970, a sports club, held land in accordance with conditions which would, subject to the provisions of this Act, have entitled it to obtain a sporting lease if this Act had then been in force, the provisions of this Act shall extend to the club, with necessary modifications, notwithstanding that its interest, occupation or possession ceased before the passing of this Act, and in particular—

(a) any reference to an immediate lessor or a superior lessor or to a landlord or other person shall be construed as including reference to the immediate lessor, superior lessor, landlord or other person as on the 3rd day of March, 1970, and his successors in title,

(b) the conditions specified in subparagraphs (ii) and (iii) of subsection (2)(a) shall be construed as if the references therein to the date of the application for a sporting lease were references to the 3rd day of March, 1970, and

(c) the time for applying for a sporting lease shall be not later than three months after the passing of this Act.

Application to obtain sporting lease.

3.—(1) A sports club may apply to its immediate lessor to obtain a sporting lease of the land— [7–03]

(a) not earlier than fifteen years before the expiration of the lease, and

(b) not later than the expiration of the lease or the expiration of three months from the service on the club by its immediate lessor or any superior lessor of notice of the expiration of the lease, whichever is the later.

(2) The notice shall be valid only if served not earlier than three months before the expiration of the lease.

(3) Where an application is made for a sporting lease before the expiration of the lease under which the applicant holds, the sporting lease, where granted, shall commence on the expiration of the previous lease or on such other date as may be agreed upon between the parties.

(4) Where an application is made for a sporting lease after the expiration of the previous lease, the sporting lease, where granted, shall commence on such date as may be agreed upon between the parties or, in default of agreement, on the date of the application.

(5) A sports club which holds land otherwise than under a lease and which is entitled to obtain a sporting lease may apply at any time to the landlord or other person from whom it holds the land for a sporting lease of the land and the sporting lease, where granted, shall commence on such date as may be agreed between the parties or, in default of agreement on the date of the application.

Restrictions on right to sporting lease.

4.—(1) A sports club shall not be entitled to a sporting lease under this Act of the land or any part of the land in respect of which that lease is sought where the immediate lessor, any superior lessor, the landlord or other person who is a necessary party to the granting of the lease satisfies the Court— [7–04]

(a) that he holds the land for a freehold estate or has an interest in reversion of not less than fifteen years, and

(b) (i) that he requires vacant possession of the land for the purpose of carrying out a scheme of development of property which includes the land and that he has obtained planning permission under Part IV of the Local Government (Planning and Development) Act, 1963, for that scheme of development, and

(ii) that it is reasonable that a sporting lease should be refused.

(2) Subsection (1) is, in relation to a sporting lease, in substitution for section 15 (1) of the Act of 1958.

(3) Section 16 of the Act of 1958 (which provides for compensation for disturbance) shall apply to a case in which a sports club would, but for the provisions of subsection (1), be entitled to a sporting lease.

Covenants under sporting lease.

[7–05] 5.—(1) A sporting lease shall contain such covenants and conditions as may be agreed upon between the parties or, in default of agreement, as may be determined by the Court.

(2) If the Court fixes the covenants and conditions of the sporting lease, the lessee shall be made liable to pay all rates for the land and to insure against fire and keep the premises in repair.

(3) Where a sports club is entitled to a sporting lease under this Act and the terms of that lease are fixed by the Court, the sporting lease shall contain the following conditions:

(a) *Omitted. Repealed by s 5(7) of the Landlord and Tenant (Amendment) Act 1984. Which Act came into force one week after the day of its passing (passed on 14th March 1984).*

(b) that, if the property demised by the sporting lease is not used for or in connection with some outdoor sport, game or recreation, the lessor shall be entitled to terminate the lease on giving three months' notice to the lessee.

Rent under sporting lease.

[7–06] 6.—(1) Where the rent under a sporting lease is to be determined by the Court, the Court shall fix a fair rent for the grant of a lease of the property for the purpose of carrying on the sport.

(2) In fixing the rent the Court shall have regard to the general intention of this Act in relation to sports clubs which is the advancement of outdoor sports, games and recreations and the preservation of open spaces for the common good and, without prejudice to such other considerations as it considers relevant, may take into account the rent or other sum previously paid for the property by the sports club and any covenants and conditions under which it was so paid, to the rent paid by other sports clubs of the same kind in the same or a comparable locality, to the contribution made by the sports club to the enhancement of the property, and to the price paid by any person who is a necessary party to the granting of the lease in the acquisition of his estate or interest.

Application of Act of 1958.

[7–07] 7.—Subject to this Act, the provisions of the Act of 1958 shall, with necessary modifications, have effect for the purposes of the preceding provisions of this Act as if in the Act of 1958 "reversionary lease" included a sporting lease and "lease" included any tenancy or other right of user, and cognate words and expressions shall be construed accordingly.

Leases deemed to be building leases.

8.—(1) Where a lease was granted in renewal of a lease which expired or was surrendered before the 31st day of March, 1931, and which, if the Act of 1958 were then in force, would have been a building lease or a proprietary lease within the meaning of that Act, and that renewed lease or new lease, as the case may be, was granted— **[7–08]**

(a) to the person entitled to the lessee's interest under the expired or surrendered lease, or

(b) at a rent less than the rateable valuation of the property at the date of the granting of the renewed or new lease,

such renewed or new lease shall be deemed to be a building lease within the meaning of the Act of 1958.

(2) *Omitted. Repeals s 10 of the Landlord and Tenant (Reversionary Leases) Act 1958.*

> **Note:** The Landlord and Tenant (Reversionary Leases) Act 1958 was repealed in full by s 11 of the Landlord and Tenant (Amendment) Act 1980.

Rights of lessees under certain expired leases.

9.—Where— **[7–09]**

(a) a lease expired within eight years before the passing of this Act, and

(b) the lessee is, at such passing, in possession of the land comprised in the expired lease under a yearly tenancy arising by implication from the acts of the parties, or under a statutory tenancy under the Rent Restrictions Acts, 1960 and 1967, or as a tenant at will or otherwise, without having obtained a new tenancy from the lessor or without having acquired the lessor's interest in the land, and

(c) no person was, immediately before such passing, entitled to be granted a reversionary lease under the Act of 1958,

the lessee shall, during the twelve months immediately after the passing of this Act, have the same rights in relation to obtaining a reversionary lease as he would have had within fifteen years before the expiration of the expired lease if this Act had then been in force.

Amendment of section 4 of Rent Restrictions (Amendment) Act 1967.

10.—*Omitted. Repealed by s 6 of the Housing (Private Rented Dwellings) Act 1982.* **[7–10]**

Amendment of section 10 of Rent Restrictions (Amendment) Act, 1967.

11.—*Omitted. Repealed by s 6 of the Housing (Private Rented Dwellings) Act 1982.* **[7–11]**

Short title, construction and collective citation.

[7-12] 12.—(1) This Act may be cited as the Landlord and Tenant (Amendment) Act, 1971.

(2) The Landlord and Tenant Acts, 1931 to 1967, and this Act shall be construed together as one Act and may be cited together as the Landlord and Tenant Acts, 1931 to 1971.

Note: As this Act has no commencement provision it commences as and from the end of the day before the date of its passing. The Act was passed on 7th December 1971 — see s 8(3) of the Interpretation Act 1937.

Chapter 8

LANDLORD AND TENANT (GROUND RENTS) ACT, 1978

(1978, No. 7)

AN ACT TO PREVENT THE CREATION OF NEW LEASES RESERVING GROUND RENTS ON DWELLINGS AND TO PROVIDE FOR RELATED MATTERS.

[16TH MAY 1978]

BE IT ENACTED BY THE OIREACHTAS AS FOLLOWS:

Note: This Act does not apply to the sale of a dwelling under s 26(1)(a)(ii) or (iii) of the Housing (Miscellaneous Provisions) Act 1992 — see s 26(11)(b) of the 1992 Act. This Act also does not apply to certain shared ownership leases granted under s 16 of the Planning and Development (Amendment) Act 2002.

Definitions.

1.—In this Act— [8–01]

"the Act of 1958" means the Landlord and Tenant (Reversionary Leases) Act, 1958;

"the Act of 1967" means the Landlord and Tenant (Ground Rents) Act, 1967;

"dwelling" does not include a separate and self-contained flat in premises divided into two or more such flats;

"person" includes his personal representatives and successors in title.

Restriction on right to create leases of dwellings.

2.—(1) Subject to subsection (2), a lease of land made after the passing of this Act shall be void if the lessee would, apart from this section, have the right under section 3 of the Act of 1967 to enlarge his interest into a fee simple and the permanent buildings are constructed for use wholly or principally as a dwelling. [8–02]

(2) Subsection (1) shall not apply where the lease is a reversionary lease under the Act of 1958.

Note: As the 1958 Act was repealed in full by the Landlord and Tenant (Amendment) Act 1980, s 30(3) of the 1980 Act re-states that s 2(1) of this Act does not apply where the lease is a reversionary lease.

(3) The construction of permanent buildings for use wholly or principally as a dwelling on land which is held under a lease made after the passing of this Act shall render the lease void if the existence of the buildings, as so constructed, immediately before the making of the lease would have rendered the lease void under subsection (1).

(4) A person who has given consideration for a lease that is void under subsection (1) shall have the right to acquire the fee simple in the land and any intermediate interests therein as if he were a person to whom section 3 of the Act of 1967 applies at the expense, as to both purchase money and costs, of the person who purported to grant the lease.

(5) (a) Where, immediately before the passing of this Act—

(i) a person holds land under a lease for a term of not less than ninety-nine years, of which at least fifty years are unexpired, and

(ii) permission exists under Part IV of the Local Government (Planning and Development) Act, 1963 (including permission granted on an outline application under regulations made under section 25 of that Act) for the development of the land, wholly or mainly by the construction of dwellings,

that person shall, during the period of one year after such passing, have the right to acquire under the Act of 1967 the fee simple in the land and any intermediate interests therein, except in a case in which he has entered into an enforceable agreement with another person for the assignment to that person of his interest under the lease or for the grant of a lease for a term of not less than ninety-nine years, in which case the latter person shall during that period of one year have such right.

(b) Section 18(1)(b) of the Act of 1967 (which refers to the maximum purchase price) shall not apply in any such case.

Note: This section disapplies s 18(1)(b) of the Act of 1967 in the circumstances outlined. However, s 18 of the Act of 1967 was repealed in full by s 7(1) of the Landlord and Tenant (Ground Rents) (No 2) Act 1978.

(6) Where the trustees of a trust established by any enactment for the provision of dwellings are prevented by reason of this section from disposing of such dwellings to their tenants by way of lease, they shall be empowered in lieu thereof to dispose of them to their tenants by the grant of the fee simple.

(7) Where a lease is rendered void under subsection (3)—

(a) a sublease of any portion of the land shall not be terminated thereby, if the buildings referred to in subsection (3) are not constructed, either wholly or in part, on that portion,

(b) the person who would, but for this subsection, become entitled by virtue of the voidance to the possession of the land comprised in the sublease shall become entitled to the reversion on the sublease and to the benefit of the rent reserved by and the covenants and conditions contained in the sublease, and

(c) the sublessee shall, from the date of the voidance, hold the land demised to him at whichever of the following rents is the greater—

(i) the rent reserved by the sublease, or

(ii) such portion of the rent reserved by the avoided lease as is fairly attributable to the land comprised in the sublease.

(8) Where a dispute arises in regard to the apportionment of the rent under subsection (7)(c)(ii), the matter shall be determined under section 17 of the Act of 1967 (which refers to the determination of certain matters by arbitration).

Note: This subsection applies s 17 of the Act of 1967 to disputes as to the apportionment of rent under subs (7)(c)(ii) above.

(9) In subsection (7), references to a sublease or sublessee include, where appropriate, references to an assignment and to an assignee, his personal representatives and successors in title.

Extension of Section 2.

3.—(1) Section 2 shall extend to a lease which would be a lease to which section 4 of the Act of 1958 applies if, in substitution for paragraph (d) of subsection (2) of that section, the following paragraph were substituted: **[8–03]**

"(d) that the lease, being a lease for a term of not less than fifty years, was made—

(i) partly in consideration of the payment of a sum of money (other than rent) by the lessee to the lessor at or immediately before the grant of the lease and for this purpose any money paid in redemption of any part of the rent reserved by the lease (whether the money was paid in pursuance of a covenant in the lease or in pursuance of an agreement made between the lessee and the lessor during the currency of the lease) shall be deemed to be part of the consideration, or

(ii) partly in consideration of the expenditure (otherwise than on decoration) of a sum of money by the lessee on the premises demised by the lease, or

(iii) partly in consideration of both that payment and that expenditure

and that the sum so paid or expended or the total of those sums was not less than fifteen times the yearly amount of the rent or the greatest rent reserved by the lease, whichever is the less."

Note: Section 2 of this Act extended to include leases which would fall within s 4 of the Act of 1958 if substituted by the revised wording. However, the Act of 1958 was repealed in full by s 11 of the Landlord and Tenant (Amendment) Act 1980.

(2) In determining, for the purposes of subsection (1) the greatest rent reserved by a lease the following provisions shall have effect:

(a) where during the currency of a lease part of the rent is redeemed by a capital payment, the reduced rent shall be deemed to be the greatest rent reserved by the lease;

(b) a penal rent payable for any breach of covenant and any exceptional rent reserved for a specified period not exceeding five years shall be disregarded.

Sales of dwelling by housing authority.

4.—*Omitted. Repealed by s 37 and the Schedule to the Housing (Miscellaneous Provisions) Act 1992.* **[8–04]**

Short title, construction and collective citation.

[8–05] 5.—(1) This Act may be cited as the Landlord and Tenant (Ground Rents) Act, 1978.

(2) The Landlord and Tenant Acts, 1931 to 1971, and this Act shall be construed together as one Act and may be cited together as the Landlord and Tenant Act 1931 to 1978.

ACTS REFERRED TO

Landlord and Tenant Act, 1931 (1931, No. 55)
Landlord and Tenant (Reversionary Leases) Act, 1958 (1958, No. 2)
Local Government (Planning and Development) Act, 1963 (1963, No. 28)
Housing Act, 1966 (1966, No. 21)
Landlord and Tenant (Ground Rents) Act, 1967 (1967, No. 3)

Note: As this Act has no commencement provision it commences as and from the end of the day before the date of its passing. The Act was passed on 16th May 1978—see s 8(3) of the Interpretation Act 1937.

Chapter 9

LANDLORD AND TENANT (GROUND RENTS) (NO 2) ACT, 1978

(1978, No. 16)

AN ACT TO PROVIDE FOR THE ACQUISITION OF THE FEE SIMPLE IN LAND BY CERTAIN LESSEES AND TENANTS AND THE CONSEQUENTIAL TERMINATION OF THEIR LIABILITY FOR THE PAYMENT OF GROUND RENT, TO AMEND IN OTHER RESPECTS THE LAW OF LANDLORD AND TENANT AND TO PROVIDE FOR OTHER MATTERS CONNECTED WITH THE MATTERS AFORESAID.

[28TH JUNE 1978]

BE IT ENACTED BY THE OIREACHTAS AS FOLLOWS:

PART I – PRELIMINARY

Short title, construction and collective citation.

1.—(1) This Act may be cited as the Landlord and Tenant (Ground Rents) (No. 2) Act, 1978. **[9–01]**

(2) The collective citation, the Landlord and Tenant Acts, 1931 to 1978, shall include this Act and those Acts and this Act shall be construed together as one Act.

Commencement.

2.—This Act shall come into operation on the 1st day of August, 1978. **[9–02]**

Definitions.

3.—In this Act, except where the context otherwise requires— **[9–03]**

"the Act of 1931" means the Landlord and Tenant Act, 1931;

"the Act of 1958" means the Landlord and Tenant (Reversionary Leases) Act, 1958;

"the Act of 1967" means the Landlord and Tenant (Ground Rents) Act, 1967;

"the Court" means the Circuit Court;

"dwelling" does not include a separate and self-contained flat in premises divided into two or more such flats;

"dwellinghouse" has the meaning assigned by section 19;

"immediate lessor" means the person for the time being entitled to the next superior interest in land held by any person whether under a lease or other contract of tenancy, or otherwise;

"lease" means an instrument in writing, whether under or not under seal, containing a contract of tenancy in respect of any land in consideration of a rent or return and includes a fee farm grant;

"lessee" includes the personal representatives and successors in title of a lessee;

"lessor" includes the personal representatives and successors in title of a lessor;

"the Minister" means the Minister for Justice;

"notice", in relation to the acquisition of the fee simple, means, where notices are required to be served under section 4 of the Act of 1967 on more than one person, the first served of those notices;

"statutory tenancy" means a statutory tenancy under the Rent Restrictions Act, 1946, or the Rent Restrictions Act, 1960.

Restriction on application to State etc.

[9–04] 4.—(1) This Act shall not bind—

(a) a Minister of the Government,

(b) the Commissioners of Public Works in Ireland,

(c) Industrial Development Agency (Ireland),

(cc) a company within the meaning of section 2 of the Harbours Act 1996,

(d) Shannon Free Airport Development Company, or

(e) Udarás na Gaeltachta.

(2) Subsection (1) is in addition to any other enactment imposing a restriction on the application of this Act.

Amendment history: Section 4 of this Act was substituted by s 2 of the Landlord and Tenant (Ground Rents) Act 2005 which Act commenced as and from the end of the day before the date of its passing (passed on 19th May 2005). Section 4 of this Act originally read: "This Act shall not bind a Minister of the Government, the Commissioners of Public Works in Ireland or the Irish Land Commission."

Subs(1)(cc) was added by s 55(1) of the Maritime Safety Act 2005. S 55(2) of the 2005 Act provides that this amendment does not affect actions taken before the commencement of the section under the Landlord and Tenant Acts 1967 to 2005.

Note: Section 3 of the Landlord and Tenant (Ground Rents) Act 2005 contains certain savers to which the amendment of s 4 herein does not apply — see s 3 of the 2005 Act.

Section 70 of the Landlord and Tenant (Amendment) Act 1980 had previously extended the application of s 4, s 16(2)(d) and s 16(2)(e) of this Act to certain public authorities.

Regulations.

[9–05] 5.—(1) The Minister may make regulations for the purpose of giving full effect to the provisions of this Act including the prescribing of forms.

(2) Every regulation made by the Minister under this Act shall be laid before each House of the Oireachtas as soon as may be after it is made and, if a resolution annulling the regulation is passed by either such House within the next subsequent twenty-one days on which that House has sat after the regulation is laid before it, the regulation shall be annulled accordingly, but without prejudice to the validity of anything previously done under the regulation.

Expenses.

6.—The expenses incurred by the Minister in the administration of this Act shall, to such extent as may be sanctioned by the Minister for Finance, be paid out of moneys provided by the Oireachtas. [9–06]

Repeals.

7.—(1) *Omitted. Repeals s 3 (except subs (5)), s 5(1), s 5(2), s 18 and s 31 of the Landlord and Tenant (Ground Rents) Act 1967.* [9–07]

(2) The reference in section 3(5) of the Act of 1967 to a certificate of the Commissioner of Valuation shall have effect as if for the reference to "paragraph (d) of subsection (2) of this section" there were substituted a reference to Part II of this Act.

PART II – PURCHASE OF FEE SIMPLE

General Right

General right to acquire fee simple.

8.—A person to whom this Part applies shall, subject to the provisions of this Part, have the right as incident to his existing interest in land to enlarge that interest into a fee simple, and for that purpose to acquire by purchase the fee simple in the land and any intermediate interests in it and the Act of 1967 shall apply accordingly. [9–08]

Lessees

Right of lessee.

9.—(1) This Part applies to a person who holds land under a lease, if the following conditions are complied with: [9–09]

(a) that there are permanent buildings on the land and that the portion of the land not covered by those buildings is subsidiary and ancillary to them;

(b) that the permanent buildings are not an improvement within the meaning of subsection (2);

(c) that the permanent buildings were not erected in contravention of a covenant in the lease; and

(d) one of the alternative conditions set out in section 10.

(2) In subsection (1)(b) "improvement" in relation to buildings means any addition to or alteration of the buildings and includes any structure which is ancillary or subsidiary to those buildings, but does not include any alteration or reconstruction of the buildings so that they lose their original identity.

> **Note:** The rights granted under s 9(1) and (2) of this Act extend to the right to a reversionary lease — see s 30(2)(b) of the Landlord and Tenant (Amendment) Act, 1980.

(3) Where it is claimed that a lease complies with this Part on the ground that the permanent buildings were erected in pursuance of an agreement for the grant of the lease on their erection but express evidence of the agreement is not available, the following provisions shall have effect:

(a) if it is proved that the buildings were erected by the person to whom the lease was subsequently made, it shall be presumed, until the contrary is proved, that the agreement was in fact made and that the buildings were erected in accordance with it;

(b) in any other case, the arbitrator may, if he so thinks proper on hearing such evidence as is available and is adduced, presume that the agreement was in fact made and that the buildings were erected in accordance with it.

(4) Permanent buildings erected by a lessee in pursuance of a covenant in his lease to reinstate the buildings comprised in the lease in the event of their destruction by fire or otherwise shall be deemed to have been erected by the person who erected the original buildings.

(5) The arbitrator may declare a person to be a person to whom this Part applies notwithstanding that the buildings were, in whole or in part, erected in contravention of a covenant, if he is of opinion that it would be unreasonable to order otherwise.

Alternative conditions to be complied with.

[9–10] 10.—The following are alternative conditions one of which must also be complied with in a case to which section 9 relates:

1. that the permanent buildings were erected by the person who at the time of their erection was entitled to the lessee's interest under the lease or were erected in pursuance of an agreement for the grant of the lease upon the erection of the permanent buildings;
2. that the lease is for a term of not less than fifty years and the yearly amount of the rent or the greatest rent reserved thereunder (whether redeemed at any time or not) is of an amount that is less than the amount of the rateable valuation of the property at the date of service under section 4 of the Act of 1967 of notice of intention to acquire the fee simple or the date of an application under Part III of this Act, as the case may be, and that the permanent buildings on the land demised by the lease were not erected by the lessor or any superior lessor or any of their predecessors in title:

   provided that it shall be presumed, until the contrary is proved, that the buildings were not so erected;

Note: The reference in condition 2 of s 10 of this Act includes an application under s 31 of the Landlord and Tenant (Amendment) Act 1980 — see s 30(2)(c) of the 1980 Act.

3. that the lease was granted by a lessor to the nominee of a person (in this paragraph referred to as the builder) to whom land was demised for the purpose of erecting buildings thereon in pursuance of an agreement between the lessor and the builder that the builder having contracted to sell the buildings would surrender his lease in consideration of the lessor granting new leases to the builder's nominees;
4. that the lease was granted by a lessor to the nominee of a person (in this paragraph referred to as the builder) in pursuance of an agreement between the lessor and the builder that the lessor, upon the erection of the buildings by the builder, would grant leases to the builder's nominees;

5. that the lease was granted, either at the time of the expiration or surrender of a previous lease or subsequent to such expiration or surrender—
   (a) at a rent less than the rateable valuation of the property at the date of the grant of the lease, or
   (b) to the person entitled to the lessee's interest under the previous lease,

   provided that the previous lease [expired or was surrendered before the 31st day of March, 1931 and that it] would have been a lease to which this Part would have applied had this Act then been in force and provided that it shall be presumed, until the contrary is proved, that the person to whom the lease was granted was so entitled;
6. that the lease is a reversionary lease granted on or after the 31st day of March, 1931, to a person entitled thereto under Part V of the Act of 1931 or the Act of 1958, whether granted on terms settled by the Court or negotiated between the parties;
7. that the lease, being a lease for a term of not less than fifty years, was made—
   (a) partly in consideration of the payment of a sum of money (other than rent) by the lessee to the lessor at or immediately before the grant of the lease and, for this purpose, any money paid in redemption of any part of the rent reserved by the lease (whether the money was paid in pursuance of a covenant in the lease or in pursuance of an agreement made between the lessee and the lessor during the currency of the lease) shall be deemed to be part of the consideration, or
   (b) partly in consideration of the expenditure (otherwise than on decoration) of a sum of money by the lessee on the premises demised by the lease, or
   (c) partly in consideration of both that payment and that expenditure,

   where the sum so paid or expended or the total of those sums was not less than fifteen times the yearly amount of the rent or the greatest rent reserved by the lease, whichever is the less.

Amendment history: The words in square brackets in s 10, condition 5 of this Act was deleted by s 71 of the Landlord and Tenant (Amendment) Act 1980.

Note: By virtue of s 72 of the Landlord and Tenant (Amendment) Act 1980, s 10, condition 7 and s 12 of this Act were extended to a lease made for a term of less than 50 years if: (a) the lease is a sublease (whether mediate or immediate) under a lease (herein referred to as the superior lease) to which Part II of this Act applies; (b) the land demised by the lease is the whole or part of the land comprised in the superior lease, and; (c) the lease is made for a term which equals or exceeds the lesser of the following periods, namely twenty years or two-thirds of the term of the superior lease, and in any case expires at the same time as or not more than 15 years before the expiration of the superior lease, and the other requirements of the condition are fulfilled.

The rights granted under s 10 of this Act extend to the right to a reversionary lease — see s 30(2)(b) of the Landlord and Tenant (Amendment) Act 1980.

Greatest rent under section 10.

[9–11] 11.—In determining for the purposes of section 10 the greatest rent reserved by a lease the following provisions shall have effect:

(a) where during the currency of a lease part of the rent is redeemed by a capital payment, the reduced rent shall be deemed to be the greatest rent reserved by the lease;

(b) a penal rent payable for any breach of covenant and any exceptional rent reserved for a specified period not exceeding five years shall be disregarded.

Note: The rights granted under s 11 of this Act extend to the right to a reversionary lease — see s 30(2)(b) of the Landlord and Tenant (Amendment) Act 1980.

Extension of section 10, condition 7.

[9–12] 12.—A lease for a term of not less than fifty years shall be deemed to comply with condition 7 in section 10 if—

(a) the lease was granted partly in consideration of an undertaking by the lessee to carry out specified works on the premises demised by the lease,

(b) the amount to be expended on the works was not specified,

(c) the works were carried out by the lessee, and

(d) it is proved that the reasonable cost of the works taken either alone or together with any fine or other payment mentioned in that condition was not less than fifteen times the yearly amount of the rent or the greatest rent reserved by the lease, whichever is the less.

Note: By virtue of s 72 of the Landlord and Tenant (Amendment) Act 1980, s 10, condition 7 and s 12 of this Act were extended to a lease made for a term of less than 50 years if: (a) the lease is a sublease (whether mediate or immediate) under a lease (herein referred to as the superior lease) to which Part II of this Act applies; (b) the land demised by the lease is the whole or part of the land comprised in the superior lease, and; (c) the lease is made for a term which equals or exceeds the lesser of the following periods, namely twenty years or two-thirds of the term of the superior lease, and in any case expires at the same time as or not more than 15 years before the expiration of the superior lease, and the other requirements of the condition are fulfilled.

The rights granted under s 12 of this Act extend to the right to a reversionary lease — see s 30(2)(b) of the Landlord and Tenant (Amendment) Act 1980.

Right of lessee under expired lease.

13.—Where— [9–13]

(a) a lease expired within ten years before the commencement of this Act, and

(b) the lessee is, at such commencement, in possession of the land comprised in the expired lease under a yearly tenancy arising by implication from the acts of the parties or under a statutory tenancy under the Rent Restrictions Acts, 1960 and 1967, or as a tenant at will or otherwise, without having obtained a new tenancy from the lessor or acquired the lessor's interest in the land, and

(c) no person was, immediately before such commencement, entitled to be granted a lease under the Act of 1958,

the lessee shall, during the twelve months after the commencement of this Act, have the same right to acquire the fee simple as he would have if his lease had not expired.

Partly-built leases.

14.—(1) Where a person holds land under a lease (in this section referred to as a partly-built lease) which would entitle him to acquire the fee simple but for the fact that the portion of the land which is not covered by the permanent buildings is not wholly subsidiary and ancillary to those buildings, the following provisions of this section shall have effect. [9–14]

(2) The partly-built lease shall, for the purposes of this Act, be deemed to comprise two separate leases as follows:

(a) one lease (in this section referred to as the built-on lease) comprising that portion of the land demised by the partly-built lease which is covered by the permanent buildings, together with so much of the land as is subsidiary and ancillary to those buildings, and

(b) the other lease (in this section referred to as the vacant lease) comprising the residue of the said land.

(3) For the purposes of the division of the partly-built lease, such portion of the rent reserved by that lease as is fairly attributable to the land comprised in the built-on lease shall be apportioned to the built-on lease and the remainder of the said rent shall be apportioned to the vacant lease, and the covenants on the lessee's part and the conditions contained in the partly-built lease shall be apportioned likewise so as to relate separately to the land comprised in the built-on lease and to the land comprised in the vacant lease.

(4) The built-on lease shall be a lease to which this Part applies.

Note: The rights granted under s 14 of this Act extend to the right to a reversionary lease — see s 30(2)(b) of the Landlord and Tenant (Amendment) Act 1980.

Yearly tenants

Right of yearly tenant.

15.—(1) This Part also applies to a person who holds land in the following circumstances— [9–15]

(a) that the land is covered wholly or partly by permanent buildings and any land not so covered is subsidiary and ancillary to those buildings;

(b) that the land is held under a contract of yearly tenancy or under a yearly tenancy arising by operation of law or by inference on the expiration of a lease, or under a statutory tenancy implied by holding over property on the expiration of a lease which reserves a yearly rent;

(c) that the land has been continuously held under any one or more of the tenancies referred to in paragraph (b) (including any expired lease) by the person or his predecessors in title for a period of not less than twenty-five years prior to the date of service by the person of notice of intention under section 4 of the Act of 1967 to acquire the fee simple or the date of an application under Part III of this Act;

(d) that, either—

(i) the yearly rent is less than the rateable valuation of the property at the date of service of that notice of intention or application, or

(ii) it is proved that the permanent buildings were erected by the tenant or a predecessor in title.

(e) that the permanent buildings were not erected by the immediate lessor or any superior lessor or any of their predecessors in title, provided, however, that it shall be presumed until the contrary is proved that the permanent buildings were not so erected;

(f) that the contract of tenancy is not a letting which is made and expressed to be made for the temporary convenience of the immediate lessor or of the person holding under the Contract and, if the letting was made after the passing of the Act of 1931, stating the nature of the temporary convenience, and

(g) that the contract of tenancy is not a letting which is made for or dependent on the continuance of the person holding under the contract in any office, employment or appointment.

(2) Where land (in this section referred to as a partly-built holding) would be land in relation to which this section applies but for the fact that the portion of the land which is not covered by the permanent buildings is not wholly subsidiary and ancillary to those buildings, subsections (3), (4) and (5) shall have effect.

(3) The partly-built holding shall, for the purposes of this Part, be deemed to comprise two separate holdings as follows:

(a) one holding (in this section referred to as the built-on holding) comprising that portion of the land which is covered by the permanent buildings, together with so much of the land as is subsidiary and ancillary to those buildings, and

(b) the other holding (in this section referred to as the vacant holding) comprising the residue of the land.

(4) For the purposes of the division of the partly-built holding, such portion of the rent for the holding as is fairly attributable to the land comprised in the built-on holding shall be apportioned to the built-on holding and the remainder of the rent shall be apportioned to the vacant holding, and the covenants on the part of the person holding the land and the conditions attached to the tenancy of the partly-built holding shall be apportioned likewise so as to relate separately to the land comprised in the built-on holding and to the land comprised in the vacant holding.

(5) The built-on holding shall be land in relation to which this section applies.

Amendment history: Section 15(1)(d) was amended and substituted by s 9 of the Landlord and Tenant (Amendment) Act 1984 which Act commenced one week after the day of its passing (passed on 14th March 1984). S 15(1)(d) originally read "that the yearly rent is less than the rateable valuation of the property at the date of the service of that notice of intention or application".

Restrictions

Restrictions on right to acquire fee simple.

16.—(1) Section 8 does not apply, in relation to any land, to a person who has been declared by virtue of section 15(1) of the Act of 1958 not to be entitled to a reversionary lease of the land under that Act and who is in possession of the land under a lease or tenancy or by virtue of subsection (2) of the said section 15. [9–16]

(2) A person shall not be entitled to acquire the fee simple under this Part if the lease on which such right is based is—

(a) a lease of land which is used for the purposes of business or includes a building divided into not less than four separate and self-contained flats being a lease which contains provisions enabling the amount of the rent reserved by the lease to be altered within twenty-six years from the commencement of the lease (not being provisions enabling such rent to be altered once only and within five years from such commencement or upon the erection after such commencement of any buildings upon the land or upon the breach of a covenant in the lease), or

(b) a lease granted before the commencement of the Act of 1967 of land which is used for the purposes of business, being a lease which contains provisions requiring the lessee to carry on business on the land which is restricted in whole or in part to dealing in commodities produced or supplied by the lessor, or

(c) a lease of land containing a covenant by the lessee to erect a building or buildings or carry out development on the land if and so long as the covenant has not been substantially complied with, or

(d) a lease made by the Commissioners of Irish Lights, or

(e) a lease made by a harbour authority, within the meaning of the Harbours Act, 1946, whether before or after the passing of that Act, or

(f) subject to subsection (3), a sublease of land granted by a lessee who is not a person to whom this Part applies—

(i) on or after 27 February 2006, or

(ii) before that date, unless before that date—

(I) a notice of intention to acquire the fee simple in the land was served by the sublessee in accordance with section 4 of the Act of 1967, or

(II) an application was made by the sublessee to the Registrar of Titles under Part III of this Act.

(3) Subsection (2)(f) does not apply where—

(a) at the date on which the sublease is granted, the sole reason why the lessee is not a person to whom this Part applies is that a covenant by the lessee to erect permanent buildings on the land has not been substantially complied with, and

(b) after that date, the covenant is substantially complied with by the sublessee.

(4) In this section "sublessee" includes the personal representatives and successors in title of a sublessee.

Amendment history: S 16 of this Act was amended by s 76 of the Registration of Deeds and Title Act 2006. By virtue of s 76 of the 2006 Act, s 16(2)(f); s 16(3); and s 16(4) were added to this Act. S 16(2)(e) was also amended to add ",or" after the original s 16(2)(e). This amendment/addition took effect upon the passing of the 2006 Act (passed 7th May 2006).

Note: Section 70 of the Landlord and Tenant (Amendment) Act 1980 extends the application of s 4, s 16(2)(d) and s 16(2)(e) of this Act to certain public authorities. But see s 4 of this Act as substituted by s 2 of the Landlord and Tenant (Ground Rents) Act 2005.

Purchase Price

Determination of purchase price by arbitration.

[9–17] 17.—*Omitted. Repealed by s 7(11) of the Landlord and Tenant (Amendment) Act 1984.*

PART III – VESTING OF FEE SIMPLE IN DWELLINGHOUSES

Note: By virtue of s 10(c) of the Registration of Deeds and Title Act 2006, the Property Registration Authority now exercises the functions of dealing with applications under Part III of this Act. The Property Registration Authority was established on 4th November 2006 — see Registration of Deeds and Title Act 2006 (Commencement) (No 2) Order 2006 (SI No 511 of 2006).

Duration of Part III.

[9–18] 18.—*Omitted. Repealed by s 1 of the Landlord and Tenant (Ground Rents) (Amendment) Act 1987.*

Amendment history: Section 18 which set a duration for the application of Part III of this Act was amended by s 1 of the Landlord and Tenant (Ground Rents) (Amendment) Act 1983 to increase the original five-year period to six years. Section 18 was again amended by s 2 of the Landlord and Tenant (Ground Rents) (Amendment) Act 1984 and the period increased to nine years. Section 18 was then repealed in full by s 1 of the Landlord and Tenant (Ground Rents) (Amendment) Act 1987.

Dwellinghouses.

19.—This Part applies to land to which Part II applies where the permanent buildings are constructed for use wholly or principally as a dwelling and are so used and such land is referred to in this Act as a dwellinghouse. **[9–19]**

Vesting by consent.

20.—A person who is entitled to acquire the fee simple in a dwellinghouse by virtue of Part II may, with the consent of every person who would be a necessary party to the conveyance to him of the fee simple free from incumbrances, apply to the Registrar of Titles to vest the premises in him under section 22. **[9–20]**

Arbitration.

21.—(1) A person who claims to be entitled to acquire the fee simple in a dwellinghouse by virtue of Part II may, without any consent referred to in section 20, apply to the Registrar of Titles to have the premises vested in him under section 22 and he shall serve notice of his application upon the immediate lessor. Service of a notice may be effected in any manner provided for by section 63 of the Act of 1931 or section 23 of the Act of 1967. **[9–21]**

(2) The Registrar may, however, dispense with service under subsection (1) where the applicant satisfies him that it is not reasonably practicable to effect such service. In any such case, the Registrar shall serve notice of the application on every person who appears to him to be the owner of any estate, interest or incumbrance which would be extinguished by the issue of a certificate under section 22(1), so far as it is reasonably practicable to ascertain such persons.

(3) The Registrar of Titles shall determine the application by arbitration.

(4) The provisions of the Act of 1967 shall apply for the purposes of this Part with the substitution, for references to the county registrar, of references to the Registrar of Titles.

(5) An appeal to the Court under section 22 of the Act of 1967 against an award, order or other decision of the Registrar as arbitrator shall be heard and determined by a Judge of the Court for the time being assigned to the circuit in which are situate the premises or any part of the premises in relation to which the appeal is taken.

Vesting certificate.

22.—(1) Where— **[9–22]**

(a) the Registrar of Titles is satisfied that an application under section 20 has been duly made, or

(b) the Registrar as arbitrator or the Court on appeal is satisfied that the applicant under section 21 is entitled to acquire the fee simple,

the Registrar shall, subject to subsection (2), issue a certificate (in this section referred to as a "vesting certificate") which shall, subject to subsection (3), operate to convey fee from incumbrances the fee simple and any intermediate interests in the dwellinghouse on the date specified in that behalf in the certificate.

> **Note:** A spelling or typographical error appears in this subsection in the Act as published. Presumably the wording "... to convey fee from incumbrances ..." ought to read "... to convey free from incumbrances ...".

(2) Before issuing a vesting certificate the Registrar shall satisfy himself that the purchase price has been paid or deposited with him, that the prescribed fees have been discharged and that rent for the dwellinghouse (other than arrears an action for the recovery of which is statute-barred) has been paid up to date.

(3) The vesting certificate shall be deemed to be a conveyance on sale for the purposes of sections 24 and 25 of the Registration of Title Act, 1964 (which provide for the extension of compulsory registration of ownership) and shall be deemed to be an instrument in the prescribed form for the purposes of section 51 of that Act (which provides for transfer of registered land).

(4) In a case to which subsection (3) relates, the Registrar shall, on being supplied with any further documents which he may require, provide for registration of the title under the Registration of Title Act, 1964.

(5) The Registrar shall serve notice of the grant of a vesting certificate on arbitration on every person who appears to him to have been the owner of any estate, interest or incumbrance extinguished by virtue of subsection (1), so far as it is reasonably practicable to ascertain such persons.

(6) A person who claims to be entitled, as the owner of any estate, interest or incumbrance extinguished by virtue of subsection (1), to payment of the purchase money or any part of it deposited with the Registrar may apply to the Registrar as arbitrator for an award and the arbitrator shall, after serving reasonable notice of the claim on each of the persons notified under subsection (5), make such award and give such directions as he thinks just for the disbursement and distribution of the purchase money.

(7) The Registrar may, if he thinks proper, lodge in Court any money deposited with him under this section and the jurisdiction conferred on him under subsection (6) shall thereupon be exercised by a Judge of the Court for the time being assigned to the circuit in which are situate the premises or any part of the premises in relation to which the money is lodged.

Fees.

[9–23] 23.—(1) The fee to be taken in the Land Registry

(a) for the issue of a vesting certificate under section 22 shall, where the applicant is in occupation of the dwellinghouse, be [£5] [£15] [£26] €30;

(b) for an arbitration under section 21 shall, where the applicant is in occupation of the dwellinghouse, be [£12] [£36] [£63] €75 which shall be in addition to the fee to be taken under paragraph (a).

Amendment history: In relation to any application under Part III of this Act, made on or after 1 August 1983, s 23 (1) of this Act has effect as if there were substituted "£15" for "£5" in paragraph (a) and "£36" for "£12" in paragraph (b) — see s 2 of the Landlord and Tenant (Ground Rents) (Amendment) Act 1983. In relation to any application under Part III of this Act made on or after 1st August 1984, s 23 (1) of this Act, as amended by section 2 of the Landlord and Tenant (Ground Rents) (Amendment) Act 1984, has effect as if there were substituted "£26" for "£15" in paragraph (a) and "£63" for "£36" in paragraph (b). By the provisions of the s 1 and the First Schedule to the Euro Changeover (Amounts) Act 2001: "£26" now equates to €30; and "£63" now equates to €75.

(2) The Minister, with the consent of the Minister for Finance, may by order fix the fees to be taken in the Land Registry for the purposes of this Part, [other than the fees mentioned in subsection (1)], and may revoke or amend any such order.

> **Note:** In subs (2), on and after 1 August 1984, the words in square brackets "other than the fees mentioned in subsection (1)" ceased to have effect — see s 3 of the Landlord and Tenant (Ground Rents) (Amendment) Act 1984.

(3) [With the exception of fees fixed in respect of the cases mentioned in subsection (1)] the fees shall, so far as possible, be so fixed as to meet the full cost of dealing with the relevant application.

> **Note:** In subs (3), on and after 1st August 1984, the words in square brackets "With the exception of fees fixed in respect of the cases mentioned in subsection (1)" ceased to have effect — see s 3 of the Landlord and Tenant (Ground Rents) (Amendment) Act 1984.

(4) The applicant shall be liable for the payment of the fee to be taken for the issue of the vesting certificate and, subject to subsection (5), he shall also be liable for the payment of the fee to be taken for the arbitration.

(5) Where the applicant is in occupation of the dwellinghouse neither he nor any other party shall be liable to make any payment, apart from the fees fixed by or under this section, to the Registrar in respect of the arbitration or vesting, save that where in the opinion of the Registrar, any party to the arbitration has behaved unreasonably (whether by act or omission) or has, without reasonable cause—

(a) refused or failed to comply with a provision of this Act or delayed in so complying, or

(b) refused or failed to reach agreement or delayed in reaching agreement in relation to any matter under this Act,

and thereby occasioned the incurring of the whole or part of the cost of dealing with the arbitration, the Registrar may direct that the whole or a specified part of such cost shall be paid by that party.

(6) Sections 9 and 19(1) of the Act of 1967 (which provide for the costs of an arbitration) shall not apply where the applicant is in occupation of the dwellinghouse.

(7) Section 14 (2) of the Registration of Title Act, 1964, shall not apply to the taking of fees in relation to the functions of the Registrar of Titles under this Act.

Duty of Registrar of Titles as to applications under Part III.

24.—(1) The Registrar of Titles shall deal with applications received under this Part in the order in which they are received so far as is consistent with the efficient discharge of all his functions as Registrar of Titles. [9–24]

(2) Where the Registrar is satisfied for reasons submitted in writing by the applicant or any other person concerned that an application is exceptional in that compliance with the duty imposed by subsection (1) in respect of it would result in serious inconvenience or substantial loss to any such person, he may deal with the application otherwise than in the order in which it was received.

(3) No action shall lie against the Registrar in relation to the duty imposed upon him under this section.

Exercise of functions of Registrar of Titles.

[9–25] 25.—All or any of the powers and duties conferred or imposed on the Registrar of Titles by this Part may be exercised and performed by such of his officers as the Minister may authorise in that behalf.

PART IV – MISCELLANEOUS

Acquisition of fee simple from housing authority.

[9–26] 26.—(1) Where a housing authority have leased to a tenant a dwelling provided by them under statutory authority, the tenant shall be entitled to acquire from them the fee simple in the dwelling subject to the provisions of this section.

(2) The terms and conditions specified in the instrument by which the lease was effected (other than a condition for the payment of rent) shall continue to apply in relation to the dwelling for the period of twenty-five years from the date of the lease or for the period during which any part of the purchase price of the leasehold interest remains unpaid, whichever is the greater.

(3) Where the rent reserved by the lease contains an element in respect of the repayment of the purchase price of the leasehold interest, the housing authority shall certify the amount of the purchase price and the amount of the rent attributable to the repayment of that amount, and the amount of such purchase price shall stand charged on the property from the date of acquisition of the fee simple.

(4) Where a housing authority have leased a dwelling provided by them under statutory authority, to a person other than a tenant thereof, the lessee shall be entitled to acquire from them the fee simple in the dwelling and any condition specified in the instrument by which the lease was effected in respect of the repayment of the purchase price of the leasehold interest or in respect of the refund of a subsidy shall attach to the fee simple.

(5) The purchase price of the fee simple shall not exceed the amount provided for under section 17(3) taking the rent referred to in that subsection as being the amount thereof less any amount attributable to the repayment of the purchase price of the leasehold interest.

> **Note:** S 17 of this Act was repealed by s 7(11) of the Landlord and Tenant (Amendment) Act 1984. Nonetheless, reference to s 17 of this Act remains in subs (5). However, the provisions of s 17(3) of this Act are substantially re-enacted in s 7(5) of the 1984 (Amendment) Act.

(6) Every term and condition attaching to the grant of the fee simple pursuant to this section shall be binding upon the purchaser thereof, his personal representatives and successors in title.

(7) A vesting of the fee simple under this section shall be effected by a transfer order under section 90 of the Housing Act, 1966.

(8) The fee to be taken by a housing authority for the issue of a transfer order pursuant to this section shall be £5.

> **Note:** In the case of an application made on or after 1st August 1984, for a transfer order pursuant to s 26 of this Act, the fee to be taken by a housing authority for the issue of the order shall, subject to subs (2),

be £20 and s 26(8) of this Act ceased to have effect in any such case — see s 4(1) of the Landlord and Tenant (Ground Rents) (Amendment) Act 1984. The Minister for the Environment is empowered by s 4(2) of the Landlord and Tenant (Ground Rents) (Amendment) Act 1984 to fix the fee (by order) to be taken from time to time for the issue of a transfer order pursuant to s 26 of this Act.

(9) Where a housing authority has not the fee simple in any land on which it has provided dwellings under statutory authority, the authority shall be entitled to acquire the fee simple and for that purpose the provisions of Part II shall apply to the authority.

(10) In this section "statutory authority" shall be construed as including the Housing Act, 1966, and any Act repealed by that Act.

(11) In this section references to a lease are to the grant of a leasehold interest in consideration of a purchase price.

Note: Section 26 does not apply in relation to a house leased under a shared ownership lease by a housing authority — see s 3(8)(b) of the Housing (Miscellaneous Provisions) Act 1992.

Covenant for re-entry for non-payment of ground rent for dwellinghouse.

27.—(1) Where a person is entitled to acquire the fee simple in a dwellinghouse by **[9–27]** virtue of Part II a covenant giving the lessor a right to re-enter and take possession of the premises where rent is in arrear shall not be enforceable against him but this shall not affect any other civil remedy of the lessor.

(2) Section 52 of the Landlord and Tenant Law Amendment Act, Ireland, 1860 (which provides for proceedings for ejectment for non-payment of a year's rent) shall not apply to a dwellinghouse to which subsection (1) relates.

Effect of acquisition of fee simple on covenants.

28.—(1) Subject to subsection (1A), where a person to whom Part II of this Act **[9–28]** applies acquires the fee simple in land under the Act of 1967 or Part III of this Act—

(a) covenants (except any of those specified in subsection (2)) affecting the land in the lease under which the person held the land thereupon cease to have effect, and

(b) no new covenant affecting the land shall be created when the fee simple is being conveyed, except with the person's agreement.

(1A) Subsection (1) has effect where the fee simple in the land concerned is acquired on or after 27 February 2006, unless before that date—

(i) a notice of intention to acquire the fee simple was served by the person in accordance with section 4 of the Act of 1967, or

(ii) an application was made by the person to the Registrar of Titles under Part III of this Act.

Amendment history: S 28(1) was amended by s 77 of the Registration of Deeds and Title Act 2006, the amendment took effect upon the passing of the 2006 Act (passed 7th May 2006). The effect of the amendment is to substitute a new subs(1) and subs (1A) for the original subs (1). S 28(1) originally read: "(1) Where a person having an interest in land acquires the fee simple in the land, all covenants subject to which he held the land, other than a covenant specified in subsection (2), shall thereupon cease to have effect and no new covenant shall be created in conveying the fee simple."

(2) In the case of a covenant—

(a) which protects or enhances the amenities of any land occupied by the immediate lessor of the grantee, or

(b) which relates to the performance of a duty imposed by statute on any such person, or

(c) which relates to a right of way over the acquired land or a right of drainage or other right necessary to secure or assist the development of other land,

the covenant shall, notwithstanding anything contained in this Act, continue in full force and effect and shall be enforceable as follows:

(i) in the case of a covenant which does not relate to a right of way, right of drainage or other right aforesaid, by any such person or his personal representatives or successors in title, as if the acquisition had not occurred, and

(ii) in the case of a covenant which does so relate, by any person aggrieved by breach of the covenant.

(3) In any case where the fee simple in land was acquired since the commencement of the Act of 1967 by a person who had an interest in the land, any covenant subject to which the grantee held the land, other than a covenant specified in subsection (2), shall be deemed to have ceased to have effect at the date of the acquisition.

(4) Section 72(1) of the Registration of Title Act, 1964 (which relates to burdens that affect land without registration) is hereby amended by the insertion of:

"(r) covenants which continue in force by virtue of section 28 of the Landlord and Tenant (Ground Rents) (No. 2) Act, 1978".

Effect of acquisition of simple on mortgages.

[9–29] 29.—Upon conveyance of the fee simple in land, under this Act or otherwise, to a person whose previous interest in the land was subject to a mortgage or charge (including a mortgage by subdemise) the mortgage or charge shall, if it has not been extinguished, be deemed to be a mortgage or charge on the fee simple in the land.

ACTS REFERRED TO

Harbours Act, 1946 (1946, No. 9)
Housing Act, 1966 (1966, No. 21)
Landlord and Tenant Act, 1931 (1931, No. 55)
Landlord and Tenant (Ground Rents) Act, 1967 (1967, No. 3)
Landlord and Tenant Law Amendment Act, Ireland, 1860 (1860 c. 154)
Landlord and Tenant (Reversionary Leases) Act, 1958 (1958, No. 2)
Registration of Title Act, 1964 (1964, No. 16)
Rent Restrictions Act, 1946 (1946, No. 4)
Rent Restrictions Act, 1960 (1960, No. 42)

Chapter 10

LANDLORD AND TENANT (AMENDMENT) ACT, 1980

(1980 No. 10)

ARRANGEMENT OF SECTIONS

PART I – PRELIMINARY

PART II – RIGHT TO NEW TENANCY

PART III – REVERSIONARY LEASES

30 Reversionary lease.
31 Application to obtain reversionary lease.
32 Persons bound to grant reversionary leases.
33 Restrictions on right to reversionary lease.
34 Terms of reversionary lease settled by Court.
35 Determination of rent.
36 Gross rent.
37 Applications to the Court.
38 Expenditure on repairs.
39 Reversionary lease a graft on former lease.
40 Right of lessee to continue in possession.
41 Evidence of agreement to build.
42 Buildings replaced under covenant.
43 Buildings erected in breach of covenant.
44 Application of Act of 1967.

PART IV – COMPENSATION

Compensation for Improvements

45 "Improvement".
46 Compensation for improvements.
47 Measure of compensation for improvements.
48 Improvement notice.
49 Works required by public authority.
50 Execution of improvement in absence of objection.
51 Rights of parties on service of improvement undertaking.
52 Rights of parties on service of improvement objection.
53 Restriction on increase of rent of controlled dwellings.
54 Restrictions on right to compensation for improvements.
55 Improvement certificate.
56 Claim for improvements.
57 Compensation for improvements a first charge.

Compensation for Disturbance

58 Compensation where tenant not entitled to new tenancy.
59 Compensation where lessee not entitled to new lease.
60 Compensation on termination of tenancy in obsolete buildings.

Consequential Provisions

61 Set-off compensation against rent, etc.
62 Payment of compensation where interest is mortgaged.
63 Protection of trustees, etc.

AN ACT TO AMEND THE LAW RELATING TO THE RENEWAL OF LEASES AND TENANCIES AND TO COMPENSATION FOR IMPROVEMENTS AND FOR DISTURBANCE OR LOSS OF TITLE AND FOR THESE AND OTHER PURPOSES TO AMEND THE LAW OF LANDLORD AND TENANT AND TO PROVIDE FOR OTHER MATTERS CONNECTED WITH THE MATTERS AFORESAID.

[9TH JUNE 1980]

BE IT ENACTED BY THE OIREACHTAS AS FOLLOWS:

PART I – PRELIMINARY

Short title, construction and collective citation.

[10–01] 1.—(1) This Act may be cited as the Landlord and Tenant (Amendment) Act, 1980.

(2) The Landlord and Tenant (Ground Rents) Act, 1967, the Landlord and Tenant (Amendment) Act, 1971, the Landlord and Tenant (Ground Rents) Act, 1978, the Landlord and Tenant (Ground Rents) (No. 2) Act, 1978, and this Act shall be construed together as one Act and may be cited together as the Landlord and Tenant Acts, 1967 to 1980.

Commencement.

[10–02] 2.—This Act shall come into operation on such day as the Minister by order appoints.

> **Note:** This Act commenced on 8th September 1980 — see Landlord and Tenant (Amendment) Act, 1980 (Commencement) Order, 1980 (SI 271 of 1980).

Interpretation.

[10–03] 3.—(1) In this Act, except where the context otherwise requires—

"Act of 1931" means the Landlord and Tenant Act, 1931;

"Act of 1958" means the Landlord and Tenant (Reversionary Leases) Act, 1958;

"Act of 1967" means the Landlord and Tenant (Ground Rents) Act, 1967;

"business" means any trade, profession or business, whether or not it is carried on for gain or reward, any activity for providing cultural, charitable, educational, social or sporting services, and also the public service and the carrying out by an authority being the council of a county, the corporation of a county or other borough, the council of an urban district, the commissioners of a town, a health board under the Health Act, 1970, or a harbour authority under the Harbours Act, 1946, of any of their functions;

"controlled dwelling" means a controlled dwelling under the Rent Restrictions Act, 1960;

"the Court" means the Circuit Court;

"covenant" includes condition and agreement and any reservation, stipulation or other similar provision in a lease or tenancy;

"development" and "development plan" have the meanings assigned by the Local Government (Planning and Development) Act, 1963;

"immediate lessor" means the person for the time being entitled to the next superior interest in premises held by any other person under a lease or other contract of tenancy or otherwise;

"improvement certificate" has the meaning assigned by section 55 (1);

"improvement consent" has the meaning assigned by section 48 (2) (a);

"improvement notice" has the meaning assigned by section 48 (1);

"improvement objection" has the meaning assigned by section 48 (2) (c);

"improvement order" has the meaning assigned by section 52 (3);

"improvement undertaking" has the meaning assigned by section 48 (2) (b);

"landlord" means the person for the time being entitled to receive (otherwise than as agent for another person) the rent paid in respect of premises by the tenant thereof and, where the context so admits, includes a person who has ceased to be so entitled by reason of the termination of his tenancy;

"lease" means an instrument in writing, whether under or not under seal, containing a contract of tenancy in respect of any land in consideration of a rent or return and includes a fee farm grant;

"lessee" includes tenant and the personal representatives and successors in title of a lessee;

"lessor" includes landlord and the personal representatives and successors in title of a lessor;

"the Minister" means the Minister for Justice;

"planning authority" has the meaning assigned by the Local Government (Planning and Development) Act, 1963;

"planning permission" means a permission for the development of land if required by and granted under Part IV of the Local Government (Planning and Development) Act, 1963, and, where regulations under section 25 of that Act make provision for outline applications, includes a permission granted on such an application;

"predecessors in title"—

(a) when used in relation to a tenant, means all previous tenants under the same tenancy as the tenant or any tenancy of which that tenancy is or is deemed to be a continuation or renewal, and

(b) when used in relation to a landlord, means all previous landlords;

"prescribed" means prescribed by regulations made by the Minister under this Act;

"Rent Restrictions Acts", when used without reference to particular years, includes, where the context so admits, a reference to the Increase of Rent and Mortgage Interest (Restrictions) Act, 1923, to the Rent Restrictions Act, 1946, and to the Rent Restrictions Acts, 1960 and 1967;

"reversionary lease" has the meaning assigned by section 30;

"state authority" means any authority being a Minister of the Government, the Commissioners of Public Works in Ireland or the Irish Land Commission;

"statutory tenancy" means a statutory tenancy under the Rent Restrictions Act, 1946, or the Rent Restrictions Act, 1960;

"tenant" means the person for the time being entitled to the occupation of premises and, where the context so admits, includes a person who has ceased to be entitled to that occupation by reason of the termination of his tenancy;

"tenement" has the meaning assigned by section 5;

"work notice" has the meaning assigned by section 49 (1);

"work undertaking" has the meaning assigned by section 49 (2).

(2) A reference in this Act to a Part or section is to a Part or section of this Act unless it is indicated that reference to some other enactment is intended.

(3) A reference in this Act to a subsection, paragraph or other division is to the subsection, paragraph or other division of the provision in which the reference occurs, unless it is indicated that reference to some other provision is intended.

(4) A reference in this Act to any enactment shall be construed as a reference to that enactment as amended by any subsequent enactment.

Restriction on application to State.

[10–04] 4.—(1) In this section "the relevant date" means the date on which a State authority acquires the interest of the lessor or immediate lessor of any premises.

(2) Subject to the following subsections, this Act shall not bind a State authority in its capacity as lessor or immediate lessor of any premises.

(3) Where a State authority acquires the interest of the lessor or immediate lessor of any premises after the commencement of this Act and neither that nor any other State authority had any previous interest in the premises as lessor or immediate lessor, section 13 shall apply as if the expressions 'at any time' and 'at that time' in subsection (1) thereof were references to the relevant date and Part II shall have effect accordingly, save that a tenant of the State authority whose tenancy of the premises is renewed under that Part as applied by this section shall not be entitled to a further renewal of his tenancy.

[(4) Subject to the provisions of this Act, in a case to which subsection (3) applies, the tenant shall be entitled to a new tenancy in the tenement beginning on the termination of the tenancy under which he holds at the relevant date but he shall not be entitled to a further renewal of his tenancy.]

Amendment history: Subs (3) was substituted and subs (4) (in square brackets) was repealed by s 14 of the Landlord and Tenant (Amendment) Act 1984, which Act came into force one week after the day of its passing (passed on 14th March 1984). Subs 3 originally read: "Where a State authority acquires the interest of the lessor or immediate lessor of any premises after the commencement of this Act, section 13 shall apply as if the expressions "at any time" and "at that time" in subsection (1) thereof were references to the relevant date and Part II shall apply accordingly."

(5) In a case to which subsection (3) applies, subsection (2) shall not apply so as to disqualify any person for payment of compensation for improvements in respect of such improvements as may have been carried out before the relevant date.

"Tenement".

[10–05] 5.—(1) In this Act "tenement" means—

(a) premises complying with the following conditions:

(i) they consist either of land covered wholly or partly by buildings or of a defined portion of a building;

(ii) if they consist of land covered in part only by buildings, the portion of the land not so covered is subsidiary and ancillary to the buildings;

(iii) they are held by the occupier thereof under a lease or other contract of tenancy express or implied or arising by statute;

(iv) such contract of tenancy is not a letting which is made and expressed to be made for the temporary convenience of the lessor or lessee and (if made after the passing of the Act of 1931) stating the nature of the temporary convenience; and

(v) such contract of tenancy is not a letting made for or dependent on the continuance in any office, employment or appointment of the person taking the letting;

or

(b) premises to which section 14 or 15 applies.

(2) For the purposes of subsection (1) (a) (iii), where a State authority holds premises under a lease or other contract of tenancy express or implied or arising by statute, the authority shall be deemed to be in exclusive occupation thereof notwithstanding that they may be occupied for the purposes of another State authority.

(3) Where—

(a) a person holds premises under a lease or other contract of tenancy express or implied or arising by statute, and

(b) that person is entitled to the occupation of the premises, and

(c) either—

(i) the premises are used with that person's permission by a private company for the purpose of carrying on a business which that person himself carried on in the premises up to the time when it began to be carried on by the private company, or

(ii) that person being a company which is another company's holding company, the premises are used for the purpose of carrying on a business by the other company, or

(iii) that person being a company which is another company's subsidiary, the premises are used for the purpose of carrying on a business by the other company, or

(iv) that person being a company which is another company's subsidiary, the premises are used for the purpose of carrying on a business by another subsidiary of the other company,

the private company, the other company or the other subsidiary (as the case may be) shall be deemed for the purposes of subsection (1) (a) (iii) to be the tenant of the premises and to be in exclusive occupation thereof.

(4) In subsection (3) "company", "private company", "holding company" and "subsidiary" have the same meanings respectively as in the Companies Act, 1963.

Premises provided by local authorities.

6.—Where premises were or are provided or deemed to be provided by a housing authority under the Housing Act, 1966, the following provisions shall, unless the premises are let for the purpose of carrying on, in all or part thereof, a business, have effect— **[10–06]**

(a) if the premises are held by the housing authority in fee simple, this Act shall not apply to the premises;

(b) if the premises are held by the housing authority under a lease or other contract of tenancy express or implied or arising by statute, the housing authority shall be deemed for the purposes of this Act to be the tenant of the premises and to be in exclusive occupation thereof.

Note: S 32 of the Housing (Miscellaneous Provisions) Act 1992 extends the application of s 6 of this Act to apply in respect of (a) a house leased under a shared ownership lease, and (b) housing accommodation by an approved body other than a local authority, subject to certain requirements.

Statutory tenancies under the Rent Restrictions Act, 1960.

[10–07] 7.—Where a person retains possession of a tenement by virtue of the Rent Restrictions Act, 1960, the tenancy arising by virtue of that Act on the retention shall, for the purposes of this Act (whether the retention began before or after the passing of this Act), be deemed to be a continuation of the tenancy on the termination of which the retention began.

Jurisdiction of Circuit Court.

[10–08] 8.—The jurisdiction conferred by this Act on the Court shall be exercised by the Judge of the Court for the time being assigned to the Circuit in which are situate the premises or any part of the premises in relation to which the jurisdiction is exercised.

Regulations.

[10–09] 9.—(1) The Minister may make regulations in relation to any matter referred to in this Act as prescribed.

(2) Every regulation made by the Minister under this Act shall be laid before each House of the Oireachtas as soon as may be after it is made and, if a resolution annulling the regulation is passed by either such House within the next subsequent twenty-one days on which that House has sat after the regulation is laid before it, the regulation shall be annulled accordingly, but without prejudice to the validity of anything previously done under the regulation.

Expenses.

[10–10] 10.—The expenses incurred by the Minister in the administration of this Act shall, to such extent as may be sanctioned by the Minister for Finance, be paid out of moneys provided by the Oireachtas.

Repeals and consequential provisions.

[10–11] 11.—(1) The enactments mentioned in the Schedule are hereby repealed to the extent specified in the third column.

(2) The Landlord and Tenant (Amendment) Act, 1971, shall have effect as if the references to provisions of the Act of 1958 were to the corresponding provisions of this Act.

Note: The Landlord and Tenant (Reversionary Leases) Act 1958 is repealed by s 11(1) of this Act. All references to provisions of that Act of 1958 in the Landlord and Tenant (Amendment) Act 1971 are deemed to have effect as if to corresponding provisions of this Act.

(3) Any notice given under an enactment repealed by this Act shall, for the purpose of making a claim under this Act, be treated as a notice under the corresponding provision of this Act as if that provision were in force when the notice was given.

(4) Subsections (2) and (3) are without prejudice to section 21 of the Interpretation Act, 1937, which, amongst other matters, provides for the continuance of pending proceedings and the preservation of existing rights and liabilities.

Rules of court.

12.—The rules of court for the purposes of any enactment repealed by this Act shall, pending the making of rules of court for the purposes of this Act, apply for such purposes with such adaptations as may be necessary. **[10–12]**

PART II – RIGHT TO NEW TENANCY

Note: Section 192 of the Residential Tenancies Act 2004 states that as and from the fifth anniversary of the relevant date (the relevant date is 1 September 2004 — see s 5 of the 2004 Act and also SI No 505 of 2004) Part II of this Act shall not apply to a dwelling to which the 2004 Act applies. However, this does not have effect in relation to a dwelling where the tenant has served a notice of intention to claim relief before the fifth anniversary of the relevant date (the relevant date is 1 September 2004 — see s 5 of the 2004 Act and also SI No 505 of 2004).

Application of Part II.

13.—(1) This Part applies to a tenement at any time if— **[10–13]**

(a) the tenement was, during the whole of the period of [three years] five years ending at that time, continuously in the occupation of the person who was the tenant immediately before that time or of his predecessors in title and bona fide used wholly or partly for the purpose of carrying on a business, or

(b) the tenement was, during the whole of the period of twenty years ending at that time, continuously in the occupation of the person who was the tenant immediately before that time or of his predecessors in title, or

(c) improvements have been made on the tenement and the tenant would, if this Part did not apply to the tenement, be entitled to compensation for those improvements under Part IV and not less than one-half of the letting value of the tenement at that time is attributable to those improvements.

Amendment history: Paragraph (a) was amended by the substitution of "five years" for "three years" by s 3 of the Landlord and Tenant (Amendment) Act 1994. That amendment has effect only in relation to a lease or other contract of tenancy the term of which commences after the commencement of the Act of 1994 — see s 3(2) of the Landlord and Tenant (Amendment) Act 1994. The Act of 1994 commenced on 10th August 1994 — see s 1(3) of that Act.

(2) For the purpose of subsection (1) (a) a temporary break in the use of the tenement shall be disregarded if the Court considers it reasonable to disregard it.

(3) (a) The occupation by a person or his predecessors in title under a lease or other contract of tenancy of a tenement in the Custom House Docks Area (within the meaning of section 41 of the Finance Act, 1986), being a tenement bona

fide used on the commencement of occupation under the lease or contract of tenancy, and expressly authorised or required by that lease or contract to be used, wholly or partly for the purpose of carrying on an activity consisting of or including a relevant trading operation within the meaning of section 39B (inserted by section 30 of the Finance Act, 1987, as amended by section 36 of the Finance Act, 1988) of the Finance Act, 1980, or bona fide used for preparing for the carrying on of such an activity, shall not be regarded as occupation for the purposes of paragraph (a) or (b) of subsection (1).

(b) Where this subsection applies by virtue of paragraph (a) in relation to occupation—

(i) it also applies to occupation under the lease or contract concerned at any time when the tenement concerned is no longer used for the purpose of carrying on an activity aforesaid, and

(ii) it applies in relation to occupation of the whole or part of the tenement under any other lease or contract of tenancy that is in force during the whole or part of the currency of, and is made after the making of, the first-mentioned lease or contract of tenancy.

(4) Subsection (3) shall have effect only in relation to a lease or other contract of tenancy the term of which commences during the period of 5 years from the passing of the Landlord and Tenant (Amendment) Act, 1989, or such longer period as may stand specified for the time being in regulations made by the Minister at any time during the said period of 5 years or during a period standing so specified.

(5) A draft of every regulation proposed to be made under this section shall be laid before each House of the Oireachtas and the regulation shall not be made until a resolution approving of the draft has been passed by each such House.

Amendment history: Subsections (3), (4) and (5) were inserted by s 1 of the Landlord and Tenant (Amendment) Act 1989. Which Act came into force on 1st March 1989. They are new provisions added to the section after subs (2).

Note The Landlord and Tenant (Amendment) Act 1980 (S 13(4)) Regulations 1994 (SI 36 of 1994) specify the period of ten years from the passing of the Landlord and Tenant (Amendment) Act 1989 as "such longer period" for the purposes of subs (4). The 1989 Act was passed on 1st March 1989, hence the relevant period can be deduced up to and including 28th February 1999.

Application of Part II to business premises decontrolled by Rent Restrictions Act, 1960.

[10–14] 14.—(1) This Part also applies to premises which, immediately before the commencement of the Rent Restrictions Act, 1960, comprised controlled business premises under the Rent Restrictions Act, 1946, the letting of which was not—

(a) a letting made and expressed to be made for the temporary convenience of the landlord or of the tenant and (if made after the passing of the Act of 1931) stating the nature of the temporary convenience, or

(b) a letting made for or dependent on the continuance of the tenant in any office, employment or appointment.

(2) Where the premises were, immediately before the commencement of the Rent Restrictions Act, 1960, held under a statutory tenancy, the tenant under that tenancy shall, on and after such commencement, be deemed to hold the premises from the landlord under a tenancy having the same terms and conditions as the statutory tenancy except that the landlord may, by not less than three months' notice to quit (expiring on any day specified in that behalf in the notice) served on the tenant, determine the tenancy.

Application of Part II to dwellings decontrolled by Rent Restrictions (Amendment) Act, 1967.

15.—(1) This Part also applies to a dwelling, being a house or a separate and self-contained flat, which immediately before the passing of the Rent Restrictions (Amendment) Act, 1967, was a controlled dwelling, the rateable valuation of which— **[10–15]**

(a) if situate in the county borough of Dublin or the borough of Dún Laoghaire, exceeds £40 (if a house) or £30 (if a flat), and

(b) in any other case, exceeds £30 (if a house) or £20 (if a flat), and the letting of which was not—

(i) a letting made and expressed to be made for the temporary convenience of the landlord or of the tenant and (if made after the passing of the Act of 1931) stating the nature of the temporary convenience, or

(ii) a letting made for or dependent on the continuance of the tenant in any office, employment or appointment.

(2) This Part also applies to a dwelling, being a house having a rateable valuation exceeding £10, of which, after the passing of the Rent Restrictions (Amendment) Act, 1967, a bachelor or spinster over the age of 21 years and under the age of 65 years has become the tenant and which, immediately before he or she became the tenant, was a controlled dwelling.

(3) Where a dwelling to which subsection (1) refers was, immediately before the passing of the Rent Restrictions (Amendment) Act, 1967, held under a statutory tenancy, the tenant under that tenancy shall, from such passing, be deemed to hold the dwelling from the landlord under a tenancy having the same terms and conditions as the statutory tenancy except that the landlord may, by not less than three months' notice to quit (expiring on any day specified in that behalf in the notice) served on the tenant, determine the tenancy.

(4) Where a dwelling to which subsection (2) refers was, immediately before the time when the person referred to in that subsection became the tenant, held under a statutory tenancy, that person shall, from that time, be deemed to hold the dwelling from the landlord under a tenancy having the same terms and conditions as the statutory tenancy except that the landlord may, by not less than three months' notice to quit (expiring on any day specified in that behalf in the notice) served on the tenant, determine the tenancy.

(5) (a) The application, by virtue of this section, of this Part to a dwelling shall cease upon the landlord's coming into possession of the dwelling.

(b) In paragraph (a) "possession" means actual possession, and a landlord shall not be deemed to have come into possession by reason only of a change of tenancy made with his consent.

Right of tenant to new tenancy.

[10–16] 16.—Subject to the provisions of this Act, where this Part applies to a tenement, the tenant shall be entitled to a new tenancy in the tenement beginning on the termination of his previous tenancy, and the new tenancy shall be on such terms as may be agreed upon between the tenant and the person or persons granting or joining in the grant of the new tenancy or, in default of agreement, as shall be fixed by the Court.

Restrictions on right to new tenancy.

[10–17] 17.—(1) (a) A tenant shall not be entitled to a new tenancy under this Part if—

(i) the tenancy has been terminated because of non-payment of rent, whether the proceedings were framed as an ejectment for non-payment of rent, an ejectment for overholding or an ejectment on the title based on a forfeiture, or

(ii) the tenancy has been terminated by ejectment, notice to quit or otherwise on account of a breach by the tenant of a covenant of the tenancy, or

(iii) the tenant has terminated the tenancy by notice of surrender or otherwise, or

(iiia) if section 13(1)(a) applies to the tenement, the terms of the tenancy provided for the use of the tenement wholly and exclusively as an office and, prior to the commencement of the tenancy, the tenant had executed, whether for or without valuable consideration, a valid renunciation of his entitlement to a new tenancy in the tenement and had received independent legal advice in relation to the renunciation, or

(iiib) if section 13(1)(b) applies to the tenement (and the tenement is a dwelling to which the Residential Tenancies Act 2004 applies), the tenant had completed and signed, whether for or without valuable consideration, a renunciation of his or her entitlement to a new tenancy in the tenement and had received independent legal advice in relation to such renunciation, or

(iv) the tenancy has been terminated by notice to quit given by the landlord for good and sufficient reason, or

(v) the tenancy terminated otherwise than by notice to quit and the landlord either refused for good and sufficient reason to renew it or would, if he had been asked to renew it, have had good and sufficient reason for refusing.

(b) In this subsection "good and sufficient reason" means a reason which emanates from or is the result of or is traceable to some action or conduct of the tenant and which, having regard to all the circumstances of the case, is in the opinion of the Court a good and sufficient reason for terminating or refusing to renew (as the case may be) the tenancy.

(2) (a) A tenant shall not be entitled to a new tenancy under this Part where it appears to the Court that—

(i) the landlord intends or has agreed to pull down and rebuild or to reconstruct the buildings or any part of the buildings included in the tenement and has planning permission for the work, or

(ii) the landlord requires vacant possession for the purpose of carrying out a scheme of development of property which includes the tenement and has planning permission for the scheme, or

(iii) the landlord being a planning authority, the tenement or any part thereof is situate in an area in respect of which the development plan indicates objectives for its development or renewal as being an obsolete area, or

(iv) the landlord, being a local authority for the purposes of the Local Government Act, 1941, will require possession, within a period of five years after the termination of the existing tenancy, for any purpose for which the local authority are entitled to acquire property compulsorily, or

(v) for any reason the creation of a new tenancy would not be consistent with good estate management.

(b) In the case of certain dwellings and business premises to which this subsection applies the tenant is entitled to compensation for disturbance under Part IV.

(3) Where the Court is satisfied—

(a) that a tenant would but for subparagraph (i), (ii), (iii) or (iv) of subsection (2) (a) be entitled to a new tenancy, and

(b) that the landlord will not require possession for the purposes mentioned in the relevant subparagraph until after the expiration of a period of at least six months,

the Court may, if the tenant so requests, continue the existing tenancy until terminated by the landlord for those purposes by the service of six months' previous notice in writing, but subject to the condition that the continuation of the tenancy shall be without prejudice to the right of the tenant to relief under this Act on the termination of the continued tenancy.

(4) Where, in a case in which an application for a new tenancy has been refused on a ground mentioned in subparagraph (i) or (ii) of subsection (2) (a), it appears to the Court that the landlord has not, within a reasonable time, carried out the intention, agreement or purpose, as the case may be, on account of which such application was refused, the Court may order the landlord to pay to the tenant such sum as it considers proper by way of punitive damages.

Amendment history: Subs (1)(a)(iiia) was added by s 4 of the Landlord and Tenant (Amendment) Act 1994, which Act came into force one the day that was one month after the date of its passing (passed 10th July 1994). Subsection (1)(a)(iiib) was added by s 191 of the Residential Tenancies Act 2004 as from 1st September 2004 (which is the date of commencement of Part IV of the 2004 Act — see s 5 of the 2004 Act and also SI No 505 of 2004).

Provisions relating to award of new tenancy.

18.—(1) This section applies where the Court, on an application for a new tenancy under this Part, finds that the tenant is entitled to a new tenancy. **[10–18]**

(2) The Court shall fix the terms of the new tenancy and make an order requiring the landlord, and any superior landlord whose joinder may be necessary, to grant or join in the grant of, and the tenant to accept, a new tenancy accordingly.

(3) Such person or persons shall grant or join in the grant of, and the tenant shall accept, a new contract of tenancy in writing in respect of the tenement on the terms specified in the order, commencing on the termination of the previous tenancy.

(4) The tenant shall not be entitled to compensation in respect of the termination of his previous tenancy.

(5) If any dispute, failure or question arises or occurs in the carrying out of the order, the Court may, on the application of any person concerned, make such order as justice may require.

Provisions where tenant not entitled to new tenancy.

[10–19] 19.—Where the Court, on an application for a new tenancy under this Part finds that the tenant is not entitled to a new tenancy—

(a) if the notice of intention to claim relief includes a claim in the alternative for compensation, the Court shall hear and determine the claim and fix the amount of any compensation;

(b) if the notice of intention to claim relief does not include a claim in the alternative for compensation, the Court may, on the application of the tenant, if having regard to all the circumstances of the case the Court thinks proper to do so, amend the notice in such terms as the Court thinks proper by inserting in it a claim in the alternative for compensation and thereupon deal with that claim in accordance with paragraph (a).

Notice of intention to claim relief.

[10–20] 20.—(1) A claim for a new tenancy under this Part shall not be maintained unless the claimant, within the time limited in subsection (2), serves on each person against whom the claim is intended to be made a notice of intention to claim relief in the prescribed form.

(2) A notice of intention to claim relief may be served—

(a) in the case of a tenancy terminating by the expiration of a term of years or other certain period or by any other certain event—

(i) before the termination of the tenancy, or

(ii) at any time thereafter but before the expiration of three months after the service (not earlier than three months before the termination of the tenancy) on the claimant by the landlord of notice in the prescribed form of the expiration of the term or period or the happening of the event;

(b) in the case of a tenancy terminating by the fall of a life or any other uncertain event—at any time but before the expiration of three months after the service on the claimant by the landlord of notice in the prescribed form of the happening of the event;

(c) in the case of a tenancy which is terminable by notice to quit—at any time but before the expiration of three months (or, in the case of premises to which section 14 or 15 applies, six months) after the service of the notice;

(d) in the case of a tenancy to which section 29 applies—within six months after the commencement of this Act.

(3) The notice may include a claim in the alternative for compensation.

Application for relief.

21.—(1) A person who serves a notice of intention to claim relief may, at any time not less than one month thereafter, apply to the Court to determine his right to relief and (as the case may be) to fix the amount of the compensation or the terms of the new tenancy to which he is found to be entitled. [10–21]

(2) If he does not do so within three months after service of the notice, any person on whom the notice was served may apply to the Court to determine the matters to which the notice relates.

(3) An application under this section may be made, heard and determined either before and in anticipation of or after the termination of the tenancy.

Offer by landlord of new tenancy in lieu of compensation.

22.—(1) Where the tenant serves on the landlord a notice of intention to claim compensation under Part IV for improvements, the landlord, any superior landlord or any two or more of such persons may, within two months, serve on the tenant a notice in the prescribed form offering him a new tenancy in the tenement on terms specified in the notice or on terms to be fixed by the Court. [10–22]

(2) Where a notice is served under subsection (1) offering the tenant a new tenancy on terms specified in the notice—

(a) the tenant may, within one month, serve on the person or persons who served the notice a notice in the prescribed form accepting the new tenancy;

(b) in that case, such person or persons shall forthwith grant, and the tenant shall forthwith accept, a new contract of tenancy in writing in respect of the tenement on the terms specified in the notice served on the tenant, commencing on the termination of the previous tenancy;

(c) the tenant may, alternatively, within one month serve on such person or persons a notice refusing the new tenancy;

(d) in that case the tenant may proceed with his application for relief by way of compensation for improvements, but—

(i) on the hearing of the application, the Court if satisfied that the tenant is entitled to that relief, may in lieu of awarding that relief make an order requiring the necessary person or persons to grant, and the tenant to accept, a new tenancy in the tenement on such terms as the Court (subject to the provisions of this Act) thinks proper and specifies in the order, and

(ii) upon the making of that order, the necessary person or persons shall forthwith grant, and the tenant shall forthwith accept, a contract of tenancy in writing in respect of the tenement on the terms specified in the order.

(3) Where a notice is served under subsection (1) offering a new tenancy on terms to be fixed by the Court—

(a) either the person or persons who served the notice or the tenant may apply to the Court for an order fixing the terms of the new tenancy;

(b) upon the making of that order, the necessary person or persons shall forthwith grant, and the tenant shall forthwith accept, a contract of tenancy in writing in respect of the tenement on the terms specified in the order.

(4) Where any person or persons and the tenant are required by this section or an order made under this section, respectively to grant and accept a new tenancy, the tenant shall not be entitled to compensation in respect of the termination of his tenancy previous to the new tenancy.

(5) Where any person or persons and the tenant are required, by this section or an order made under this section, respectively to grant and accept a new tenancy and any dispute, failure or question arises or occurs in the granting and accepting of the tenancy, the Court, on the application of any person concerned, may make such order as justice may require.

Fixing of terms of new tenancy by Court.

[10–23] 23.—(1) This section applies where the Court fixes the terms of a new tenancy under this Part.

(2) The Court shall fix the duration of the tenancy at thirty-five years or such less term as the tenant may nominate save, where the right to a new tenancy arises in respect of a tenement referred to in section 13(1)(a) (as amended by section 3 of the Landlord and Tenant (Amendment) Act, 1994), the duration of the tenancy shall be fixed at twenty years or such less term as the tenant may nominate provided that it shall not be fixed for a term of less than five years without the landlord's agreement.

> **Amendment history:** Subs (2) was substituted by s 5 of the Landlord and Tenant (Amendment) Act 1994, which Act came into force on the day that was one month after the date of its passing (passed on 10th July 1994). The original subs (2) read as follows: "The Court shall fix the duration of the tenancy at thirty-five years or such less term as the tenant may nominate."

(3) The rent payable by the tenant under the new tenancy shall not be less than (as the case may require) the rent payable by the landlord in respect of the tenement or such proportion of the rent payable by the landlord in respect of the tenement and other property as is in the opinion of the Court fairly apportionable to the tenement.

(4) Subject to subsection (3), the rent shall be the gross rent reduced, where appropriate, by the allowance for improvements provided for by subsection (6).

(5) The gross rent shall be the rent which in the opinion of the Court a willing lessee not already in occupation would give and a willing lessor would take for the tenement, in each case on the basis of vacant possession being given, and having regard to the other terms of the tenancy and to the letting values of tenements of a similar character to the tenement and situate in a comparable area but without regard to any goodwill which may exist in respect of the tenement.

(6) The allowance for improvements shall be such proportion of the gross rent as is, in the opinion of the Court, attributable to improvements made by the tenant or his predecessors in title and in respect of which the tenant would have been entitled to compensation for improvements if (as the case may be) this Part did not apply to the tenement or the new tenancy had not been created.

(7) The Court may, as one of the terms of the new tenancy, require the intended tenant to expend, within such time as the Court thinks proper, a specified sum of money in the execution of specified repairs (including painting for purposes of preservation but not painting for purposes of mere decoration) to the tenement and

authorise the postponement of the grant of the new tenancy until the requirement has been complied with.

(8) If the intended tenant refuses or fails to comply with a requirement under subsection (7), the Court shall have power to declare him to have forfeited his right to a new tenancy and to discharge any order granting it to him.

(9) The new tenancy shall be subject to such covenants as may be agreed upon between the parties or, in default of agreement, as may be determined by the Court.

Review of rent.

24.—*Omitted. Repealed by s 15(7) of the Landlord and Tenant (Amendment) Act 1984. Which Act came into force one week after the day of its passing (passed on 14th March 1984). Please see s 15 of the Landlord and Tenant (Amendment) Act, 1984 for review of rent provisions.* **[10–24]**

Modification of sections 23 and 24 in case of dwellings to which section 15 relates.

25.—(1) In the case of a dwelling to which section 15 relates, sections 23 and 24 shall apply subject to the provisions of this section. **[10–25]**

(2) If the terms of a new tenancy for the dwelling have not on any previous occasion been fixed by the Court under the Act of 1931 or under this Part and the Court is satisfied that payment of the rent which, apart from this provision, would be fixed would cause hardship to the tenant, the Court shall fix the rent payable by the tenant under the new tenancy at a sum (not below the existing rent) which the Court is satisfied that, having regard to all the circumstances of the case, including any hardship to the landlord, the tenant should be required to pay and section 23 (2) shall have effect as if "not more than ten years" were substituted for "thirty-five years or such less term as the tenant may nominate" and section 24 shall not apply to the rent so fixed.

(3) In any other case, section 23 (6) shall have effect as if for "and in respect of which the tenant would have been entitled to compensation for improvements if (as the case may be) this Part did not apply to the tenement or the new tenancy had not been created" there were substituted "(whether before or after the commencement of this Act or the passing of the Act of 1931 or the Rent Restrictions (Amendment) Act, 1967) which, at the time of the application to the Court, add to the letting value and are suitable to the character of the tenement".

Termination of tenancy after order for new tenancy.

26.—Where, following the making of an order under this Part or the Act of 1931 for a new tenancy, the existing tenancy is terminated in such manner that the tenant would under section 17 (1) not be entitled to a new tenancy, then— **[10–26]**

(a) if the new tenancy has not been granted, the obligation to grant it shall cease, and

(b) if it has been granted, it shall be void.

Continuation of existing tenancies.

27.—Where a tenancy is continued or renewed or a new tenancy is created under this Part, the continued, renewed or new tenancy shall for the purposes of this Act be or be deemed to be a continuation of the tenancy previously existing and shall for all purposes be deemed to be a graft upon that tenancy, and the interest of the tenant thereunder shall be subject to any rights or equities arising from its being such graft. **[10–27]**

Right of tenant to continue in occupation pending decision.

[10–28] 28.—Where an application is pending under this Part for a new tenancy or to fix the terms of a new tenancy and the pre-existing tenancy was terminated otherwise than by ejectment or surrender the tenant may, if he so desires, continue in occupation of the tenement from the termination of the tenancy until the application is determined by the Court or, in the event of an appeal, by the final appellate court, and the tenant shall while so continuing be subject to the terms (including the payment of rent) of such tenancy, but without prejudice to such recoupments and readjustments as may be necessary in the event of a new tenancy being granted to commence from such termination.

Tenancy terminated before commencement of this Act.

[10–29] 29.—Where, the tenancy of a tenement having terminated before the commencement of this Act, the tenant is at such commencement in possession of the tenement under a tenancy arising by implication from the acts of the parties or under a statutory tenancy under the Rents Restrictions Acts, 1960 and 1967, or as a tenant at will or otherwise, without having obtained a new tenancy, the tenancy shall for the purposes of this Act be deemed to terminate immediately after such commencement and this Act shall apply accordingly.

PART III – REVERSIONARY LEASES

Reversionary lease.

[10–30] 30.—(1) In this Act "reversionary lease" means a lease under this Part.

(2) (a) A person who holds or has held land under a lease shall subject to section 33 be entitled to a reversionary lease of the land if the conditions specified in section 9 of the Landlord and Tenant (Ground Rents) (No. 2) Act, 1978 (which provides for the acquisition of the fee simple by lessees) are complied with.

(b) Section 9(1) (2) and sections 10 to 12 and 14 of that Act shall extend to the right to a reversionary lease.

(c) The reference in condition 2 of section 10 of that Act to an application shall include an application under section 31 and the reference in condition 6 of the said section 10 to a reversionary lease shall include a reversionary lease within the meaning of this section.

(3) Section 2 (1) of the Landlord and Tenant (Ground Rents) Act, 1978 (which restricts the right to create leases of dwellings) shall not apply where the lease is a reversionary lease.

Note: This section gives entitlement to a reversionary lease subject to conditions in s 9 of the Landlord and Tenant (Ground Rents) (No 2) Act 1978 being complied with. It extends s 9(1)and (2) and ss 10-12 and 14 of the No 2 Act of 1978 to the right to a reversionary lease. It also states that s 2(1) of the Landlord and Tenant (Ground Rents) Act 1978 does not apply where the lease is a reversionary lease.

Application to obtain reversionary lease.

31.—(1) A person who is entitled to a reversionary lease may apply to his immediate lessor to obtain from that lessor a reversionary lease of the land held by him— [10–31]

(a) not earlier than fifteen years before the expiration of his existing lease, and

(b) not later than the expiration of the lease or the expiration of three months from the service on him by his immediate lessor or any superior lessor of notice of the expiration of the lease, whichever is the later.

(2) The notice shall be valid only if served not earlier than three months before the expiration of the lease,

(3) Where an application is made for a reversionary lease before the expiration of the lease under which the applicant holds, the lease if granted shall commence on the expiration of the previous lease or on such other date as may be agreed upon between the parties.

(4) In any other case, the reversionary lease shall commence on such date as may be agreed upon between the parties or, in default of agreement, on the date of the application for the lease.

Note: By virtue of s 4 of the Landlord and Tenant (Amendment) Act 1984 where: (a) after 13 November 1980, and before the commencement of the Act of 1984, a person was entitled to obtain a reversionary lease of land under Part III of this Act; and (b) at that commencement he was no longer so entitled by virtue of s 31 of this Act but was in possession of the land without having obtained a new tenancy and without having acquired the interest in the land of the immediate lessor, that person during the 12 months after that commencement had the same right to obtain a reversionary lease as he would have had if his lease had not expired, and s 40 of this Act applied accordingly. Furthermore, a reversionary lease granted in such a manner commenced on the expiration of the lease to which it is reversionary or on such other date as may have been agreed upon between the parties

Persons bound to grant reversionary leases.

32.—(1) Where a person is entitled to a reversionary lease his immediate lessor shall be bound to grant the lease to him. [10–32]

(2) If the immediate lessor holds the land for a term which is less than the term for which the reversionary lease is to be granted, his immediate lessor and such (if any) superior lessors as may be necessary shall be bound to join in the grant of the lease.

Restrictions on right to reversionary lease.

33.—(1) A person shall not be entitled to a reversionary lease of the land or any part of the land where a necessary party to the granting of the lease satisfies the Court— [10–33]

(a) that his interest in reversion in the land is a freehold estate or is for a term of not less than fifteen years, and

(b) (i) that he intends or has agreed to pull down and rebuild or to reconstruct the whole or a substantial portion of the buildings on the land and has planning permission for the work, or

(ii) that he requires vacant possession of the land for the purpose of carrying out a scheme of development of property which includes the land and has planning permission for the scheme, or

(iii) that for any reason the grant of a reversionary lease would not be consistent with good estate management.

(2) A person shall not be entitled to a reversionary lease where a planning authority, being a necessary party to the granting of the lease, satisfies the Court that, in case the reversionary lease would be a lease of the whole of the land, the land or any part of the land is situate in an area in respect of which the development plan indicates objectives for its development or renewal as being an obsolete area or that, in case the reversionary lease would be a lease of part of the land, that part or any part of that part is situate in such an area.

(3) A person shall not be entitled to a reversionary lease of land used wholly or partly for the purpose of carrying on a business where a local authority for the purposes of the Local Government Act, 1941, being a necessary party to the granting of the lease, will require possession within a period of five years after the termination of the existing lease for any purpose for which the local authority are entitled to acquire property compulsorily.

(4) A person who has been declared under subsection (1), (2) or (3) not to be entitled to a reversionary lease shall be entitled to remain in possession of the land, upon such terms as the Court may think proper, until the person who successfully objected to the grant of the lease or his successor in title becomes entitled to possession of the land.

(5) Where a lease has been refused under subsection (1), (2) or (3) and it appears to the Court, on application by the person who has been refused, that the intention, agreement or purpose, as the case may be, on account of which the application was refused has not been carried out within a reasonable time the Court may order the person concerned to pay such sum as it considers proper by way of punitive damages.

(6) Where a lease has been refused under subsection (1), (2) or (3), compensation in lieu of the lease shall be paid in accordance with section 59.

Terms of reversionary lease settled by Court.

[10–34] 34.—(1) Where the terms of a reversionary lease are settled by the Court the subsequent provisions of this section shall have effect.

(2) The lease shall be for a term expiring ninety-nine years after the expiration of the lease to which it is reversionary.

(3) Subject to subsection (5), the rent reserved by the reversionary lease shall be not less than the rent reserved by the previous lease or than the rent reserved by any superior lease the lessor under which is required to join in the grant of the reversionary lease.

(4) Where the land to be comprised in a reversionary lease is part only of the land comprised in the previous lease or of the land comprised in any superior lease the lessor under which is required to join in the grant of the reversionary lease, such proportion of the rent reserved by any such lease as is fairly apportionable to the land to be comprised in the reversionary lease shall, for the purpose of subsection (3), be deemed to be the rent reserved by that lease in respect of the land to be comprised in the reversionary lease.

(5) If any new covenant restricting the lessee's rights is included in the reversionary lease, the Court may, if it so thinks proper, fix a lower rent.

(6) If the Court fixes the covenants of the lease, the lessee shall be made liable to pay all rates and taxes in respect of the land and to insure against fire and keep the premises in repair.

Determination of rent.

35.—(1) Subject to section 34 (3) and this section, the rent to be reserved by a reversionary lease the terms of which are settled by the Court shall be one-eighth of the gross rent. For this purpose the gross rent shall be reduced, where appropriate, by the special allowance provided for by subsection (2). **[10–35]**

(2) The special allowance for the purpose of subsection (1) shall be such proportion of the gross rent as, in the opinion of the Court, is attributable to works of construction, reconstruction or alteration carried out by the lessee or any of his predecessors in title which add to the letting value of the land, other than works carried out wholly or partly in consideration of the grant of a lease or repairs and maintenance during the currency of the lease.

(3) (a) The Minister may by order amend subsection (1) by substituting for the fraction standing specified for the time being therein another fraction.

(b) An order under this subsection shall not come into force unless approved by resolution of each House of the Oireachtas but, upon being so approved, shall come into force forthwith.

Gross rent.

36.—(1) The gross rent shall be the rent which, in the opinion of the Court, a willing lessee not already in occupation would give and a willing lessor would take for the land comprised in the reversionary lease— **[10–36]**

(a) on the basis that vacant possession is given and that the lessee pays rates and taxes in respect of the land and is liable to insure against fire and to keep the premises in repair, and

(b) having regard to the other terms of the reversionary lease and to the letting values of land of a similar character to and situate in the vicinity of the land comprised in the lease or in a comparable area but without having regard to any goodwill which may exist in respect of the land.

(2) If the Court requires or the parties have agreed upon the expenditure by the applicant for a reversionary lease of a specified sum of money on repairs to the premises or the execution by him of specified repairs as a condition precedent to the execution of the lease, the gross rent shall be assessed—

(a) if under the previous lease the lessee is obliged to keep or deliver up the premises in repair, having regard to the condition in which the premises will be after the repairs have been carried out, or

(b) if there is no such obligation, having regard to the actual condition of the premises at the date of the application for the reversionary lease.

(3) If the premises are, in whole or in part, controlled dwellings (other than premises controlled under section 2 (6) of the Rent Restrictions (Amendment) Act, 1967) the Court in determining the gross rent shall have regard to the restrictions imposed by the Rent Restrictions Acts, 1960 and 1967, on the rents which tenants of such premises would be liable to pay.

Applications to the Court.

[10–37] 37.—If any dispute, question or difficulty arises in regard to the right of any person to a reversionary lease, his failure to proceed with an application for such lease, the terms on which such lease is to be granted, or otherwise in relation to the grant of such lease, any person concerned may apply to the Court and the Court may make such order as justice shall require and, in particular, may fix the terms on which such lease is to be granted.

Expenditure on repairs.

[10–38] 38.—(1) The Court may require an applicant for a reversionary lease to expend, within such time as the Court thinks proper, a specified sum of money on repairs or to execute specified repairs to the buildings to be comprised in the lease and may authorise the postponement of the execution of the lease until the requirement has been complied with.

(2) If the applicant refuses or fails to comply with the requirement of the Court, the Court may declare forfeit his right to a reversionary lease and discharge any order granting it to him.

Reversionary lease a graft on former lease.

[10–39] 39.—A reversionary lease, whether granted on terms settled under this Part or negotiated between the parties, shall be deemed to be a graft for all purposes on, and a continuation of, the lease under which the lessee previously held the land and the lessee's interest shall be subject to any rights or equities arising from that lease being a graft.

Right of lessee to continue in possession.

[10–40] 40.—(1) A person who is entitled to obtain a reversionary lease and whose interest in the land has expired shall continue to be entitled to hold the land until either he is declared not to be entitled to obtain a reversionary lease or a lease is executed by his immediate lessor and such (if any) superior lessors as may be necessary, in terms agreed upon between the parties or settled under this Part and, during such period, he shall hold the land on the terms (so far as applicable) on which he previously held them, subject to any recoupments or adjustments that may be made under the reversionary lease if granted to him.

(2) Where an application is made in relation to the grant of a reversionary lease and the interest of the applicant in the land expires before the application is heard and determined, the applicant shall be entitled to remain in possession of the land until the application is finally heard and determined on the terms (so far as applicable) on which he previously held them, subject to such recoupments or adjustments as the Court thinks proper.

Evidence of agreement to build.

[10–41] 41.—Where it is claimed that a lease complies with this Part on the ground that the permanent buildings were erected in pursuance of an agreement for the grant of the lease on their erection but express evidence of the agreement is not available, the following provisions shall have effect:

(a) if it is proved that the buildings were erected by the person to whom the lease was subsequently made, it shall he presumed, until the contrary is proved, that the agreement was in fact made and that the buildings were erected in accordance with it;

(b) in any other case, the Court may, if it so thinks proper on hearing such evidence as is available and is adduced, presume that the agreement was in fact made and that the buildings were erected in accordance with it.

Buildings replaced under covenant.

42.—Permanent buildings erected by a lessee in pursuance of a covenant in his lease to reinstate the buildings comprised in the lease in the event of their destruction by fire or otherwise shall be deemed to have been erected by the person who erected the original buildings. **[10–42]**

Buildings erected in breach of covenant.

43.—The Court may declare a person to be entitled to a reversionary lease notwithstanding that the buildings were, in whole or in part, erected in contravention of a covenant, if the Court is of opinion that it would be unreasonable to order otherwise. **[10–43]**

Application of Act of 1967.

44.—Subject to this Act, the provisions of the Act of 1967 shall, with necessary modifications, have effect as if the references to a building lease or a proprietary lease were to a lease which gives rise to a right to a reversionary lease. **[10–44]**

Note: This section extends the Landlord and Tenant (Ground Rents) Act 1967 to reversionary leases.

PART IV – COMPENSATION

Compensation for Improvements

Note: Where compensation is paid under s 15(4) of the Housing (Private Rented Dwellings) Act 1982 in respect of a dwelling, no right to compensation for improvements to that dwelling lies under Part IV of this Act.

"Improvement".

45.—For the purposes of sections 46 to 57, "improvement" in relation to a tenement means any addition to or alteration of the buildings comprised in the tenement and includes any structure erected on the tenement which is ancillary or subsidiary to those buildings and also includes the installation in the tenement of conduits for the supply of water, gas or electricity but does not include work consisting only of repairing, painting and decorating, or any of them. **[10–45]**

Compensation for improvements.

46.—(1) (a) Subject to the provisions of this Act, where a tenant quits a tenement because of the termination of his tenancy, he shall be entitled to be paid by the landlord compensation (in this Act referred to as compensation for improvements) in accordance with this Act for every improvement made on the tenement by the tenant or any of his predecessors in title (whether before **[10–46]** or after the commencement of this Act) which, at the termination of the tenancy, adds to the letting value and is suitable to the character of the tenement.

(b) Paragraph (a) does not apply where—

(i) the tenant has terminated the tenancy by notice of surrender or otherwise, or

(ii) the tenancy is terminated because of non-payment of rent, whether the proceedings are framed as an ejectment for non-payment of rent, an ejectment for overholding or an ejectment on the title based on a forfeiture.

(2) Subject to the provisions of this Act, where a landlord holds a tenement under a lease or other contract of tenancy, he shall be entitled, on giving up possession of the tenement because of the expiration of the lease or tenancy, to be paid by his immediate superior landlord compensation (in this Act included in the expression compensation for improvements) for every improvement which was made (whether before or after the commencement of this Act) on the tenement by a tenant thereof and in respect of which the landlord or any of his predecessors in title has given consideration whether by reduction of rent, by payment of compensation under the Town Tenants (Ireland) Act, 1906, by payment of compensation under section 10 of the Act of 1931, by payment of compensation for improvements under this Act, or in any other way.

(3) Compensation for improvements payable by a landlord under subsection (1) shall, subject to this Act, be payable on—

(a) the expiration of one month from the date of the fixing, by agreement or by the Court, of its amount, or

(b) the delivery to the landlord by the tenant of clear possession of the tenement,

whichever is the later.

Measure of compensation for improvements.

[10–47] 47.—(1) The amount of compensation for improvements shall be such sum as may be agreed on between the landlord and the tenant or, in default of agreement, shall (subject to the provisions of this section) be the capitalised value of such addition to the letting value of the tenement at the termination of the tenancy as the Court determines to be attributable to the improvements.

(2) Where compensation for improvements is payable to the tenant by the landlord and the Court is satisfied that the tenant and (where applicable) his predecessors in title or any of them has or have received from the landlord benefits by way of reduction of rent or otherwise in consideration, expressly or impliedly, of the improvements being or having been made, the Court shall deduct from the compensation as ascertained under subsection (1) such sum as the Court thinks proper for the benefits.

(3) Where compensation for improvements is payable to the landlord by his superior landlord, the Court shall make such deduction (if any) from the compensation as ascertained under subsection (1) as the Court thinks proper for benefits received by the landlord and (where applicable) his predecessors in title or any of them by way of increased rent or otherwise on account of the improvements.

(4) The capitalised value for the purposes of this section of an addition to the letting value of a tenement shall be fixed by the Court having regard to the probable duration of

such addition, the probable life of the improvement and all other relevant circumstances but shall not in any case exceed fifteen times the annual amount of the addition.

Improvement notice.

48.—(1) Where a tenant proposes to make an improvement to his tenement, he may serve on his landlord a notice in the prescribed form (in this Act referred to as an improvement notice) together with— **[10–48]**

(a) in every case—

(i) a statement of the works proposed for making the improvement, and

(ii) an estimate, verified by an architect, surveyor or building contractor, of the cost of making the improvement, and

(b) if the improvement is development for which planning permission is required, a copy of the permission.

(2) Where an improvement notice is served, the landlord may, within one month, serve on the tenant any one of the following notices:

(a) a notice (in this Act referred to as an improvement consent) in the prescribed form consenting to the making of the improvement,

(b) a notice (in this Act referred to as an improvement undertaking) in the prescribed form undertaking to execute the improvement in consideration of either (as the landlord states in the notice) a specified increase of rent or an increase of rent to be fixed by the Court,

(c) subject to subsection (3), a notice (in this Act referred to as an improvement objection) in the prescribed form objecting to the improvement on grounds specified in the notice.

(3) An improvement objection may be served only where the grounds of the objection are—

(a) that the tenant holds the tenement otherwise than under a lease for a term of which at least five years are unexpired at the time when the improvement notice is served, and

(b) that the tenant would, on any of the grounds specified in section 17 (2) (a), not be entitled under Part II to a new tenancy.

(4) Where an improvement notice is served in a case in which the landlord holds the tenement—

(a) under a lease for a life or lives in being (either without a term of years or with a concurrent term of which less than twenty-five years are unexpired), or

(b) under a lease for a term of which less than twenty-five years are unexpired at the date of the service of such notice, or

(c) under a tenancy from year to year or any lesser tenancy,

the landlord shall, within one week, serve the notice or a copy thereof on his immediate superior landlord, endorsed with a statement of the date on which the notice was served on him, and the superior landlord may, within one month after the date of the service of the improvement notice by the tenant on the landlord, serve on the landlord and on the tenant either an improvement consent or an improvement objection.

(5) Every superior landlord on whom an improvement notice or a copy thereof is served under this section (including this subsection) and who holds the tenement—

(a) under a lease of which less than twenty-five years are unexpired at the date of such service, or

(b) under a tenancy from year to year or any lesser tenancy,

shall, within one week, serve the improvement notice or a copy thereof as endorsed under subsection (4) on his next superior landlord, and that superior landlord shall have the like right of serving an improvement consent or an improvement objection as the first-mentioned superior landlord has under this section.

Works required by public authority.

[10–49] 49.—(1) Where a sanitary authority serves under the Local Government (Sanitary Services) Acts, 1878 to 1964, or a housing authority serves under the Housing Act, 1966, a notice on the tenant of a tenement requiring him to execute an improvement, the tenant shall, within three days, serve on the landlord a notice in writing (in this Act referred to as a work notice) stating the fact of the service of the notice by that authority and stating the material portions of that notice.

(2) Where a work notice is served, the landlord may, within three days, serve on the tenant a notice (in this Act referred to as a work undertaking) in the prescribed form undertaking to execute the work in consideration of either (as the landlord states in the notice) a specified increase of rent or an increase of rent to be fixed by the Court.

(3) In the case of works required to a controlled dwelling the increase of rent shall not exceed the allowance provided for by section 10(2)(*g*) of the Rent Restrictions Act, 1960, inserted by section 6(2) of the Rent Restrictions (Amendment) Act, 1967.

(4) The service of a work undertaking shall have the same effect as the service on the tenant of an improvement undertaking, and the provisions of this Act in relation to an improvement undertaking shall apply accordingly.

(5) A copy of a work undertaking may be served by the tenant on the authority and thereupon the obligation to comply with the notice served by the authority and the liability for failure to comply with it shall become the obligation and liability of the landlord in exoneration of the tenant.

(6) Where a work notice is served and, within three days, the landlord does not serve a work undertaking, the tenant shall be entitled to execute the improvement mentioned in the notice by the authority which occasioned the work notice.

Execution of improvement in absence of objection.

[10–50] 50.—Where an improvement notice is served and, within one month, the landlord does not serve an improvement undertaking and neither the landlord nor any superior landlord serves an improvement objection, the tenant shall be entitled to execute at any time within one year after such service (whether an improvement consent has or has not been served by the landlord or superior landlord) the improvement specified in the improvement notice in accordance in all respects with the notice.

Rights of parties on service of improvement undertaking.

[10–51] 51.—(1) Where an improvement notice is served and, within one month, the landlord serves an improvement undertaking and no superior landlord serves an improvement objection the tenant may, by notice in writing served on the landlord within fourteen days after the service of the undertaking, either accept it or withdraw the improvement notice or, where the undertaking specifies an increase of rent, object to its amount.

(2) Where the tenant does not serve a notice under subsection (1) or accepts under that subsection the improvement undertaking, the landlord shall, as soon as may be,

and in any case not later than six months after the expiration of such fourteen days, execute and complete at his own expense and in accordance with the improvement undertaking the improvement mentioned therein and may for that purpose enter on the tenement at all reasonable times and there do all things necessary for or incidental to the execution of the improvement.

(3) If the tenant withdraws the improvement notice, that notice shall be deemed never to have been served.

(4) Where the tenant objects to the amount of the increase of rent specified in the improvement undertaking, then—

(a) the landlord and the tenant may either fix by agreement the amount of the increase of rent or agree that its amount shall be fixed by the Court, and thereupon the improvement undertaking shall have effect in accordance with that agreement and be deemed to have been duly accepted by the tenant, or

(b) either the landlord or the tenant may apply to the Court and, upon the hearing of the application, the Court may, as it thinks proper, either fix the amount of the increase of rent or deem the improvement undertaking to be an improvement objection and deal with it accordingly or make such other order as justice may require.

(5) Where the improvement undertaking is, by its terms or by subsequent agreement, made subject to an increase of rent of an amount to be fixed by the Court, the landlord or the tenant may, when the improvement has been duly executed by the landlord, apply to the Court to fix the amount of the increase of rent.

(6) Upon the completion of the improvement by the landlord in accordance with the improvement undertaking and this section, the rent payable by the tenant to the landlord shall, from the date of completion, be increased in accordance with the undertaking or the order of the Court (as the case may be), and any dispute as to the amount or commencement of or otherwise in relation to the increase shall be determined by the Court on the application of the landlord or the tenant.

(7) Where the landlord is bound under this section to execute the improvement in accordance with the improvement undertaking but refuses or fails to execute and complete it within the time limited in that behalf by this section, the tenant may apply to the Court and the Court may make such order in the matter as justice may require.

Rights of parties on service of improvement objection.

52.—(1) Where an improvement notice is served and, within one month, either the landlord or a superior landlord serves an improvement objection, the tenant may, save as is otherwise provided in this section, within one month after the service of the improvement objection, either— **[10–52]**

(a) by notice in writing served on the landlord or on the landlord and the superior landlord (as the case may require) withdraw the improvement notice, or

(b) apply to the Court under this section.

(2) Where a tenant so withdraws an improvement notice, the notice shall be deemed never to have been served.

(3) On an application under this section the Court shall, subject to subsection (4), make an order (in this Act referred to as an improvement order) authorising the tenant to make the improvement in accordance with the improvement notice either

without modification or with such modifications as the Court thinks proper and, if the Court so thinks fit, specifying a time within which the improvement shall be completed.

(4) The Court shall reject the application if it is satisfied that the tenant holds the tenement otherwise than under a lease for a term of which at least five years were unexpired at the time when the improvement notice was served and would, on any of the grounds specified in section 17 (2) (a), not be entitled under Part II to a new tenancy.

(5) Where an improvement order has been made and the tenant refuses or fails to execute and complete in accordance with the order the improvement thereby authorised within the time limited in that behalf by the order or, where no such time is so limited, within a reasonable time, the landlord or any superior landlord may apply to the Court and, on the hearing of the application, the Court may make such order as justice may require.

Restriction on increase of rent of controlled dwellings.

[10–53] 53.—Nothing in this Part shall authorise the charging, in the case of a controlled dwelling, of a rent exceeding the lawful rent of the dwelling as defined by section 11 of the Rent Restrictions Act, 1960.

Restrictions on right to compensation for improvements.

[10–54] 54.—(1) A tenant shall not be entitled to compensation for improvements in respect of an improvement made before the passing of the Act of 1931 in contravention of the lease or other contract of tenancy under which the tenement was held.

(2) A tenant shall not be entitled to compensation for improvements in respect of an improvement made after the passing of the Act of 1931 (whether before or after the commencement of this Act) unless a notice under section 12 (1) of the Act of 1931 or an improvement notice was served or, where no such notice was served, if the landlord, or where appropriate, a superior landlord, satisfies the Court that—

(a) he has been prejudiced by the notice not having been served, or

(b) the improvement is in contravention of any covenant contained in the contract of tenancy, or

(c) the improvement injures the amenity or convenience of the neighbourhood.

(3) A landlord shall not be entitled to compensation for improvements in respect of an improvement made after the passing of the Act of 1931 (whether before or after the commencement of this Act) in respect of which a notice under section 12(1) of the Act of 1931 or an improvement notice was served unless the notice or a copy thereof was served under section 12(3) of the Act of 1931 or under section 48(4) of this Act or, where no such notice was served, if the superior landlord satisfies the Court that—

(a) he has been prejudiced by such service not having been effected, or

(b) the improvement is a contravention of any covenant in the contract of tenancy under which the landlord holds the tenement, or

(c) the improvement injures the amenity or convenience of the neighbourhood.

(4) Neither subsection (2) nor (3) applies to an improvement which is—

(a) a work in relation to which section 17(5) of the Act of 1931 applied, or

(b) any other work executed in pursuance of an order of a sanitary authority under the Local Government (Sanitary Services) Acts, 1878 to 1964, or of a housing authority under the Housing Act, 1966,

but the tenant shall not be entitled to compensation in respect of such work unless—

(i) in the case of a work specified in paragraph (a), the tenant served on the landlord a notice under section 13(1) of the Act of 1931 and became entitled under that Act to execute the work as an improvement, or

(ii) in the case of a work specified in paragraph (b), the tenant served on the landlord a work notice in respect of the work and became entitled under this Act to execute the work as an improvement:

Provided that the failure to serve notice shall not deprive the tenant of his right (if any) to compensation in respect of the work if the tenant satisfies the Court that the landlord did not suffer loss or damage by reason of the failure.

Improvement certificate.

55.—(1) Where— [10–55]

(a) in a case in which an improvement notice is served but no improvement undertaking or improvement objection is served, the tenant executes and completes in accordance with the notice the improvement mentioned therein within one year from the service of the notice, or

(b) in a case in which an improvement order is made, the tenant completes the improvement within the time limited in that behalf by the order or, where no such time is so limited, within a reasonable time,

the landlord shall, on the application of the tenant within six months after the completion of the improvement, give to the tenant a certificate (in this section referred to as an improvement certificate) in the prescribed form certifying that the improvement has been duly completed in accordance with the improvement notice or order.

(2) Where an improvement certificate is applied for under subsection (1) and is not given within one month thereafter, the tenant may apply to the Court and, on the hearing of that application, the Court may make such order as justice may require, including an order declaring that the improvement was duly made in accordance with the improvement notice or order.

(3) An improvement certificate shall, as against the landlord by whom it is given, his personal representatives and his successors in title, be conclusive evidence that the improvement was duly executed and completed by the tenant and that all relevant provisions of this Act or any order or notice thereunder were duly complied with by him.

(4) Where, in a case in which work executed on a tenement is an improvement, the work is executed by the tenant in pursuance of an order of a sanitary authority under the Local Government (Sanitary Services) Acts, 1878 to 1964, or a housing authority under the Housing Act, 1966, the tenant shall not be entitled to an improvement certificate but shall be entitled to obtain from the authority, within six months after the due completion of the work in accordance with the order, a certificate (in this section referred to as a sanitary improvement certificate) in the prescribed form certifying that the work was executed in pursuance of and completed in accordance with an order of the authority.

(5) A sanitary improvement certificate shall, as against the landlord of the tenement, be *prima facie* evidence of the matters which it purports to certify.

(6) A landlord or authority to whom an application for an improvement certificate or sanitary improvement certificate (as the case may be) is made may, as a condition of giving the certificate, require payment of his or their reasonable expenses of giving the certificate.

Claim for improvements.

[10–56] 56.—(1) A claim for relief limited to a claim for compensation for improvements shall not be maintained unless, within the time limited under section 20(2), a notice of intention to claim relief in the prescribed form is served on the person against whom the claim is intended to be made.

(2) Section 21 shall apply accordingly.

Compensation for improvements a first charge.

[10–57] 57.—Compensation for improvements payable to a tenant shall be a first charge (in priority to all other mortgages, charges and incumbrances whatsoever) on the interest of the landlord or superior landlord (as the case may be) in the tenement.

Compensation for Disturbance

Compensation where tenant not entitled to new tenancy.

[10–58] 58.—(1) Where the Court is satisfied—

(a) that a tenant would, but for section 17(2), be entitled to a new tenancy under Part II, and

(b) that section 13(1)(a) or section 13(1)(b) applies to the tenement,

the tenant shall, in lieu of a new tenancy, be entitled, on quitting the tenement on the termination of the tenancy, to be paid by the landlord compensation for disturbance.

> **Amendment history:** Subsection (1)(b) was amended by s 199(1) of the Residential Tenancies Act 2004 which section commenced on 1st September 2004. Subs (1)(b) originally read: "that section 13(1)(a) applies to the tenement,"

(2) Subject to subsection (3), the measure of the compensation shall be the pecuniary loss, damage or expense which the tenant sustains or incurs or will sustain or incur by reason of his quitting the tenement and which is the direct consequence of that quitting.

(3) In the case of a dwelling to which section 15 applies, the measure of the compensation shall be whichever of the following is the greater, namely, the amount provided for by subsection (2) or such sum as the Court thinks proper to enable the tenant without hardship to secure appropriate alternative accommodation, being not less than three years' rent, including rates, whether or not payable by the tenant.

(4) Compensation shall, subject to section 61, be payable on—

(a) the expiration of one month from the date of the fixing, by agreement or by the Court, of its amount, or

(b) the delivery to the landlord by the tenant of clear possession of the tenement,

whichever is the later.

(5) Where compensation awarded under this section is not paid within the time limited by this Act, the tenant shall be entitled, after the expiration of that time and before the payment of the compensation, to renew his application for a new tenancy under Part II, and section 17(2)(a) and 17(3) shall not apply to that application and the granting of the application shall operate as a discharge of the award of compensation for disturbance.

Compensation where lessee not entitled to new lease.

59.—(1) Where the Court is satisfied that a person (in this section referred to as the disentitled person) would, but for section 33(1), 33(2) or 33(3) be entitled to a lease under Part III, compensation in lieu of the lease shall be paid in accordance with this section. **[10–59]**

(2) The compensation shall be paid by the successful objector or if there is more than one successful objector by them in such proportions as the Court may determine.

(3) The measure of compensation under this section shall be the pecuniary loss, damage or expense which will, in the opinion of the Court, be suffered by the disentitled person as a direct consequence of the disentitled person having been declared not to be entitled to a lease.

(4) The compensation payable to a disentitled person shall become due and payable on the occurrence of whichever of the following events is the later, that is to say, the expiration of one month after the amount of the compensation is fixed or the date on which the disentitled person's lease terminates either by effluxion of time or by agreement between the parties to it.

(5) Where the compensation awarded under this section is not paid within the time specified in subsection (4) or within such extended time as the Court may allow, the following provisions shall have effect:

- (a) any disentitled person shall thereupon become entitled to obtain from his immediate lessor a lease under Part III of the relevant land,
- (b) the provisions of sections 31 (1) and 33 shall not apply,
- (c) the granting of the lease shall operate as a discharge of the award of compensation, and
- (d) the Court may make an order for the payment by the successful objector of such other compensation as it considers proper for the pecuniary loss, damage or expense which the disentitled person has suffered as a direct consequence of the declaration of disentitlement to a lease.

(6) In this section "successful objector" shall, where the context so admits, be construed as including the personal representatives and successors in title of the objector.

Compensation on termination of tenancy in obsolete buildings.

60.—(1) In this section— **[10–60]**

"the relevant building" means—

- (a) in relation to a tenement consisting of land covered wholly or partly by buildings—those buildings, and
- (b) in relation to a tenement consisting of a defined portion of a building—that building;

["obsolete area" has the meaning assigned to it by the Local Government (Planning and Development) Act, 1963.]

"integrated area plan" has the meaning assigned to it by section 7 of the Urban Renewal Act 1988.

(2) Where, in the case of a tenement—

(a) either the relevant building is situate in an [obsolete area] area to which an integrated area plan relates or, having regard to the age, condition and character of the building—

(i) the repairing of the building would involve expenditure which would be excessive in relation to the value of the tenement, or

(ii) the building could not profitably be used unless it were reconstructed or altered to a substantial extent or rebuilt, and

(b) the landlord has a scheme for the development of property which includes the tenement, being development for which planning permission has been granted,

the Court may, by order made on the application of the landlord on at least six months' notice in the prescribed form to the tenant, terminate the tenancy if it considers it reasonable to do so:

Provided that the lease or other contract of tenancy under which the tenant, at the time the notice is served on him, holds the tenement is for a term of which not less than three and not more than twenty-five years are unexpired.

(3) Where a tenancy is terminated under this section the tenant shall be entitled, on quitting the tenement, to be paid by the landlord compensation for the termination of the tenancy in accordance with this section.

(4) Where a tenancy is terminated under this section, the tenant may continue in occupation until the expiration of the period beginning on the day on which the order of the Court is made and ending on the expiration of one year from that day or on the day on which compensation for the termination of the tenancy is paid (whichever is the later) and, so long as he does so, he shall be subject to the terms (including payment of rent) of the tenancy.

(5) Where the Court awards compensation for the termination of a tenancy under this section, the measure of the compensation shall primarily be the pecuniary loss, damage or expense which the tenant sustains or incurs or will sustain or incur by reason of his quitting the tenement and which is the direct consequence of such quitting, but

(a) such amount as the Court considers reasonable shall be added for the pecuniary benefit accruing to the landlord which is referable to his getting possession of the tenement earlier than he was entitled to under the lease or other contract of tenancy, and

(b) such amount as the Court considers reasonable shall be added for any further hardship which the tenant sustains through the making of the order terminating the tenancy.

(6) This section does not apply where the tenant of the tenement is entitled to a reversionary lease of the tenement or would be so entitled but for section 33.

Amendment history: Subs (1) and (2) were amended by s 199(2) of the Residential Tenancies Act 2004 by the deletion of "obsolete area" and its replacement with "area to which an integrated area plan relates", which provision came into force on 1st September 2004.

Consequential Provisions

Set-off compensation against rent, etc.

61.—(1) Where compensation under this Part is payable by one person to another and money is due and owing to him by the latter under or in respect of the latter's lease or other interest in the premises, either person may set off, so far as may be, the one amount against the other. [10–61]

(2) Where compensation under this Part is payable by one person to another and he claims that money is payable to him by the latter under or in respect of the latter's lease or other interest in the premises and the claim or the amount thereof is disputed or the amount of the claim is unliquidated, he may pay the amount of the compensation into Court, and thereupon the Court may, on the application of either party, make such order in relation to the amount paid into Court as justice may require and, in particular, may retain that amount or any part thereof until the validity of the claim or the amount thereof has been determined.

Payment of compensation where interest is mortgaged.

62.—(1) Where compensation under this Part is payable and the interest in the premises of the Person to whom the compensation is payable is subject to a mortgage or charge, the mortgage or charge shall extend and attach to the compensation. [10–62]

(2) Where a person by whom the compensation is payable has actual notice of a mortgage or charge which by virtue of this section or otherwise affects the compensation, he shall either—

(a) with the consent of the person to whom the compensation is due, pay the compensation to the owner of the mortgage or charge, or

(b) with the consent of that owner, pay the compensation to the person to whom it is due, or

(c) where the owner and that person direct that the compensation shall be paid in a particular manner, pay it in that manner, or

(d) where no such consent or direction is given, pay the compensation into Court.

(3) Where the compensation is paid into Court the Court may, on the application of any person interested, make such order in regard to it as justice may require.

Protection of trustees, etc.

63.—(1) Where a person (in this section referred to as a trustee) is entitled to receive the rents and profits of premises as trustee or in any character otherwise than for his own benefit and money is due by the trustee for compensation under this Part or for costs, charges or expenses in relation to a claim for that compensation— [10–63]

(a) the money shall not be recoverable personally against the trustee nor shall he be under any liability to pay it, but it shall be a charge on and recoverable only against the premises and all property, real or personal, held by the trustee on the same trusts or in the same character as the premises;

(b) the trustee shall, either before or after having paid the money, be entitled to obtain from the Court a charge on the premises and all property, real or personal, held by him on the same trusts or in the same character as the premises to the amount of the money and of all costs properly incurred by him in obtaining the charge or raising the amount thereof;

(c) if the trustee refuses or fails to pay the money within one month after the person to whom it is due has quitted the premises, that person shall be entitled to obtain from the Court a charge on the premises and all property, real or personal, held by the trustee on the same trusts or in the same character as the premises to the amount of the money or of so much thereof as is then unpaid and of all costs properly incurred by him in obtaining the charge or in raising the amount thereof.

(2) Any company incorporated by statute and having power to advance money for the improvement of land may take an assignment of any charge made by the Court under this section, and such company may assign any charge so assigned to them to any person or persons whatsoever.

PART V – COVENANTS IN LEASES OF TENEMENTS

"Lease".

[10–64] 64.—In this Part, "lease" includes a yearly tenancy arising by operation of law or by inference on the expiration of a lease and a statutory tenancy implied by holding over premises on the expiration of a lease.

Damages for breach of covenants to repair.

[10–65] 65.—(1) Where a lease (whether made before or after the commencement of this Act) of a tenement contains a covenant (whether express or implied and whether general or specific) on the part of the lessee to put or to keep the tenement in repair during the currency of the lease or to leave or put the tenement in repair at the expiration of the lease and there has been a breach of the covenant, the subsequent provisions of this section shall have effect.

(2) The damages recoverable in any court for the breach shall not in any case exceed the amount (if any) by which the value of the reversion (whether mediate or immediate) in the tenement is diminished owing to the breach.

(3) Save where the want of repair is shown to be due, wholly or substantially, to wilful damage or wilful waste committed by the lessee no damages shall be recoverable in any court for the breach if it is shown—

(a) that, having regard to the age and condition of the tenement, its repair in accordance with the covenant is physically impossible, or

(b) that, having regard to the age, condition, character and situation of the tenement, its repair in accordance with the covenant would involve expenditure which is excessive in proportion to the value of the tenement, or

(c) that, having regard to the character and situation of the tenement, the tenement could not when so repaired be profitably used or could not be profitably used unless it were re-built, re-constructed or structurally altered to a substantial extent.

Covenants against alienation.

[10–66] 66.—(1) A covenant in a lease (whether made before or after the commencement of this Act) of a tenement absolutely prohibiting or restricting the alienation of the tenement, either generally or in any particular manner, shall have effect as if it were a covenant prohibiting or restricting such alienation without the licence or consent of the lessor.

(2) In every lease (whether made before or after the commencement of this Act) in which there is contained or in which there is implied by virtue of the British Statute passed on the 5th day of May, 1826, and entitled "An Act to amend the Law of Ireland respecting the Assignment and Sub-letting of Lands and Tenements" or by virtue of subsection (1) a covenant prohibiting or restricting the alienation, either generally or in any particular manner, of the tenement without the licence or consent of the lessor, the covenant shall, notwithstanding any express provision to the contrary, be subject—

(a) to a proviso that the licence or consent shall not be unreasonably withheld, but this proviso shall not preclude the lessor from requiring payment of a reasonable sum in respect of legal or other expenses incurred by him in connection with the licence or consent, and

(b) where the lease is made for a term of more than forty years and is made in consideration wholly or partially of the erection or substantial addition to or improvement or alteration of buildings, to a proviso to the effect that, in the case of any alienation of the tenement in contravention of the covenant effected more than seven years before the end of the term, no such licence or consent shall be required if notice in writing of the transaction is given to the lessor within one month after the transaction is effected, and

(c) where such alienation would cause a transfer or increase of any rates, taxes or other burden to or of the lessor, to a proviso that all expenditure incurred by the lessor by reason of the transfer or increase shall be reimbursed by the lessee to the lessor as and when so incurred and shall be recoverable from the lessee as rent under the lease.

Note: Certain different considerations apply to any premises within the Temple Bar area under s 11(1) of the Temple Bar Renewal and Development Act 1991.

This section does not apply to a dwelling to which the Residential Tenancies Act 2004 applies—see s 193(d) of the 2004 Act.

Covenants restrictive of user.

67.—(1) A covenant in a lease (whether made before or after the commencement of this Act) of a tenement absolutely prohibiting the alteration of the user of the tenement shall have effect as if it were a covenant prohibiting such alteration without the licence or consent of the lessor. **[10–67]**

(2) In every lease (whether made before or after the commencement of this Act) of a tenement in which there is contained a covenant prohibiting either expressly or by virtue of subsection (1) the alteration of the user of the tenement without the licence or consent of the lessor, the covenant shall, notwithstanding any express provision to the contrary, be subject—

(a) to a proviso to the effect that the licence or consent shall not be unreasonably withheld, but this proviso shall not preclude the lessor from requiring payment of a reasonable sum in respect of legal or other expenses incurred by him in connection with the licence or consent, and

(b) unless the alteration involves the erection, provision or reconstruction (otherwise than as an improvement within the meaning of subsection (3)) of any building or structure, to a proviso that no fine or sum of money in the nature of a fine (other than any sum authorised by this section) nor any increase of rent shall be payable for or in respect of the licence or consent, and

(c) if the alteration would cause a transfer or increase of any rates, taxes or other burden to or of the lessor, to a proviso that all expenditure incurred by the lessor by reason of the transfer or increase shall be reimbursed by the lessee to the lessor as and when so incurred and shall be recoverable from the lessee by the lessor as rent under the lease.

(3) In this section and section 68, "improvement" means any addition to or alteration of a building or structure and includes any structure which is ancillary or subsidiary thereto but does not include any alteration or reconstruction of a building or structure so that it loses its original identity.

(4) The references in section 29 of the Act of 1967 to an improvement shall be construed as references to an improvement within the meaning of subsection (3).

Note: This section does not apply to a dwelling to which the Residential Tenancies Act 2004 applies —see s 193(d) of the 2004 Act.

Covenants against making improvements.

[10–68] 68.—(1) A covenant in a lease (whether made before or after the commencement of this Act) of a tenement absolutely prohibiting the making of any improvement within the meaning of section 67(3) on the tenement shall have effect as if it were a covenant prohibiting the making of the improvement without the licence or consent of the lessor.

(2) In every lease (whether made before or after the commencement of this Act) of a tenement in which there is contained a covenant prohibiting either expressly or by virtue of subsection (1), the making of any improvement within the meaning of section 67(3) on the tenement without the licence or consent of the lessor, the covenant shall, notwithstanding any express provision to the contrary, be subject—

(a) to a proviso that the licence or consent shall not be unreasonably withheld, and

(b) to a proviso that no fine or sum of money in the nature of a fine (other than a reasonable sum in respect of legal or other expenses incurred by him in connection with the licence or consent) nor any increase of rent shall be payable for or in respect of the licence or consent.

Note: This section does not apply to a dwelling to which the Residential Tenancies Act 2004 applies —see s 193(d) of the 2004 Act.

Consent of lessor who cannot be found.

[10–69] 69.—Where—

(a) a lease (whether made before or after the commencement of this Act) of a tenement contains a covenant prohibiting or restricting the doing by the lessee of any particular thing without the licence or consent of the lessor, and

(b) the rent reserved by the lease has not been paid for five or more years, and

(c) the lessor is not known to and cannot be found by the lessee, the Court may, on the application of the lessee and after the publication of such (if any) advertisements as the Court directs, authorise the lessee, subject to such (if any) conditions as the Court thinks fit to impose, to do the particular thing so prohibited or restricted and thereupon it shall be lawful for the lessee to do such particular thing without the licence or consent of the lessor, in accordance with the conditions (if any) so imposed.

PART VI – MISCELLANEOUS

Application of Landlord and Tenant (Ground Rents) (No. 2) Act, 1978, to certain public authorities.

70.—A person who, but for section 4 of the Landlord and Tenant (Ground Rents) (No. 2) Act, 1978, or section 16(2)(d) or 16(2)(e) of that Act, would be entitled to acquire the fee simple of a dwellinghouse shall, notwithstanding those provisions, be entitled to acquire that fee simple save where— [10–70]

(a) in a case to which section 4 of that Act applies—the appropriate State authority, or

(b) in a case to which section 16(2)(d) or 16(2)(e) of that Act applies—the Minister for Transport,

is satisfied that such acquisition would not be in the public interest and so certifies.

Note: This section modifies and extends the application of s 4, s 16(2)(d) and s 16(2)(e) of the Landlord and Tenant (Ground Rents) (No 2) Act, 1978 to certain public authorities.

Amendment of section 10, condition 5 of Landlord and Tenant (Ground Rents) (No. 2) Act, 1978.

71.—*Omitted. Amends s 10 of the Landlord and Tenant (Ground Rents) (No 2) Act 1978.* [10–71]

Extension of sections 10 and 12 of Landlord and Tenant (Ground Rents) (No. 2) Act, 1978, to certain subleases for less than 50 years.

72.—Condition 7 in section 10 of the Landlord and Tenant (Ground Rents) (No. 2) Act, 1978, and section 12 of that Act shall extend to a lease made for a term of less than fifty years if [10–72]

(a) the lease is a sublease (whether mediate or immediate) under a lease (in this section referred to as the superior lease) to which Part II of that Act applies,

(b) the land demised by the lease is the whole or part of the land comprised in the superior lease, and

(c) the lease is made for a term which equals or exceeds the lesser of the following periods, namely twenty years or two-thirds of the term of the superior lease, and in any case expires at the same time as or not more than fifteen years before the expiration of the superior lease,

and the other requirements of the condition are fulfilled.

Note: This section extends ss 10 and 12 of the Landlord and Tenant (Ground Rents) (No 2) Act 1978 to certain subleases by extending condition 7 of s 12 of that Act.

Preservation of pre-existing rights.

[10–73] 73.—Where, immediately before the commencement of the Landlord and Tenant (Ground Rents) (No. 2) Act, 1978, a person was as respects any land, a person to whom section 3 of the Act of 1967 applied or would have been such a person if he had served a notice under section 4 of that Act, he shall as from such commencement be a person to whom Part II of the Landlord and Tenant (Ground Rents) (No. 2) Act, 1978, applies.

Note: This section preserves certain rights existing before the commencement of the No. 2 Act of 1978.

Conversion of leases for lives into fee simple.

[10–74] 74.—A person entitled to an interest in land the title to which interest originated under a lease for lives renewable forever which was created prior to the 1st day of August, 1849, and was not converted into a fee farm grant under the Renewable Leasehold Conversion Act, 1849, shall from the commencement of this Act hold the land for an estate in fee simple. The said estate shall be deemed to be a graft upon the previous interest and shall be subject to any rights or equities arising from its being such graft.

Sale of houses for which letting grants were paid to public utility societies.

[10–75] 75.—(1) This section applies to a house which was erected by a public utility society within the meaning of section 2 (1) of the Housing Act, 1966, and in relation to which erection a grant was made under the Housing (Financial and Miscellaneous Provisions) Acts, 1932 to 1962, and there is a subsisting undertaking, given by the public utility society in consideration of the grant, that the house would not be sold.

(2) The Minister for the Environment (in this section referred to as the Minister) may grant his consent to the sale of a house to which this section applies.

(3) Where the Minister grants his consent to the sale of a house to which this section applies, then, notwithstanding any undertaking of the kind described in subsection (1) or any limitation which may apply by virtue of section 121 of the Housing Act, 1966, the house may be sold and the sale shall operate to vest the premises in the purchaser freed and discharged from any such undertaking.

(4) The Minister may, in relation to the sale of a house to which this section applies which was effected prior to the commencement of this section, grant his consent to such sale and where the Minister so grants his consent the fact that the sale was effected prior to the commencement of this section shall not affect and shall be deemed never to have affected the validity of the sale and such sale shall be deemed for all purposes to have been effected in accordance with subsection (3).

(5) In this section, "grant", in relation to a house, means a grant of land as a site for such house or a grant of money in respect of such house or a grant made partly in one such way and partly in the other such way.

Necessary party to deed, etc., under disability or failing to act.

76.—(1) In this section "necessary party" means a person who is required under this Act to grant or join in the grant of a lease or tenancy and "requirement" refers to anything so required. [10–76]

(2) Where a necessary party is, by reason of having a fiduciary capacity or a limited estate or by reason of restrictive covenants in a lease or tenancy under which he holds, unable to comply with a requirement the Court may, on the application of any person concerned, empower him to do so.

(3) Where a necessary party is an infant or a person of unsound mind or cannot be found or refuses or fails to execute or join in the execution of a lease or tenancy, the Court may, on the application of any person concerned, appoint and empower an officer of the Court to execute it or join in the execution thereof on behalf of the necessary party.

(4) Where, in relation to a lease or tenancy, a necessary party is unknown or unascertained, the Court may, on the application of any person concerned, appoint any person who is receiving the rent in respect of the applicant's interest in the premises, or such other person as the Court may think fit, to represent such unknown or unascertained person in all proceedings in connection therewith and may appoint and empower an officer of the Court to execute the lease or tenancy on behalf of the necessary party.

(5) Where an officer of the Court is appointed under subsection (3) or (4) to execute or join in the execution of a lease or tenancy the Court may order the rent payable under the lease or tenancy to be paid into Court or may make such order or give such direction in regard to the payment of the rent as it thinks proper.

(6) Where a person upon whom a notice under any provision of this Act is required to be served cannot be found or ascertained, that person shall be deemed to be a necessary party for the purposes of this section and the provisions of this section shall apply accordingly with the necessary modifications.

(7) A power conferred on the Court by this section shall be exercised in relation to a ward of court only by leave of the court of which he is a ward.

Survival of rights on death.

77.—On the death of a person who has claimed any right under this Act his personal representative or successor in title may act in his place for the purposes of all matters consequential upon the claim. [10–77]

Lease terminating by ejectment or re-entry.

78.—(1) Where a lease or other contract of tenancy (in this section referred to as the terminated lease or contract) is terminated before its normal expiration— [10–78]

(a) a lease or other contract of tenancy or any premises comprised in the terminated lease or contract shall not, if it is a lease or contract, to which any Part of this Act applies, inferior to the terminated lease or contract, be terminated by the termination;

(b) the person who would, but for this subsection, become entitled by virtue of the termination of the terminated lease or contract to the possession of the premises shall become entitled to the reversion on the inferior lease or contract;

(c) that person shall, subject to subsection (2), become entitled to the benefit of the rent reserved by and the covenants contained in the inferior lease or contract and shall be regarded for the purposes of this Act as having become the immediate lessor of the premises.

(2) The person holding premises under an inferior lease or other contract of tenancy to which subsection (1)(a) applies shall, from the date of the termination of the terminated lease or contract, hold the premises at whichever of the following rents is the greater—

(a) the rent reserved by the inferior lease or contract,

(b) such portion of the rent reserved by the terminated lease or contract as is fairly attributable to the premises.

Application of Settled Land Acts.

[10–79] 79.—(1) The powers of granting leases conferred on a tenant for life by section 6 of the Settled Land Act, 1882, apply to the grant of any lease or tenancy which is required to be granted under this Act.

(2) Capital money arising under the Settled Land Acts, 1882 to 1890, may be applied—

(a) in payment of any sum payable to a person for compensation or damages awarded under this Act and any related costs, charges and expenses, or

(b) in payment, as for an improvement authorised by the said Acts, of any money expended or costs incurred under this Act in or about the execution of an improvement, or

(c) in payment of any costs, charges and expenses incurred in relation to an application under this Act.

(3) The payment of compensation or damages awarded under this Act shall be included among the purposes for which a tenant for life may raise money under section 18 of the Settled Land Act, 1882.

(4) (a) Where a person liable to pay compensation under this Act is a tenant for life or in a fiduciary position, he may require the sum payable for compensation and any related damages, costs, charges and expenses to be paid out of capital money held on the same trusts as the settled land.

(b) In this subsection "capital money" includes personal estate held on the same trusts as the land, and "settled land" includes land held on trust for sale.

Mortgages.

[10–80] 80.—(1) For the purposes of the application to any person of the provisions of this Act relating to the grant to him of any estate or interest in land, the existence of a mortgage on the interest of that person shall be disregarded.

(2) Where, either before or after the commencement of this Act—

(a) a lessee executes a mortgage by subdemise of the whole or part of the land comprised in his lease, retaining a nominal reversion therein, and

(b) the land comprised in the subdemise is sold for the enforcement of the mortgage,

the purchaser shall, for the purposes of this Act, be deemed to have acquired the interest of the lessee in the demised land for the entire of the unexpired term of the lease, including the period of the nominal reversion.

Valuation by Commissioner of Valuation.

[10–81] 81.—(1) The Court may, and if so requested by any party concerned shall, cause to be sent to the Commissioner of Valuation a request for a valuation, estimate or statement in respect of any particular matter relevant to proceedings under this Act and may for that purpose adjourn the proceedings.

(2) The Commissioner shall thereupon cause such valuation, estimate or statement to be prepared and sent to the Court and may charge therefor a fee calculated in accordance with regulations made by the Minister for Finance.

(3) Where a request is sent to the Commissioner under this section, the Court shall have regard to the valuation, estimate or statement furnished by the Commissioner.

(4) Any party concerned shall be entitled to obtain from the Circuit Court Office a copy of a valuation, estimate or statement furnished by the Commissioner under this section, subject to payment therefor at the rate for the time being chargeable by law for copies of documents obtained from the office.

(5) A fee payable under this section shall be borne and paid to the county registrar by such party or by such parties in such proportions as the Court directs, and shall be paid by the county registrar into or disposed of by him for the benefit of the Exchequer in such manner as the Minister for Finance directs.

Evidence and apportionment of rateable valuation.

82.—(1) The inclusion in the certificate signed by or on behalf of the Commissioner of Valuation on an extract from the valuation list issued under section 9 of the Annual Revision of Rateable Property (Ireland) Amendment Act, 1860, of a statement that a valuation shown in the extract is the rateable valuation obtaining on a date specified in the certificate shall for the purposes of this Act be evidence of that fact. **[10–82]**

(2) Where land does not on a particular date bear a separate rateable valuation, the Commissioner of Valuation may for the purposes of this Act apportion the rateable valuation or valuations of the properties in which the land was comprised on that date and may charge a fee for the apportionment.

(3) Every fee charged by the Commissioner of Valuation under this section shall be determined, accounted for and applied in the same manner as the fees charged by the Commissioner under section 9 of the Annual Revision of Rateable Property (Ireland) Amendment Act, 1860.

Extension of times limited by this Act.

83.—Where a person fails to do any act or thing in the time provided for by or under this Act, the Court may, on such terms as it thinks proper (and shall unless satisfied that injustice would be caused) extend the time where it is shown that the failure was occasioned by disability, mistake, absence from the State, inability to obtain requisite information or any other reasonable cause. **[10–83]**

Notices requiring information.

84.—(1) A person seeking any estate or interest in any premises under this Act may, in order to secure the joinder of all necessary parties in the grant, serve a notice in the prescribed form upon his immediate lessor requiring information as to the nature and duration of the reversion of that lessor, and the name and address of the person for the time being entitled to the next superior interest and may also serve a similar notice on each other person holding a superior interest. **[10–84]**

(2) Where a person upon whom a notice is to be served under subsection (1) cannot be found or ascertained, a notice in the prescribed form may be served upon the person receiving the rent for the premises requiring the name and address of the

person to whom the rent is paid by the person upon whom the notice is served and any other information reasonably necessary for the purpose specified in subsection (1).

(3) It shall be the duty of a person on whom a notice is served under this section to give or send in writing, within one month of service, such required information as is within his possession or procurement.

(4) Where a person has served a notice under this section and the person on whom it is served refuses or fails to provide the information as required by this section, the person who served the notice may apply to the Court which may make such order as justice may require to compel the person on whom the notice was served to provide the information.

Void contracts.

[10–85] 85.—So much of any contract, whether made before or after the commencement of this Act, as provides that any provision of this Act shall not apply in relation to a person or that the application of any such provision shall be varied, modified or restricted in any way in relation to a person shall be void.

(2) Subsection (1) does not apply to a renunciation referred to in—

(a) subparagraph (iiia) (inserted by section 4 of the Landlord and Tenant (Amendment) Act 1994), or

(b) subparagraph (iiib) (inserted by section 191 of the Residential Tenancies Act 2004),of section 17(1)(a)

Amendment history: Section 85 was amended by s 6 of the Landlord and Tenant (Amendment) Act 1994. It was subsequently amended by s 191(3) of the Residential Tenancies Act 2004. However, the 1994 Act added subs (2) to follow "subsection (1)". The original s 85 had no subsection divisions. In those circumstances subs (2) merely follows the original text of s 85.

Rights of entry and inspection.

[10–86] 86.—Where an improvement notice or a notice of intention to claim relief under Part II or IV has been served, the landlord and every superior landlord on whom the notice or a copy thereof has been served under this Act, and every person authorised by the landlord or any such superior landlord, shall be entitled to enter at all reasonable times on the premises and there to make such inspection and examination and take such measurements as are necessary or proper for the determination by the landlord or superior landlord (as the case may be) of the course he will adopt in relation to the notice.

Set-off against rent for cost of repairs.

[10–87] 87.—(1) Where a landlord refuses or fails to execute repairs to a tenement which he is bound by covenant or otherwise by law to execute and has been called upon by the tenant to execute, and the tenant executes the repairs at his own expense, the tenant may set off the expenditure against any subsequent gale or gales of rent until it is recouped.

(2) Where a set-off is made under this section against the whole or part of a gale of rent, the landlord entitled to receive the rent shall on receiving evidence of the expenditure of the amount so set off, be bound to give the like receipt for the gale of rent as he would be bound to give if the gale or part of the gale had been paid in money.

Service of notices.

88.—(1) Service of a notice or other document under this Act may be effected by post and, if so effected, shall be by registered post. [10–88]

(2) Any notice or other document required or authorised by this Act to be served by a lessee on his lessor may be so served by sending it by registered post addressed to the person to whom the lessee pays the rent of the premises to which the notice or document relates at the place at or to which he pays or sends the rent.

(3) Any notice or other document required or authorised by this Act to be served on a lessee may be so served by sending it by registered post addressed to him at the premises to which the notice or document relates.

(4) Service of a notice or other document under this Act on behalf of a person shall be deemed, for the purposes of this Act, to be service of the notice or document by the person.

SCHEDULE

Repeal of Enactments (Section 11)

Landlord and Tenant Act, 1931 (1931, No. 55)	The whole Act.
Landlord and Tenant (Reversionary Leases) Act, 1958 (1958, No. 2)	The whole Act.
Rent Restrictions Act, 1960 (1960, No. 42)	Section 54.
Rent Restrictions (Amendment) Act, 1967 (1967, No. 10)	Section 13.

ACTS REFERRED TO

An Act to amend the Law of Ireland respecting the Assignment and Sub-Letting of Lands and Tenements (1826, c. 29)
Annual Revisions of Rateable Property (Ireland) Amendment Act, 1860 (1860, c. 4)
Companies Act, 1963 (1963, No. 33)
Harbours Act, 1946 (1946, No. 9)
Health Act, 1970 (1970, No. 1)
Housing Act, 1966 (1966, No. 21)
Increase of Rent and Mortgage Interest (Restrictions) Act, 1923 (1923, No. 19)
Interpretation Act, 1937 (1937, No. 38)
Landlord and Tenant Act, 1931 (1931, No. 55)
Landlord and Tenant (Amendment) Act, 1971 (1971, No. 30)
Landlord and Tenant (Ground Rents) Act, 1967 (1967, No. 3)
Landlord and Tenant (Ground Rents) Act, 1978 (1978, No. 7)
Landlord and Tenant (Ground Rents) (No. 2) Act, 1978 (1978, No. 16)
Landlord and Tenant (Reversionary Leases) Act, 1958 (1958, No. 2)
Local Government Act, 1941 (1941, No. 23)
Local Government (Planning and Development) Act, 1963 (1963, No. 28)
Local Government (Sanitary Services) Acts, 1878 to 1964
Rent Restrictions Act, 1946 (1946, No. 16)
Rent Restrictions Act, 1960 (1960, No. 42)
Rent Restrictions (Amendment) Act, 1967 (1967, No. 10)
Settled Land Act, 1882 (1882, c. 32)
Town Tenants (Ireland) Act, 1906 (1906, c. 54)

Chapter 11

LANDLORD AND TENANT (GROUND RENTS) (AMENDMENT) ACT, 1983

(1983, No. 20)

AN ACT TO EXTEND THE PERIOD DURING WHICH APPLICATIONS MAY BE MADE UNDER PART III OF THE LANDLORD AND TENANT (GROUND RENTS) (NO. 2) ACT, 1978, AND TO PROVIDE FOR THE INCREASE OF CERTAIN FEES UNDER THAT PART.

[29TH JUNE, 1983]

BE IT ENACTED BY THE OIREACHTAS AS FOLLOWS:

Duration of Part III of Landlord and Tenant (Ground Rents) (No. 2) Act, 1978.

1.—*Omitted. Amends s 18 of the Landlord and Tenant (Ground Rents) (No 2) Act 1978.* [11–01]

Amendment of section 23 of Landlord and Tenant (Ground Rents) (No. 2) Act, 1978.

2.—*Omitted. Amends s 23 of the Landlord and Tenant (Ground Rents) (No 2) Act 1978.* [11–02]

Short title, construction and collective citation.

3.—(1) This Act may be cited as the Landlord and Tenant (Ground Rents) (Amendment) Act, 1983. [11–03]

(2) The Landlord and Tenant Acts, 1967 to 1980, and this Act shall be construed together as one Act and may be cited together as the Landlord and Tenant Acts, 1967 to 1983.

ACT REFERRED TO

Landlord and Tenant (Ground Rents) (No. 2) Act, 1978 (1978, No. 16)

Note: As this Act has no commencement provision it commences as and from the end of the day before the date of its passing. The Act was passed on 29th June 1983 — see s 8(3) of the Interpretation Act 1937.

Chapter 12

LANDLORD AND TENANT (AMENDMENT) ACT, 1984

(1984 No. 4)

ARRANGEMENT OF SECTIONS

AN ACT TO MAKE PROVISION FOR THE PERIODICAL REVIEW OF RENTS PAYABLE UNDER REVERSIONARY LEASES AND SPORTING LEASES AND FOR THE DETERMINATION OF THE PURCHASE PRICE OF THE FEE SIMPLE AND OTHER INTERESTS IN LAND IN CERTAIN CASES AND FOR THESE AND OTHER PURPOSES TO AMEND THE LAW OF LANDLORD AND TENANT AND TO PROVIDE FOR OTHER MATTERS CONNECTED WITH THE MATTERS AFORESAID.

[14TH MARCH 1984]

BE IT ENACTED BY THE OIREACHTAS AS FOLLOWS:

Commencement.

[12–01] 1. —This Act shall come into operation one week after the day of its passing.

Interpretation.

[12–02] 2. —(1) In this Act, except where the context otherwise requires—

"Act of 1967" means the Landlord and Tenant (Ground Rents) Act, 1967;

"Act of 1971" means the Landlord and Tenant (Amendment) Act, 1971;

"Act (No. 2) of 1978" means the Landlord and Tenant (Ground Rents) (No. 2) Act, 1978;

"Act of 1980" means the Landlord and Tenant (Amendment) Act, 1980;

"the Court" means the Circuit Court.

(2) A reference in this Act to a section is to a section of this Act unless it is indicated that reference to some other enactment is intended.

(3) A reference in this Act to a subsection or paragraph is to the subsection or paragraph of the provision in which the reference occurs, unless it is indicated that reference to some other provision is intended.

(4) A reference in this Act to any other enactment shall, except so far as the context otherwise requires, be construed as a reference to that enactment as amended or applied by or under any other enactment including this Act.

Reversionary Leases

Review of rent.

[12–03] 3. —(1) Where, after the commencement of this Act, the terms of a reversionary lease are settled by the Court under Part III of the Act of 1980 the lessor or the lessee shall be entitled to have the rent reviewed in accordance with this section.

(2) The person seeking the review shall serve on the other party notice of his intention to have the rent reviewed.

(3) The notice may be served—

(a) where the rent has not previously been reviewed—not earlier than one month before the fifth anniversary of the date on which the terms of the lease were settled,

(b) where the rent has previously been reviewed—not earlier than the fifth anniversary of the date of service of the notice for the preceding review.

(4) In default of agreement on the rent, the person seeking the review shall be entitled to apply to the Court to have the rent reviewed not earlier than one month after service of the notice.

(5) In default of agreement, the rent fixed upon the review shall become payable on whichever of the following dates is the later—

(a) the first gale day after service of the notice under subsection (2),

(b) (i) where the rent has not previously been reviewed, the first gale day following the fifth anniversary of the date on which the terms of the lease were settled,

(ii) where the rent has previously been reviewed, the first gale day following the fifth anniversary of the date of service of the notice for the preceding review.

(6) On a review of the rent by the Court the rent shall be fixed in accordance with the relevant provisions of sections 34, 35 and 36 of the Act of 1980 by reference to the date of service of the notice on which the application to the Court is based.

Temporary extension of right to reversionary lease.

4. —(1) Where— [12–04]

(a) after the 13th day of November, 1980, and before the commencement of this Act a person was entitled to obtain a reversionary lease of land under Part III of the Act of 1980, and

(b) at that commencement he is no longer so entitled by virtue of section 31 of the Act of 1980 but is in possession of the land without having obtained a new tenancy and without having acquired the interest in the land of the immediate lessor,

that person shall during the twelve months after that commencement have the same right to obtain a reversionary lease as he would have had if his lease had not expired, and section 40 of that Act shall apply accordingly.

(2) A reversionary lease granted by virtue of subsection (1) shall commence on the expiration of the lease to which it is reversionary or on such other date as may be agreed upon between the parties.

Sporting Leases

Review of rent.

5. —(1) Where, after the commencement of this Act, the rent under a sporting lease is fixed by the Court under the Act of 1971 the lessor or the lessee shall be entitled to have the rent reviewed in accordance with this section. [12–05]

(2) The person seeking the review shall serve on the other party notice of his intention to have the rent reviewed.

(3) The notice may be served—

(a) where the rent has not previously been reviewed—not earlier than one month before the fifth anniversary of the date on which the rent under the lease was fixed,

(b) where the rent has previously been reviewed—not earlier than the fifth anniversary of the date of service of the notice for the preceding review.

(4) In default of agreement on the rent, the person seeking the review shall be entitled to apply to the Court to have the rent reviewed not earlier than one month after service of the notice.

(5) In default of agreement, the rent fixed upon the review shall become payable on whichever of the following dates is the later—

(a) the first gale day after service of the notice under subsection (2),

(b) (i) where the rent has not previously been reviewed, the first gale day following the fifth anniversary of the date on which the rent under the lease was fixed,

(ii) where the rent has previously been reviewed, the first gale day following the fifth anniversary of the date of service of the notice for the preceding review.

(6) On a review of the rent by the Court the rent shall be fixed in accordance with the relevant provisions of section 6 of the Act of 1971 by reference to the date of service of the notice on which the application to the Court is based.

(7) *Omitted. Repeals s 5(3)(a) of the Landlord and Tenant (Amendment) Act 1971.*

Effect of covenant restricting user of land to sporting purposes.

[12–06] 6.—For the avoidance of doubt, it is hereby declared that, in a lease to a sports club, a condition providing for a right to terminate the lease where the property is not used for or in connection with sporting purposes, whether inserted in pursuance of section 5 (3) (b) of the Act of 1971 or by agreement between the parties, is not a covenant to which section 29 of the Act of 1967 or section 67 of the Act of 1980 applies.

Purchase of Fee Simple

Determination of purchase price by arbitration.

[12–07] 7.—(1) In this section, "the relevant date" in relation to any land means the date of service of the notice under section 4 of the Act of 1967 or of the application under Part III of Act (No. 2) of 1978, as the case may be.

(2) This section applies to the determination of the purchase price of the fee simple or any other interest by arbitration under the Act of 1967 including an arbitration conducted by the Registrar of Titles in pursuance of section 21 of Act (No. 2) of 1978.

(3) Subject to the provisions of this section, the purchase price shall be the sum which, in the opinion of the arbitrator, a willing purchaser would give and a willing vendor would accept for the fee simple or other interest at the relevant date having had regard to—

(a) the rent payable for the land by the person acquiring the fee simple,

(b) where, at the relevant date, the land is held under a lease which provides for an increased rent payable within fifteen years after that date, the amount of that increase and the time when it becomes payable,

(c) the current interest yields on securities of the Government issued for subscription in the State,

(d) if the land is used for the purposes of business, or exceeds one acre in area and is not used for the purposes of business, the area and nature of the land, its location and user and the state of repair of any buildings or structures thereon,

(e) the price paid for the fee simple or any other interest in the land on a sale taking place on or after the 22nd day of May, 1964,

(f) any mortgage or other charge on the interest in the land of any person from whom, mediately or immediately, the person acquiring the fee simple holds the land,

(g) the costs and expenses which, in the opinion of the arbitrator, would be reasonably incurred by the persons from whom, mediately or immediately, the person acquiring the fee simple holds the land, in investing the purchase money payable in respect of the acquisition of the fee simple,

(h) the costs and expenses which, in the opinion of the arbitrator, have been incurred by a person acquiring the fee simple who holds the land under a lease by reason of the failure of the lessor to maintain any amenities which he is required to maintain under a covenant in the lease,

(i) the current price of the immediate lessor's interest in land held under leases or yearly tenancies similar to the lease or yearly tenancy, as the case may be, under which the land is held by the person acquiring the fee simple, and

(j) such other matters as are, in the opinion of the arbitrator, relevant to the determination of the purchase price.

(4) (a) Where, at the relevant date, the land is held under a lease that has expired or is held at a rent which, whether under the terms of the lease or by operation of a statute, is subject to a review which is due but has not been made, the purchase price of the fee simple shall, subject to the other provisions of this section, be a sum equal to one eighth of the amount which, at that date, a willing purchaser would give and a willing vendor would accept for the land in fee simple free of all estates, interests and incumbrances, but having regard to any covenant which continues in force by virtue of section 28 of Act (No. 2) of 1978, and assuming that the lessee has complied with any other covenants or conditions in his lease that could affect the price.

(b) A deduction shall be made from that amount equal to the value of the goodwill, if any, in the premises of the person acquiring the fee simple.

(c) A deduction shall also be made from that amount equal to any addition to the value of the premises resulting from such works as would qualify for the special allowance mentioned in section 35 of the Act of 1980.

(d) In determining the amount referred to in paragraph (a) any addition to value deriving from contemplation of substantial rebuilding or a scheme of development (such as are mentioned in section 33 (1) (b) (i) and (ii) of the Act of 1980) shall be disregarded.

(5) If the land—

(a) is not used for the purposes of business,

(b) is held by the person acquiring the fee simple under a contract of yearly tenancy, or under a yearly tenancy arising by operation of law or by inference on the expiration of a lease or under a lease which will not expire within fifteen years after the relevant date, and

(c) does not exceed one acre in area,

then, subject to subsections (6) and (7), the purchase price shall not exceed the amount which, if invested on the date of the award in the security of the Government which was issued last before that date for subscription in the State and is redeemable not less than fifteen years after the date of issue, would produce annually in gross interest an amount equal to the amount of the rent payable under the lease or yearly tenancy, as the case may be, during the year immediately preceding the relevant date.

(6) Where the cost of extinguishing a rent or charge out of or on land the fee simple in which is being acquired under Act (No. 2) of 1978 or the Act of 1967 is fixed by statute, allowance shall be made for such cost in determining the purchase price of the fee simple under this section.

(7) Subsection (5) shall not apply to a case where, whether under the lease or by virtue of the operation of a statute, an increased rent is or may become payable, or the rent is subject to review, within fifteen years after the relevant date.

(8) If the land—

(a) is not used for the purposes of business,

(b) is held by the person acquiring the fee simple under a lease, and—

(i) the lease will expire within fifteen years after the relevant date, or

(ii) the rent is subject to review within that period, under the lease or by virtue of any statute, and

(c) does not exceed one acre in area,

the purchase price shall not exceed the amount which would be determined under subsection (5) if the land were land to which the subsection applied, together with, in respect of each year by which the unexpired term (reckoned from that date) of the lease falls short of fifteen years, one fifteenth of the difference between that price and the price that would be determined under subsection (4) if the lease had expired.

(9) Subject to subsection (8), where, at the relevant date, the land is held under a lease that will expire within fifteen years after that date or where the rent is subject to review within that time, under the lease or by virtue of any statute, then—

(a) the length of time to run from that date to the expiration of the lease or to the earliest date from which the rent as so reviewed may become payable, as the case may be, and

(b) the provisions as to price that would apply if, as the case may be, the lease had already expired or the review of rent were already due,

shall be among the matters to which, pursuant to subsection (3), the arbitrator shall have regard in determining the purchase price.

(10) The arbitrator shall, if so requested by a party to the arbitration, specify the matters (if any) to which he has had regard under subsection (3) (j).

(11) *Omitted. Repeals s 17 of the Landlord and Tenant (Ground Rents) (No 2) Act 1978.*

Restrictions on right to acquire fee simple.

[12–08] 8.—A right to acquire the fee simple under Part II of Act (No. 2) of 1978 existing at the commencement of this Act shall, notwithstanding anything in section 16 (2) (a) of that Act, not be excluded by reason only of any provision in a reversionary lease granted after that commencement for a review of the rent reserved by the lease.

Buildings erected by yearly tenant.

[12–09] 9.—*Omitted. Amends s 15 of the Landlord and Tenant (Ground Rents) (No 2) Act 1978.*

Failure to provide information regarding title to land.

[12–10] 10.—*Omitted. Amends s 7 of the Landlord and Tenant (Ground Rents) Act 1967.*

Nomination of county registrar to arbitrate.

[12–11] 11. —If, during any period, the office of county registrar for a particular area is vacant or the county registrar for a particular area is unable owing to illness or for any other reason to transact the business of his office, the Minister may nominate any county registrar to hear and determine by arbitration under section 17 of the Act of 1967 a particular dispute, question or difficulty to which that section applies arising in that area or any dispute, question or difficulty to which that section applies so arising and the matter may be heard and determined accordingly.

Right of lessee to continue in possession.

12. —(1) A person to whom Part II of Act (No. 2) of 1978 applies by virtue of section 73 of the Act of 1980 and whose interest in the land has expired shall continue to be entitled to hold the land until either he is declared not to be entitled to acquire the fee simple or a grant to him of the fee simple is duly made and, during such period, he shall hold the land on the terms (so far as applicable) on which he previously held it, subject to all proper recoupments or adjustments. [12–12]

(2) Where an application is made in relation to the acquisition of the fee simple and the interest of the applicant in the land expires before the application is heard and determined, the applicant shall be entitled to remain in possession of the land until the application is finally heard and determined on the terms (so far as applicable) on which he previously held it, subject to all proper recoupments or adjustments.

Temporary extension of right to acquire fee simple.

13. —(1) Where an application under section 31 of the Act of 1980 was made after the 13th day of November, 1980, and before the commencement of this Act and at that commencement the application has not been determined, the following provisions shall apply during the period of twelve months following that commencement: [12–13]

(a) the applicant may by notice served on his immediate lessor withdraw that application and shall in that event be liable for the reasonable costs and expenses actually and necessarily incurred on foot of that application by the immediate lessor and any superior lessors;

(b) where a notice under paragraph (a) is served the applicant shall, notwithstanding that his interest in the land has expired, have the same right to acquire the fee simple as he would have had if that interest had not expired.

(2) Section 12 shall apply in relation to any case in which a notice is served under section 4 of the Act of 1967 or an application is made under section 20 or 21 of Act (No. 2) of 1978 by virtue of subsection (1)(b).

(3) Where—

(a) after the 13th day of November, 1980, and before the commencement of this Act, a person was entitled to acquire the fee simple of land by virtue of Part II of Act (No. 2) of 1978, and

(b) at that commencement, he is no longer so entitled but is in possession of the land without having obtained a new tenancy and without having acquired the interest in the land of the immediate lessor,

that person shall during the twelve months after that commencement have the same right to acquire the fee simple as he would have had if his interest had not expired, and section 12 shall apply accordingly.

New Tenancies

Restriction on application of Act 1980 to State.

14.—*Omitted. Amends and partly substitutes s 4 of the Landlord and Tenant (Amendment) Act 1980.* [12–14]

Review of rent.

[12–15] 15. —(1) Where the terms of a new tenancy are fixed by the Court under Part II of the Act of 1980 the landlord or the tenant shall be entitled to have the rent reviewed in accordance with this section.

(2) The person seeking the review shall serve on the other party notice of his intention to have the rent reviewed.

(3) The notice may be served—

(a) where the rent has not previously been reviewed—not earlier than one month before the fifth anniversary of the date on which the terms of the tenancy were fixed,

(b) where the rent has previously been reviewed—not earlier than the fifth anniversary of the date of service of the notice for the preceding review.

(4) In default of agreement on the rent, the person seeking the review shall be entitled to apply to the Court to have the rent reviewed not earlier than one month after service of the notice.

(5) In default of agreement, the rent fixed upon the review shall become payable on whichever of the following dates is the later—

(a) the first gale day after service of the notice under subsection (2),

(b) (i) where the rent has not previously been reviewed, the first gale day following the fifth anniversary of the date on which the terms of the tenancy were fixed,

(ii) where the rent has previously been reviewed, the first gale day following the fifth anniversary of the date of service of the notice for the preceding review.

(6) On a review of the rent by the Court the rent shall be fixed in accordance with the relevant provisions of section 23 of the Act of 1980 by reference to the date of service of the notice on which the application to the Court is based.

(7) *Omitted. Repeals s 24 of the Landlord and Tenant (Amendment) Act, 1980.*

Short title, construction and collective citation.

[12–16] 16. —(1) This Act may be cited as the Landlord and Tenant (Amendment) Act, 1984.

(2) The Landlord and Tenant Acts, 1967 to 1983, and this Act shall be construed together as one Act and may be cited together as the Landlord and Tenant Acts, 1967 to 1984.

ACTS REFERRED TO

Landlord and Tenant (Ground Rents) Act, 1967 (1967, No. 3)
Landlord and Tenant (Amendment) Act, 1971 (1971, No. 30)
Landlord and Tenant (Ground Rents) (No. 2) Act, 1978 (1978, No. 16)
Landlord and Tenant (Amendment) Act, 1980 (1980, No. 10)

Chapter 13

LANDLORD AND TENANT (GROUND RENTS) (AMENDMENT) ACT, 1984

(1984, No. 15)

ARRANGEMENT OF SECTIONS

AN ACT TO EXTEND THE PERIOD DURING WHICH APPLICATIONS MAY BE MADE UNDER PART III OF THE LANDLORD AND TENANT (GROUND RENTS) (NO. 2) ACT, 1978, AND TO PROVIDE FOR THE INCREASE OF CERTAIN FEES UNDER THAT ACT.

[10TH JULY 1984]

BE IT ENACTED BY THE OIREACHTAS AS FOLLOWS:

Definitions.

1.—In this Act— **[13–01]**

"Act (No. 2) of 1978" means the Landlord and Tenant (Ground Rents) (No. 2) Act, 1978;

"the Act of 1983" means the Landlord and Tenant (Ground Rents) (Amendment) Act, 1983.

Duration of Part III of Act (No. 2) of 1978.

2.—*Omitted. Amends s 18 of the Landlord and Tenant (Ground Rents) (No. 2) Act 1978.* **[13–02]**

Amendment of section 23 of Act (No. 2) of 1978.

3.—*Omitted. Amends s 23 of the Landlord and Tenant (Ground Rents) (No 2) Act 1978.* **[13–03]**

Amendment of section 26 of Act (No. 2) of 1978.

4.—(1) *Omitted. Amends s 26 of the Landlord and Tenant (Ground Rents) (No 2) Act 1978.* **[13–03]**

(2) The Minister for the Environment may, with the consent of the Minister for Finance, by order fix the fee to be taken from time to time for the issue of a transfer order pursuant to section 26 of Act (No. 2) of 1978.

Short title, collective citation and construction.

[13–04] 5.—(1) This Act may be cited as the Landlord and Tenant (Ground Rents) (Amendment) Act, 1984.

(2) The collective citation, the Landlord and Tenant Acts, 1967 to 1984, shall include this Act and those Acts and this Act shall be construed together as one Act.

ACTS REFERRED TO

Landlord and Tenant (Ground Rents) (No. 2) Act, 1978 (1978, No. 16)
Landlord and Tenant (Ground Rents) (Amendment) Act, 1983 (1983, No. 20)

> **Note:** As this Act has no commencement provision it commences as and from the end of the day before the date of its passing. The Act was passed on 10th July 1984 — see s 8(3) of the Interpretation Act 1937.

Chapter 14

LANDLORD AND TENANT (GROUND RENTS) (AMENDMENT) ACT, 1987

(1987, No. 12)

ARRANGEMENT OF SECTIONS

AN ACT TO AMEND THE LANDLORD AND TENANT (GROUND RENTS) (NO. 2) ACT, 1978, BY REPEALING THE PROVISION OF THAT ACT WHICH LIMITS THE PERIOD WITHIN WHICH APPLICATIONS MAY BE MADE UNDER PART III OF THAT ACT.

[14TH JULY 1987]

BE IT ENACTED BY THE OIREACHTAS AS FOLLOWS:

Repeal.

1.—*Omitted. Repeals s 18 of the Landlord and Tenant (Ground Rents) (No 2) Act 1978.* **[14–01]**

Short title, construction and collective citation.

2.— (1) This Act may be cited as the Landlord and Tenant (Ground Rents) (Amendment) Act, 1987. **[14–02]**

(2) The Landlord and Tenant Acts, 1967 to 1984, and this Act shall be construed together as one Act and may be cited together as the Landlord and Tenant Acts, 1967 to 1987.

ACTS REFERRED TO

Landlord and Tenant (Ground Rents) (No. 2) Act, 1978 (1978, No. 16)
Landlord and Tenant (Ground Rents) (Amendment) Act, 1984 (1984, No. 15)

Note: As this Act has no commencement provision it commences as and from the end of the day before the date of its passing. The Act was passed on 14th July 1987 —see s 8(3) of the Interpretation Act 1937.

Chapter 15

LANDLORD AND TENANT (AMENDMENT) ACT, 1989

(1989, No. 2)

AN ACT TO AMEND SECTION 13 OF THE LANDLORD AND TENANT (AMENDMENT) ACT, 1980, SO AS TO RESTRICT ITS APPLICATION IN RELATION TO CERTAIN TENEMENTS IN THE CUSTOM HOUSE DOCKS AREA.

[1ST MARCH 1989].

BE IT ENACTED BY THE OIREACHTAS AS FOLLOWS:

Amendment of section 13 of Landlord and Tenant (Amendment) Act, 1980.

1.—*Omitted. Amends s 13 of the Landlord and Tenant (Amendment) Act 1980.* **[15–01]**

Short title, construction and collective citation.

2.—(1) This Act may be cited as the Landlord and Tenant (Amendment) Act, 1989. **[15–02]**

(2) The Landlord and Tenant Acts, 1967 to 1987, and this Act shall be construed together as one Act and may be cited together as the Landlord and Tenant Acts, 1967 to 1989.

Note: As this Act has no commencement provision it commences as and from the end of the day before the date of its passing. The Act was passed on 1st March 1989 — see s 8(3) of the Interpretation Act 1937.

Chapter 16

HOUSING (MISCELLANEOUS PROVISIONS) ACT, 1992

[Extracts]

(1992 No. 18)

Minimum notice to quit, etc.

16. — *Omitted. S.193(e) of the Residential Tenancies Act, 2004 provides that s.16 of this Act does not apply to a dwelling to which the 2004 Act applies.* **[16–01]**

Rent books.

17.—(1) The Minister may make regulations requiring the landlord of a house let for rent or other valuable consideration to provide the tenant of such a house with a rent book or other documentation to the like effect (in this section referred to as "other documentation"). **[16–02]**

(2) Regulations under this section may, in particular, but without prejudice to the generality of subsection (1), make provision in relation to all or any one or more of the following:

(a) the class or classes of houses or tenancies in respect of which rent books or other documentation shall be provided;

(b) the particulars to be contained in a rent book or other documentation, including information relating to—

(i) the house,

(ii) the landlord,

(iii) the tenant,

(iv) the terms of the tenancy and the rights and obligations of the tenant and the landlord,

(v) the deposit (if any) paid,

(vi) the rent reserved under the tenancy;

(c) the manner in which payments of rent are recorded or acknowledged;

(d) requirements regarding the proper use of a rent book or other documentation;

(e) such other matters as the Minister considers necessary.

(3) A person authorised by a housing authority for the purposes of this section may, in relation to a house to which regulations under this section apply—

(a) require the tenant to furnish or cause to be furnished to him at a specified time and place such document (if any) purporting to be the rent book or other documentation provided by the landlord;

(b) at all reasonable times enter and inspect the house as respects any particulars required by the regulations to be contained in the rent book or other documentation;

(c) require the landlord to furnish or cause to be furnished to him at a specified time and place the landlord's books, documents or other records (whether legible or in a machine readable form) relating to the house and the tenancy thereof.

Standards for rented houses.

[16–03] 18.—(1) The Minister may make regulations prescribing standards for houses (including any common areas, works and services appurtenant thereto and enjoyed therewith) let for rent or other valuable consideration and it shall be the duty of the landlord of such a house to ensure that the house complies with the requirements of such regulations.

(2) A person authorised by a housing authority for the purposes of this section may at all reasonable times enter and inspect a house to which regulations under this section apply.

(3) Where, in the opinion of a housing authority, a requirement of a regulation is not being complied with, the authority may, after giving not less than 21 days notice in writing to the landlord of the house concerned, carry out or arrange the carrying out of any work necessary to ensure that the house complies with the requirements of the regulations.

(4) Where a housing authority give a notice under subsection (3), they shall at the same time send a copy of the notice to the tenant of the house concerned.

(5) Any expenses reasonably incurred by a housing authority under subsection (3) shall be repaid by the landlord and may be—

(a) secured by—

(i) charging the house under the Registration of Title Act, 1964, or

(ii) an instrument vesting the ownership of the house in the authority subject to a right of redemption by the landlord;

(b) without prejudice to paragraph (a), recovered from the landlord as a simple contract debt in any court of competent jurisdiction.

(6) A landlord upon whom a notice is served under subsection (3) may, before the expiry of such notice, appeal to the District Court in the District Court district in which the house concerned is situate to have the notice set aside and a housing authority shall not carry out or arrange the carrying out of any work under that subsection until the appeal is determined.

(7) Regulations under this section may, in particular, but without prejudice to the generality of subsection (1), make provision in relation to all or any one or more of the following:

(a) the class or classes of houses or tenancies in respect of which the prescribed standards shall apply;

(b) the maintenance of the house in a proper state of structural repair and in good general repair;

(c) the quality and condition of the accommodation, any common areas, furnishings and appliances;

(d) ventilation and lighting;

(e) water supplies, sanitary facilities and drainage;

(f) facilities for heating and cooking;

(g) facilities for the storage and the preparation of food.

(8) For the purposes of subsection (7)(b) "a proper state of structural repair" means essentially sound, with roof, floors, ceilings, walls and stairs in good repair and not subject to serious dampness or liable to collapse because they are rotted or otherwise defective.

Prohibition on distress for rent of dwelling.

19.—No distress shall be levied for the rent (including rent-charge) of any premises let solely as a dwelling. **[16–04]**

Registration of rented houses.

20.—(1) The Minister may make regulations requiring a landlord of a house let for rent or other valuable consideration to register the tenancy of such a house with the housing authority in whose functional area the house is situate and to furnish such particulars as the regulations may specify, including in each case the name and address of the landlord and of the tenant and the amount of the rent or the value or nature of the other consideration, as the case may be. **[16–05]**

(2) Regulations under subsection (1) may be expressed to apply to houses or tenancies of a particular class or classes and may contain such provisions as the Minister considers necessary for the purposes of this section.

> **Note:** Regulations were made in 1996 by the Minister — see the Housing (Registration of Rented Houses) Regulations 1996 (SI No 30 of 1996). However, these Regulations were revoked by s 10(2) of the Residential Tenancies Act 2004.

(3) *Omitted. Repealed by s 4(1) and the First Schedule to the Local Government Act 1994.*

(4) A housing authority shall keep a register (in this section referred to as "the register") for the purposes of this section in respect of all houses in their functional area to which regulations under this section relate and shall make all such entries therein as may from time to time be appropriate in accordance with this section and such regulations.

(5) The register shall be kept at an office of the housing authority designated by them and shall be available for inspection by any person during normal office hours.

(6) (a) A copy of an entry in the register purporting to be certified by an authorised officer of the housing authority shall, in the absence of any evidence to the contrary, be deemed to have been so certified by the authority and shall be received in evidence accordingly.

(b) Evidence of an entry in the register may be given by the production of a copy thereof certified in accordance with paragraph (a) and it shall not be necessary to produce the register.

(7) Where an application is made to a housing authority for a copy of an entry in the register, the copy shall be issued to the applicant on payment by him of such fee (if any) in respect of each entry as the Minister may, from time to time, prescribe by regulations or as may be determined by the authority where not so prescribed.

(8) All fees received by a housing authority by virtue of any requirement on landlords relating to the registration of tenancies shall be paid, as appropriate, into the county fund or the municipal fund.

Amendment history: Subsection (8) was amended by s 200(2) of the Residential Tenancies Act 2004 which provision came into effect on 1st September 2004. The original subs (8) read: "All fees received by a housing authority under this section shall be paid, as appropriate, into the county fund or the municipal fund."

(9) A person authorised by a housing authority for the purposes of this section may at all reasonable times enter into and inspect a house to which regulations under this section apply as respects any particulars required by the regulations to be furnished to the authority.

(10) References in section 11 of the Housing (Private Rented Dwellings) Act 1982, and in section 7 of the Housing (Private Rented Dwellings) (Amendment) Act, 1983, to regulations under section 24 of the Housing (Private Rented Dwellings) Act, 1982, shall be construed as references to regulations made or deemed by virtue of section 37 to have been made under this section.

20A.—The Minister may make regulations requiring the landlord of a house, let for rent or other valuable consideration to pay to the housing authority such annual or other fee as may be prescribed in relation to the functions of the authority under section 17, 18 or 20.

Note: Section 20A was added by s 4(2) and the Second Schedule to the Local Government Act 1994, which provision came into force on 1st July 1994 — see Local Government Act, 1994 Commencement (No 2) Order, 1994 (SI 171 of 1994).

Chapter 17

LANDLORD AND TENANT (AMENDMENT) ACT, 1994

(1994 No. 20)

AN ACT TO AMEND THE LAW RELATING TO THE RENEWAL OF LEASES AND TENANCIES AND TO AMEND THE LAWS OF LANDLORD AND TENANT.

[10TH JULY 1994]

BE IT ENACTED BY THE OIREACHTAS AS FOLLOWS:

Short title, construction, collective citation and commencement.

1.—(1) This Act maybe cited as the Landlord and Tenant (Amendment Act, 1994). **[17–01]**

(2) The Landlord and Tenant (Ground Rents) Act, 1967, the Landlord and Tenant (Amendment) Act, 1971, the Landlord and Tenant (Ground Rents) Act, 1978, the Landlord and Tenant (Ground Rents) (No. 2) Act, 1978, the Landlord and Tenant (Amendment) Act, 1980, the Landlord and Tenant (Amendment) Act 1989, and this Act shall be construed together as one Act and may be cited together as the Landlord and Tenant Acts, 1967 to 1994.

(3) This Act shall come into operation on the day that is one month after the date of its passing.

Definition.

2.—In this Act, "the Act of 1980" means the Landlord and Tenant (Amendment) Act, 1980. **[17–02]**

Amendment of section 13 of Act of 1980.

3.—(1) *Omitted. Amends s 13 of the Landlord and Tenant (Amendment) Act 1980.* **[17–03]**

(2) Subsection (1) shall have effect only in relation to a lease or other contract of tenancy the term of which commences after the commencement of this Act.

Amendment of section 17 of Act of 1980.

4.—*Omitted. Amends s 17 of the Landlord and Tenant (Amendment) Act 1980.* **[17–04]**

Amendment of section 23 of Act of 1980.

5.—*Omitted. Substitutes s 23(2) of the Landlord and Tenant (Amendment) Act 1980.* **[17–05]**

Amendment of section 85 of Act of 1980.

6.—*Omitted. Amends s 85 of the Landlord and Tenant (Amendment) Act 1980.* **[17–06]**

ACTS REFERRED TO

Landlord and Tenant (Amendment) Act, 1971 (1971, No. 30)
Landlord and Tenant (Amendment) Act, 1980 (1980, No. 10)
Landlord and Tenant (Amendment) Act, 1989 (1989, No. 2)
Landlord and Tenant (Ground Rents) Act, 1967 (1967, No. 3)
Landlord and Tenant (Ground Rents) Act, 1978 (1978, No. 7)
Landlord and Tenant (Ground Rents) (No. 2) Act, 1978 (1978, No. 16)

Chapter 18

RESIDENTIAL TENANCIES ACT 2004

(2004 No. 27)

ARRANGEMENT OF SECTIONS

PART I – PRELIMINARY AND GENERAL

PART 2 – TENANCY OBLIGATIONS OF LANDLORDS AND TENANTS

CHAPTER 1 – PROVISIONS REGARDING LANDLORD'S OBLIGATIONS

CHAPTER 2 – PROVISIONS REGARDING TENANT'S OBLIGATIONS

PART 3 – RENT AND RENT REVIEWS

PART 4 – SECURITY OF TENURE

Chapter 7 – Miscellaneous

PART 5 – TENANCY TERMINATIONS – NOTICE PERIODS AND OTHER PROCEDURAL REQUIREMENTS

Chapter 1 – Scope of Part and Interpretation Provisions

Chapter 2 – What a Valid Notice of Termination Must Contain

Chapter 3 – Period of Notice to be Given

Chapter 4 – Additional Requirements and Procedures Where Tenancy Sub-Let

Chapter 5 – Miscellaneous

PART 6 – DISPUTE RESOLUTION

Chapter 1 – Referral of Matters to Board for Resolution

Chapter 2 – Relationship between Part and Certain Other Dispute Resolution Mechanisms

Chapter 3 – Preliminary Steps by Board (Include Power to Refer Matter to Tribunal)

Chapter 4 – Mediation and Adjudication

Chapter 5 – Tenancy Tribunal

Chapter 2 – Procedure for Registration

Chapter 3 – Updating of Register and Enforcement of Requirement to Register

Chapter 4 – Data Exchange – Private Residential Tenancies

PART 8 – PRIVATE RESIDENTIAL TENANCIES BOARD

Chapter 1 – Establishment and Principal Functions of Board

Chapter 2 – Composition of Board

Chapter 3 – Meetings and Committees

ACTS REFERRED TO

Adoption Acts 1952 to 1998
Arbitration Act 1954 (1954, No. 26)
Civil Liability Act 1961 (1961, No. 41)
Civil Service Commissioners Act 1956 (1956, No. 45)
Civil Service Regulation Acts 1956 to 1996
Companies Acts 1963 to 2003
Comptroller and Auditor General (Amendment) Act 1993 (1993, No. 8)
Conveyancing Act 1881 (1881, c. 41)
Conveyancing and Law of Property Act 1892 (1892, c. 13)
Criminal Law Amendment Act 1912 (1912, c. 20)
Equal Status Act 2000 (2000, No. 8)
European Parliament Elections Act 1997 (1997, No. 2)
Finance Act 1999 (1999, No. 2)
Health Act 1970 (1970, No. 1)
Health (Eastern Regional Health Authority) Act 1999 (1999, No. 13)
Housing Act 1966 (1966, No. 21)
Housing Act 1988 (1988, No. 28)
Housing Acts 1966 to 1997
Housing Acts 1966 to 2002
Housing (Miscellaneous Provisions) Act 1992 (1992, No. 18)
Housing (Miscellaneous Provisions) Act 1997 (1997, No. 21)
Housing (Miscellaneous Provisions) Act 2002 (2002, No. 9)
Housing (Private Rented Dwellings) Act 1982 (1982, No. 6)
Housing (Traveller Accommodation) Act 1998 (1998, No. 33)
Interpretation Act 1937 (1937, No. 38)
Landlord and Tenant Act 1931 (1931, No. 55)
Landlord and Tenant (Amendment) Act 1980 (1980, No. 10)

Landlord and Tenant (Amendment) Act 1994 (1994, No. 20)
Landlord and Tenant (Ground Rents) (No. 2) Act 1978 (1978, No. 7)
Landlord and Tenant Law Amendment Act Ireland 1860 (1860, c. 154)
Local Government Act 2001 (2001, No. 37)
Organisation of Working Time Act 1997 (1997, No. 20)
Petty Sessions (Ireland) Act 1851 (1851, c. 93)
Planning and Development Act 2000 (2000, No. 30)
Public Offices Fees Act 1879 (1879, c. 58)
Social Welfare (Consolidation) Act 1993 (1993, No. 27)
Statute of Limitations 1957 (1957, No. 6)
Succession Act 1965 (1965, No. 27)
Taxes Consolidation Act 1997 (1997, No. 39)
Urban Renewal Act 1998 (1998, No. 27)

AN ACT TO PROVIDE—

(a) IN ACCORDANCE WITH THE EXIGENCIES OF THE COMMON GOOD, FOR A MEASURE OF SECURITY OF TENURE FOR TENANTS OF CERTAIN DWELLINGS,

(b) FOR AMENDMENTS OF THE LAW OF LANDLORD AND TENANT IN RELATION TO THE BASIC RIGHTS AND OBLIGATIONS OF EACH OF THE PARTIES TO TENANCIES OF CERTAIN DWELLINGS,

(c) WITH THE AIM OF ALLOWING DISPUTES BETWEEN SUCH PARTIES TO BE RESOLVED CHEAPLY AND SPEEDILY, FOR THE ESTABLISHMENT OF A BODY TO BE KNOWN AS AN BORD UM THIONÓNTACHTAÍ CÓNAITHE PRÍOBHÁIDEACHA OR, IN THE ENGLISH LANGUAGE, THE PRIVATE RESIDENTIAL TENANCIES BOARD AND THE CONFERRAL ON IT OF POWERS AND FUNCTIONS OF A LIMITED NATURE IN RELATION TO THE RESOLUTION OF SUCH DISPUTES,

(d) FOR THE REGISTRATION OF TENANCIES OF CERTAIN DWELLINGS, AND

(e) FOR RELATED MATTERS.

[19TH JULY 2004]

BE IT ENACTED BY THE OIREACHTAS AS FOLLOWS:

PART 1 – PRELIMINARY AND GENERAL

Short Title.

1.—This Act may be cited as the Residential Tenancies Act 2004. **[18–01]**

Commencement.

2.—This Act shall come into operation on such day or days as the Minister may appoint by order or orders either generally or with reference to any particular purpose or provision and different days may be so appointed for different purposes or different provisions. **[18–02]**

Note: Part 1, Part 4, Part 5 (other than ss 71 and 72), Part 7, Part 8 (other than s 159(1)), Part 9 (other than ss 182, 189, 190, 193(a), 193(d), 195(4), and 195(5)), and the Schedule to this Act came into operation on 1 September 2004 — see the Residential Tenancies Act 2004 (Commencement) Order 2004 (SI No 505 of 2004).

All other Parts and provisions of this Act came into operation on 6 December 2004 — see the Residential Tenancies Act 2004 (Commencement) (No 2) Order 2004 (SI No 750 of 2004).

Application of Act.

[18–03] 3.—(1) Subject to subsection (2), this Act applies to every dwelling, the subject of a tenancy (including a tenancy created before the passing of this Act).

(2) Subject to section 4(2), this Act does not apply to any of the following dwellings—

(a) a dwelling that is used wholly or partly for the purpose of carrying on a business, such that the occupier could, after the tenancy has lasted 5 years, make an application under section 13(1)(a) of the Landlord and Tenant (Amendment) Act 1980 in respect of it,

(b) a dwelling to which Part II of the Housing (Private Rented Dwellings) Act 1982 applies,

(c) a dwelling let by or to—

(i) a public authority, or

(ii) a body standing approved for the purposes of section 6 of the Housing (Miscellaneous Provisions) Act 1992 and which is occupied by a person referred to in section 9(2) of the Housing Act 1988,

(d) a dwelling, the occupier of which is entitled to acquire, under Part II of the Landlord and Tenant (Ground Rents) (No. 2) Act 1978, the fee simple in respect of it,

(e) a dwelling occupied under a shared ownership lease,

(f) a dwelling let to a person whose entitlement to occupation is for the purpose of a holiday only,

(g) a dwelling within which the landlord also resides,

(h) a dwelling within which the spouse, parent or child of the landlord resides and no lease or tenancy agreement in writing has been entered into by any person resident in the dwelling,

(i) a dwelling the subject of a tenancy granted under Part II of the Landlord and Tenant (Amendment) Act 1980 or under Part III of the Landlord and Tenant Act 1931 or which is the subject of an application made under section 21 of the Landlord and Tenant (Amendment) Act 1980 and the court has yet to make its determination in the matter.

Interpretation generally.

[18–04] 4.—(1) In this Act, unless the context otherwise requires—

"adjudicator" shall be construed in accordance with section 164(2);

"authorised agent" shall be construed in accordance with section 12(1)(e);

"Board" shall be construed in accordance with section 150(1);

"child" includes a person who is no longer a minor and cognate words shall be construed accordingly;

"company" means a company within the meaning of the Companies Acts 1963 to 2003;

"contract of tenancy" does not include an agreement to create a tenancy;

"Director" shall be construed in accordance with section 160(1);

"Dispute Resolution Committee" shall be construed in accordance with section 157(2);

"dwelling" means, subject to subsection (2), a property let for rent or valuable consideration as a self-contained residential unit and includes any building or part of a building used as a dwelling and any out office, yard, garden or other land appurtenant to it or usually enjoyed with it and, where the context so admits, includes a property available for letting but excludes a structure that is not permanently attached to the ground and a vessel and a vehicle (whether mobile or not);

"establishment day" means the day appointed under section 149;

"functions" includes powers and duties and references to the performance of functions include, as respects powers and duties, references to the exercise of the powers and the carrying out of the duties;

"further Part 4 tenancy" shall be construed in accordance with section 41(2) or 45(2), as appropriate;

"local authority" means a local authority for the purposes of the Local Government Act 2001;

"management company", in relation to an apartment complex, means the company in which functions are vested with respect to the management of the apartment complex;

"mediator" shall be construed in accordance with section 164(1);

"Minister" means the Minister for the Environment, Heritage and Local Government;

"Part 4 tenancy" shall be construed in accordance with section 29;

"personal representative" has the same meaning as it has in the Succession Act 1965;

"planning permission" means a permission under section 34 of the Planning and Development Act 2000;

"prescribed" means prescribed by regulations made by the Minister under this Act;

"public authority" means—

(a) a Minister of the Government or a body under the aegis of a Minister of the Government,

(b) the Commissioners of Public Works in Ireland,

(c) a local authority,

(d) the Health Service Executive established under section 6 of the Health Act 2004,

(f) a voluntary body standing approved of by the Minister for Health and Children or by the Health Service Executive for the purpose of providing accommodation for elderly persons or persons with a mental handicap or psychiatric disorder,

Amendment history: Subs (1)(d), (e) and (f) were amended by s 75 of the Health Act 2004, which amendment came into force on the 1st January 2005 (see Health Act 2004 (Commencement) (No 2) Order 2004 (SI No 887 of 2004)). The original subs (1)(d) and (e) were both substituted by the new subs (1)(d). Subs (1)(d), (e) and (f) originally stated: "(d) a health board established under the Health Act 1970, (e) the Eastern Regional Health Authority or an area health board established under the Health (Eastern Regional Health Authority) Act 1999, (f) a voluntary body standing approved of by the Minister for Health and Children or by a health board or an authority mentioned in paragraph (e) of this definition for the purpose of providing accommodation for elderly persons or persons with a mental handicap or psychiatric disorder".

(g) a recognised educational institution, namely, any university, technical college, regional technical college, secondary or technical college or other institution or body of persons approved of, for the purpose of providing an approved course of study, by the Minister for Education and Science, or

(h) the Shannon Free Airport Development Company;

"remuneration" includes fees, allowances for expenses, benefits-inkind and superannuation;

"required period of notice", in relation to a notice of termination, means the period of notice required by Part 4 or 5 or, if greater, by the lease or tenancy agreement concerned;

"self-contained residential unit" includes the form of accommodation commonly known as "bedsit" accommodation;

"shared ownership lease" has the meaning assigned to it by section 2 of the Housing (Miscellaneous Provisions) Act 1992;

"superannuation benefit" means a pension, gratuity or other allowance payable on resignation, retirement or death;

"tenancy agreement" includes an oral tenancy agreement;

"Tribunal" shall be construed in accordance with section 102(2).

(2) The definition of "dwelling" in subsection (1) shall not apply in relation to the construction of references to "dwelling" to which this subsection applies; each such reference shall be construed as a reference to any building or part of a building used as a dwelling (whether or not a dwelling let for rent or valuable consideration) and any out office, yard, garden or other land appurtenant to it or usually enjoyed with it.

(3) Subsection (2) applies to the following references to "dwelling" (whether in the singular or plural form) in this Act, namely—

(a) the second of the references in section 12(1)(h),

(b) the first and last of the references in paragraph (c)(ii) and paragraph (c)(iii) of the definition of "behave in a way that is anti-social" in section 17(1),

(c) the reference in subsection (2)(a) of section 25 to whichever of the dwellings mentioned in that subsection is not the subject of the tenancy mentioned in subsection (1) of that section,

(d) the references in subsection (2)(b) and (c) of section 25, and

(e) the second of the references in sections 136(h), 187(1) and 188(1).

(4) In this Act—

(a) a reference to a section or Part is a reference to a section or Part of this Act unless it is indicated that reference to some other enactment is intended,

(b) a reference to a Chapter is a reference to the Chapter of the Part in which the reference occurs, unless it is indicated that reference to some other provision is intended,

(c) a reference to a subsection, paragraph or subparagraph is a reference to the subsection, paragraph or subparagraph of the provision in which the reference occurs, unless it is indicated that reference to some other provision is intended, and

(d) a reference to any other enactment is a reference to that enactment as amended or extended by or under any subsequent enactment.

"relevant date", "landlord", "tenant", "lease", etc

5.—(1) In this Act— [18–05]

"landlord" means the person for the time being entitled to receive (otherwise than as agent for another person) the rent paid in respect of a dwelling by the tenant thereof and, where the context so admits, includes a person who has ceased to be so entitled by reason of the termination of the tenancy;

"lease" means an instrument in writing, whether or not under seal, containing a contract of tenancy in respect of a dwelling;

"relevant date" means the date on which Part 4 is commenced;

> **Note:** The "relevant date" is 1st September 2004, being the date Part 4 of this Act commenced — see s 5(1) of this Act and the Residential Tenancies Act 2004 (Commencement) Order 2004 (SI No 505 of 2004).

"tenancy" includes a periodic tenancy and a tenancy for a fixed term, whether oral or in writing or implied, and, where the context so admits, includes a sub-tenancy and a tenancy or sub-tenancy that has been terminated;

"tenant" means the person for the time being entitled to the occupation of a dwelling under a tenancy and, where the context so admits, includes a person who has ceased to be entitled to that occupation by reason of the termination of his or her tenancy.

(2) A reference in this Act to—

(a) the landlord of a dwelling is a reference to the landlord under a tenancy of the dwelling, and

(b) the tenant of a dwelling is a reference to the tenant under a tenancy of the dwelling.

(3) Subject to subsection (4), in this Act "costs", in relation to a matter being dealt with by the Board, a mediator, an adjudicator or the Tribunal or a determination or direction made or given by it or him or her, does not include—

(a) legal costs or expenses, or

(b) costs or expenses of any other professional kind or of employing any person with technical expertise that are connected wholly or mainly with the provision of evidence for, or the presentation of one or more issues at, the proceedings.

(4) Despite subsection (3), the Board or, with the consent of the Board, a mediator, an adjudicator or the Tribunal may if, in its or his or her opinion the exceptional circumstances of the matter so warrant, determine that any element of costs the subject of a determination or direction made or given by it or him or her shall include costs referred to in paragraph (a) or (b) of that subsection.

Service of notices.

[18–06] 6.—(1) A notice required or authorised to be served or given by or under this Act shall, subject to subsection (2), be addressed to the person concerned by name and may be served on or given to the person in one of the following ways:

(a) by delivering it to the person;

(b) by leaving it at the address at which the person ordinarily resides or, in a case in which an address for service has been furnished, at that address;

(c) by sending it by post in a prepaid letter to the address at which the person ordinarily resides or, in a case in which an address for service has been furnished, to that address;

(d) where the notice relates to a dwelling and it appears that no person is in actual occupation of the dwelling, by affixing it in a conspicuous position on the outside of the dwelling or the property containing the dwelling.

(2) Where the notice concerned is to be served on or given to a person who is the owner, landlord, tenant or occupier of a dwelling and the name of the person cannot be ascertained by reasonable inquiry it may be addressed to the person by using the words the owner, the landlord, the tenant or the occupier, as the case may require.

(3) For the purposes of this section, a company shall be deemed to be ordinarily resident at its registered office, and every other body corporate and every unincorporated body shall be deemed to be ordinarily resident at its principal office or place of business

(4) A person shall not, at any time during the period of 3 months after a notice is affixed under subsection (1)(d) remove, damage or deface the notice without lawful authority.

(5) A person who contravenes subsection (4) is guilty of an offence.

(6) Where, in proceedings under Part 6, it is shown that a notice was served or given in accordance with the provisions of this section and on the date that it is alleged it was served or given, the onus shall be on the recipient to establish to the Board, the adjudicator or Tribunal's satisfaction that the notice was not received in sufficient time to enable compliance with the relevant time limit specified by or under this Act.

Service or giving of notice on behalf of another.

7.—Where a notice required or authorised to be served or given by or under this Act is served or given on behalf of a person, the notice shall be deemed to be served or given by that person. [18–07]

Regulations or orders.

8.—(1) The Minister may make regulations prescribing any matter or thing which is referred to in this Act as prescribed or to be prescribed. [18–08]

(2) Every order (other than an order made under section 2 or 149) and regulation made by the Minister under this Act shall be laid before each House of the Oireachtas as soon as may be after it is made and, if a resolution annulling the order or regulation is passed by either such House within the next 21 days on which that House has sat after the order or regulation is laid before it, the order or regulation shall be annulled accordingly but without prejudice to the validity of anything previously done thereunder.

(3) The Minister may by order amend or revoke an order under this Act (other than an order under section 2 or 149).

(4) An order under subsection (3) shall be made in the like manner and its making shall be subject to the like (if any) consents and conditions as the order that it is amending or revoking.

Offences.

9.—(1) A person guilty of an offence under this Act shall be liable on summary conviction to a fine not exceeding €3,000 or imprisonment for a term not exceeding 6 months or both. [18–09]

(2) If the contravention in respect of which a person is convicted of an offence under this Act is continued after the conviction, the person is guilty of a further offence on every day on which the contravention continues and for each such offence the person shall be liable on summary conviction to a fine not exceeding €250.

(3) Proceedings in relation to an offence under this Act may be brought and prosecuted by the Board.

(4) Notwithstanding section 10(4) of the Petty Sessions (Ireland) Act 1851, proceedings for an offence under this Act may be instituted at any time within one year after the date of the offence.

(5) Where a person is convicted of an offence under this Act the court shall, unless it is satisfied that there are special and substantial reasons for not so doing, order the person to pay to the Board the costs and expenses, measured by the court, incurred by the Board in relation to the investigation, detection and prosecution of the offence.

Repeal and revocation.

10.—(1) *Omitted. Repeals s 5 of the Criminal Law Amendment Act 1912.* [18–10]

(2) *Omitted. Revokes the Housing (Registration of Rented Houses) Regulations 1996 (SI No 30 of 1996).*

Expenses.

11.—The expenses incurred by the Minister in the administration of this Act shall, to such extent as may be sanctioned by the Minister for Finance, be paid out of moneys provided by the Oireachtas. [18–11]

PART 2 – TENANCY OBLIGATIONS OF LANDLORDS AND TENANTS

CHAPTER 1

Provisions regarding landlord's obligations

Obligations of landlords.

[18–12] 12.—(1) In addition to the obligations arising by or under any other enactment, a landlord of a dwelling shall—

(a) allow the tenant of the dwelling to enjoy peaceful and exclusive occupation of the dwelling,

(b) subject to subsection (2), carry out to—

(i) the structure of the dwelling all such repairs as are, from time to time, necessary and ensure that the structure complies with any standards for houses for the time being prescribed under section 18 of the Housing (Miscellaneous Provisions) Act 1992, and

(ii) the interior of the dwelling all such repairs and replacement of fittings as are, from time to time, necessary so that that interior and those fittings are maintained in, at least, the condition in which they were at the commencement of the tenancy and in compliance with any such standards for the time being prescribed,

(c) subject to subsection (3), effect and maintain a policy of insurance in respect of the structure of the dwelling, that is to say a policy—

(i) that insures the landlord against damage to, and loss and destruction of, the dwelling, and

(ii) that indemnifies, to an amount of at least €250,000, the landlord against any liability on his or her part arising out of the ownership, possession and use of the dwelling,

(d) subject to subsection (4), return or repay promptly any deposit paid by the tenant to the landlord on entering into the agreement for the tenancy or lease,

(e) notify the tenant of the name of the person, if any, (the "authorised agent") who is authorised by the landlord to act on his or her behalf in relation to the tenancy for the time being,

(f) provide to the tenant particulars of the means by which the tenant may, at all reasonable times, contact him or her or his or her authorised agent,

(g) without prejudice to any other liability attaching in this case, reimburse the tenant in respect of all reasonable and vouched for expenses that may be incurred by the tenant in carrying out repairs to the structure or interior of the dwelling for which the landlord is responsible under paragraph (b) where the following conditions are satisfied—

(i) the landlord has refused or failed to carry out the repairs at the time the tenant requests him or her to do so, and

(ii) the postponement of the repairs to some subsequent date would have been unreasonable having regard to either—

(I) a significant risk the matters calling for repair posed to the health or safety of the tenant or other lawful occupants of the dwelling, or

(II) a significant reduction that those matters caused in the quality of the tenant's or other such occupants' living environment,

(h) if the dwelling is one of a number of dwellings comprising an apartment complex—

(i) forward to the management company, if any, of the complex any complaint notified in writing by the tenant to him or her concerning the performance by the company of its functions in relation to the complex,

(ii) forward to the tenant any initial response by the management company to that complaint, and

(iii) forward to the tenant any statement in writing of the kind referred to in section 187(2) made by the management company in relation to that complaint.

(2) Subsection (1)(b) does not apply to any repairs that are necessary due to the failure of the tenant to comply with section 16(f).

(3) The obligation under subsection (1)(c) does not apply at any particular time during the term of the tenancy concerned if, at that time, a policy of insurance of the kind referred to in that provision is not obtainable, or is not obtainable at a reasonable cost, by the landlord in respect of the dwelling.

(4) Subsection (1)(d) applies and has effect subject to the following provisions:

(a) no amount of the deposit concerned shall be required to be returned or repaid if, at the date of the request for return or repayment, there is a default in—

(i) the payment of rent and the amount of rent that is in arrears is equal to or greater than the amount of the deposit, or

(ii) compliance with section 16(f) and the amount of the costs that would be incurred by the landlord, were he or she to take them, in taking such steps as are reasonable for the purposes of restoring the dwelling to the condition mentioned in section 16(f) is equal to or greater than the amount of the deposit,

(b) where, at the date of the request for return or repayment, there is a default in the payment of rent or compliance with section 16(f) and subparagraph (i) or (ii), as the case may be, of paragraph (a) does not apply, then there shall only be required to be returned or repaid under subsection (1)(d) the difference between the amount of rent that is in arrears or, as appropriate, the amount of the costs that would be incurred in taking steps of the kind referred to in paragraph (a)(ii).

(5) For the avoidance of doubt, the condition in subsection (1)(g)(i) is satisfied if, after all reasonable attempts, the landlord or his or her authorised agent could not be contacted to make the request concerned.

Section 12(1)(b) supplemental regulations.

[18–13] 13.—(1) The Board, with the consent of the Minister, may make regulations specifying that particular parts of dwellings shall, for the purposes of section 12(1)(b), be regarded as parts of the interior, or as parts of the structure, of dwellings.

(2) In making regulations under this section, the Board—

(a) may invite submissions in relation to the matter from any persons or organisations appearing to the Board to be representative of the interests of landlords and of tenants and consider any submissions from those persons or organisations made on foot of that invitation,

(b) shall not specify a part of a dwelling as being part of its structure or, as the case may be, part of its interior if, to do so, would, in its opinion, result in unreasonably burdensome obligations being imposed on landlords.

(3) Different regulations may be made under this section in respect of different classes of dwelling.

Prohibition of penalisation of tenants.

[18–14] 14.—(1) A landlord of a dwelling shall not penalise a tenant for—

(a) referring any dispute between the tenant and the landlord to the Board for resolution under Part 6,

(b) giving evidence in any proceedings under Part 6 to which the landlord is a party (whether the tenant is a party to them or not),

(c) making a complaint to a member of the Garda Síochána or to a public authority in relation to any matter arising out of, or in connection with, the occupation of the dwelling or making an application regarding such a matter to a public authority, or

(d) giving notice of his or her intention to do any or all of the things referred to in the preceding paragraphs.

(2) For the purposes of this section a tenant is penalised if the tenant is subjected to any action that adversely affects his or her enjoying peaceful occupation of the dwelling concerned.

(3) Such action may constitute penalisation even though it consists of steps taken by the landlord in the exercise of any rights conferred on him or her by or under this Act, any other enactment or the lease or tenancy agreement concerned if, having regard to—

(a) the frequency or extent to which the right is exercised in relation to the tenant,

(b) the proximity in time of its being so exercised to the tenant's doing the relevant thing referred to in subsection (1), and

(c) any other relevant circumstances,

it is a reasonable inference that the action was intended to penalise the tenant for doing that thing.

(4) This section is without prejudice to any other liability (civil or criminal) the landlord may be subject to for doing a thing prohibited by this section.

Duty owed to certain third parties to enforce tenant's obligations.

[18–15] 15.—(1) A landlord of a dwelling owes to each person who could be potentially affected a duty to enforce the obligations of the tenant under the tenancy.

(2) In subsection (1) "person who could be potentially affected" means a person who, it is reasonably foreseeable, would be directly and adversely affected by a failure to enforce an obligation of the tenant were such a failure to occur and includes any other tenant under the tenancy mentioned in that subsection.

(3) This section does not confer on any person a right of action maintainable in proceedings before a court for breach of the duty created by it; the sole remedy for such a breach is by means of making a complaint (where the conditions specified in section 77 for doing so are satisfied) to the Board under Part 6.

(4) Nothing in subsection (3) affects any duty of care, and the remedies available for its breach, that exist apart from this section.

Chapter 2

Provisions regarding tenant's obligations

Obligations of tenants.

16.—In addition to the obligations arising by or under any other enactment, a tenant of a dwelling shall— **[18–16]**

(a) pay to the landlord or his or her authorised agent (or any other person where required to do so by any enactment)—

(i) the rent provided for under the tenancy concerned on the date it falls due for payment, and

(ii) where the lease or tenancy agreement provides that any charges or taxes are payable by the tenant, pay those charges or taxes in accordance with the lease or tenancy agreement (unless provision to that effect in the lease or tenancy agreement is unlawful or contravenes any other enactment),

(b) ensure that no act or omission by the tenant results in there not being complied with the obligations of the landlord, under any enactment, in relation to the dwelling or the tenancy (and in particular, the landlord's obligations under regulations under section 18 of the Housing (Miscellaneous Provisions) Act 1992),

(c) allow, at reasonable intervals, the landlord, or any person or persons acting on the landlord's behalf, access to the dwelling (on a date and time agreed in advance with the tenant) for the purposes of inspecting the dwelling,

(d) notify the landlord or his or her authorised agent of any defect that arises in the dwelling that requires to be repaired so as to enable the landlord comply with his or her obligations, in relation to the dwelling or the tenancy, under any enactment,

(e) allow the landlord, or any person or persons acting on the landlord's behalf, reasonable access to the dwelling for the purposes of allowing any works (the responsibility for the carrying out of which is that of the landlord) to be carried out,

(f) not do any act that would cause a deterioration in the condition the dwelling was in at the commencement of the tenancy, but there shall be disregarded, in determining whether this obligation has been complied with at a particular time, any deterioration in that condition owing to normal wear and tear, that is to say wear and tear that is normal having regard to—

(i) the time that has elapsed from the commencement of the tenancy,

(ii) the extent of occupation of the dwelling the landlord must have reasonably foreseen would occur since that commencement, and

(iii) any other relevant matters,

(g) if paragraph (f) is not complied with, take such steps as the landlord may reasonably require to be taken for the purpose of restoring the dwelling to the condition mentioned in paragraph (f) or to defray any costs incurred by the landlord in his or her taking such steps as are reasonable for that purpose,

(h) not behave within the dwelling, or in the vicinity of it, in a way that is anti-social or allow other occupiers of, or visitors to, the dwelling to behave within it, or in the vicinity of it, in such a way,

(i) not act or allow other occupiers of, or visitors to, the dwelling to act in a way which would result in the invalidation of a policy of insurance in force in relation to the dwelling,

(j) if any act of the tenant's, or any act of another occupier of, or visitor to, the dwelling which the tenant has allowed to be done, results in an increase in the premium payable under a policy of insurance in force in relation to the dwelling, pay to the landlord an amount equal to the amount of that increase ("the increased element") (and that obligation to pay such an amount shall apply in respect of each further premium falling due for payment under the policy that includes the increased element),

(k) not assign or sub-let the tenancy without the written consent of the landlord (which consent the landlord may, in his or her discretion, withhold),

(l) not alter or improve the dwelling without the written consent of the landlord which consent the landlord—

(i) in case the alteration or improvement consists only of repairing, painting and decorating, or any of those things, may not unreasonably withhold,

(ii) in any other case, may, in his or her discretion, withhold,

(m) not use the dwelling or cause it to be used for any purpose other than as a dwelling without the written consent of the landlord (which consent the landlord may, in his or her discretion, withhold), and

(n) notify in writing the landlord of the identity of each person (other than a multiple tenant) who, for the time being, resides ordinarily in the dwelling.

Section 16: interpretation and supplemental.

[18–17] 17.—(1) In section 16—

"alter or improve", in relation to a dwelling, includes—

(a) alter a locking system on a door giving entry to the dwelling, and

(b) make an addition to, or alteration of, a building or structure (including any building or structure subsidiary or ancillary to the dwelling), "behave in a way that is anti-social" means—

(a) engage in behaviour that constitutes the commission of an offence, being an offence the commission of which is reasonably likely to affect directly the well-being or welfare of others,

(b) engage in behaviour that causes or could cause fear, danger, injury, damage or loss to any person living, working or otherwise lawfully in the dwelling concerned or its vicinity and, without prejudice to the generality of the foregoing, includes violence, intimidation, coercion, harassment or obstruction of, or threats to, any such person, or

(c) engage, persistently, in behaviour that prevents or interferes with the peaceful occupation—

(i) by any other person residing in the dwelling concerned, of that dwelling,

(ii) by any person residing in any other dwelling contained in the property containing the dwelling concerned, of that other dwelling, or

(iii) by any person residing in a dwelling ("neighbourhood dwelling") in the vicinity of the dwelling or the property containing the dwelling concerned, of that neighbourhood dwelling.

(2) The reference in section 16(b) to an act or omission by the tenant shall be deemed to include a reference to an act or omission by any other person who, at the time of the doing of the act or the making of the omission, is in the dwelling concerned with the consent of the tenant.

(3) The landlord shall be entitled to be reimbursed by the tenant any costs or expenses reasonably incurred by him or her in deciding upon a request for consent in relation to the tenant's doing a thing referred to in paragraph (k), (l) or (m) of section 16 (whether the consent is granted or refused).

(4) If the amount of the premium referred to in section 16(j) is, apart for the reason mentioned in that provision, subsequently increased or reduced then the reference in that provision to the increased element shall be construed as a reference to the amount concerned as proportionately adjusted in line with the increase or reduction.

No contracting out from terms of section 12 or 16 permitted, etc.

18.—(1) Subject to subsections (2) and (3), no provision of any lease, tenancy agreement, contract or other agreement (whether entered into before, on or after the commencement of this Part) may operate to vary, modify or restrict in any way section 12 or 16. **[18–18]**

(2) Subsection (1) does not prevent more favourable terms for the tenant than those that apply by virtue of section 12 being provided for in the lease or tenancy agreement concerned.

(3) Obligations additional to those specified in section 16 may be imposed on the tenant by the lease or tenancy agreement concerned but only if those obligations are consistent with this Act.

PART 3 – RENT AND RENT REVIEWS

Setting of rent above market rent prohibited.

[18–19] 19.—(1) In setting, at any particular time, the rent under the tenancy of a dwelling, an amount of rent shall not be provided for that is greater than the amount of the market rent for that tenancy at that time.

(2) The reference in this section to the setting of the rent under a tenancy is a reference to—

(a) the initial setting of the rent under the tenancy, and

(b) any subsequent setting of the rent under the tenancy by way of a review of that rent.

Frequency with which rent reviews may occur.

[18–20] 20.—(1) Subject to subsection (3), a review of the rent under the tenancy of a dwelling may not occur—

(a) more frequently than once in each period of 12 months, nor

(b) in the period of 12 months beginning on the commencement of the tenancy.

(2) Subsection (1) has effect notwithstanding any provision to the contrary in the lease or tenancy agreement concerned.

(3) Subsection (1) does not apply despite the fact that a period of less than 12 months has elapsed from—

(a) the last review of the rent under the tenancy, or

(b) the commencement of the tenancy, if, in that period—

(i) a substantial change in the nature of the accommodation provided under the tenancy occurs, and

(ii) the rent under the tenancy, were it to be set immediately after that change, would, by virtue of that change, be different to what was the market rent for the tenancy at the time of that last review or the commencement of the tenancy, as the case may be.

Right to review of rent where none provided.

[18–21] 21.—If the lease or tenancy agreement concerned does not provide for such a review or the tenancy concerned is an implied one, either party may, subject to section 20, require a review of the rent under the tenancy to be carried out and a new rent, if appropriate, set on foot of that review.

Tenant to be notified of new rent.

[18–22] 22.—(1) The setting of a rent (the "new rent") pursuant to a review of the rent under a tenancy of a dwelling and which is otherwise lawful under this Part shall not have effect unless and until the condition specified in subsection (2) is satisfied.

(2) That condition is that, at least 28 days before the date from which the new rent is to have effect, a notice in writing is served by the landlord on the tenant stating the amount of the new rent and the date from which it is to have effect.

(3) Where that condition is satisfied, a dispute in relation to a rent falling within subsection (1) must be referred to the Board under Part 6 before—

(a) the date stated in the notice under subsection (2) as the date from which that rent is to have effect, or

(b) the expiry of 28 days from the receipt by the tenant of that notice, whichever is the later.

Proceedings for rent arrears.

23.—Every person entitled to any rent in arrears or to be paid other charges under a tenancy of a dwelling (whether in his or her own right or as personal representative of a deceased landlord) shall be entitled to recover, under Part 6, such arrears or charges from the person who occupied the dwelling as a tenant in the period in which the arrears accrued or the charges arose or, as may be appropriate, from the person's personal representative. **[18–23]**

"Market rent", references to rent reviews, etc.

24.—(1) In this Part "market rent", in relation to the tenancy of a dwelling, means the rent which a willing tenant not already in occupation would give and a willing landlord would take for the dwelling, in each case on the basis of vacant possession being given, and having regard to— **[18–24]**

(a) the other terms of the tenancy, and

(b) the letting values of dwellings of a similar size, type and character to the dwelling and situated in a comparable area to that in which it is situated.

(2) References in this Part to a review of a rent include references to—

(a) any procedure (however it is described) for determining whether, and to what extent, a reduction or increase in the amount of the rent for the time being payable under the tenancy concerned ought to have effect, and

(b) the effect of the operation of a provision of a lease or tenancy agreement providing that, by reference to any formula, happening of any event or other matter whatsoever (and whether any act, decision or exercise of discretion on the part of any person is involved or not), such a reduction or increase shall have effect,

and, in the case of a provision of the kind referred to in paragraph (b), any prohibition under this Part on a review of rent occurring is to be read as a prohibition on the provision operating to have the foregoing effect.

(3) References in this Part to the setting of a rent are references to the oral agreeing of the rent or to its being provided for in a lease or tenancy agreement or, in the context of a review of rent—

(a) the oral agreeing of the rent,

(b) the oral or written notification of the rent, or

(c) in the case of a provision of the kind referred to in subsection (2)(b), the rent being set by virtue of the operation of that provision.

PART 4 – SECURITY OF TENURE

Chapter 1

Preliminary

Non-application of Part.

25.—(1) This Part does not apply to a tenancy of a dwelling where the conditions specified in subsection (2) are satisfied if the landlord of the dwelling opts, in accordance with subsection (3), for this Part not to apply to it. **[18–25]**

(2) Those conditions are—

(a) the dwelling concerned is one of 2 dwellings within a building,

(b) that building, as originally constructed, comprised a single dwelling, and

(c) the landlord resides in the other dwelling.

(3) A landlord's opting as mentioned in subsection (1) shall be signified in writing in a notice served by him or her on the tenant before the commencement of the tenancy.

(4) This Part does not apply to a tenancy of a dwelling—

(a) if the landlord of the dwelling is entitled, in relation to expenditure incurred on the construction of, conversion into, or, as the case may be, refurbishment of, the dwelling, to a deduction of the kind referred to in section 380B(2), 380C(4) or 380D(2) (inserted by the Finance Act 1999) of the Taxes Consolidation Act 1997, or

(b) if the entitlement of the tenant to occupy the dwelling is connected with his or her continuance in any office, appointment or employment.

Greater security of tenure not affected.

[18–26] 26.—Nothing in this Part operates to derogate from any rights the tenant enjoys for the time being (by reason of the tenancy concerned) that are more beneficial for the tenant than those created by this Part.

Chapter 2

Statement of essential protection enjoyed by tenants

Periods of occupancy before relevant date to be disregarded.

[18–27] 27.—In this Part "continuous period of 6 months" means a continuous period of 6 months that commences on or after the relevant date.

Note: The "relevant date" is 1st September 2004, being the date Part 4 of this Act commenced — see s 5(1) of this Act and the Residential Tenancies Act 2004 (Commencement) Order 2004 (SI No 505 of 2004).

Statutory protection - "Part 4 tenancy" - after 6 months occupation.

[18–28] 28.—(1) Where a person has, under a tenancy, been in occupation of a dwelling for a continuous period of 6 months then, if the condition specified in subsection (3) is satisfied, the following protection applies for the benefit of that person.

(2) That protection is that, subject to Chapter 3, the tenancy mentioned in subsection (1) shall (if it would not or might not do so otherwise) continue in being—

(a) unless paragraph (b) applies, for the period of 4 years from—

(i) the commencement of the tenancy, or

(ii) the relevant date,

whichever is the later,

or

(b) if a notice of termination under section 34(b) is served in respect of the tenancy giving a period of notice that expires after the period of 4 years mentioned in paragraph (a), until the expiry of that period of notice.

Note: The "relevant date" is 1st September 2004, being the date Part 4 of this Act commenced — see s 5(1) of this Act and the Residential Tenancies Act 2004 (Commencement) Order 2004 (SI No 505 of 2004).

(3) The condition mentioned in subsection (1) is that no notice of termination (giving the required period of notice) has been served in respect of the tenancy before the expiry of the period of 6 months mentioned in that subsection.

(4) Despite the fact that such a notice of termination has been so served, that condition shall be regarded as satisfied if the notice is subsequently withdrawn.

"Part 4 tenancy" - meaning of that expression.

29.—A tenancy continued in being by section 28 shall be known, and is in this Act referred to, as a "Part 4 tenancy". **[18–29]**

Terms of Part 4 tenancy.

30.—(1) Subject to subsections (2) and (3), the terms of a Part 4 tenancy shall be those of the tenancy mentioned in section 28 of which it is a continuation. **[18–30]**

(2) At any time during the period of a Part 4 tenancy, the parties may, by agreement, vary its terms.

(3) Neither—

(a) any term of the tenancy of which the Part 4 tenancy is a continuation, nor

(b) any term purported to be provided for by a variation under subsection (2),

shall be a term of a Part 4 tenancy if the term is inconsistent with this or any other Part of this Act.

Sections 28 and 30: special cases.

31.—(1) The reference in section 28(1) to a continuous period of occupation under a tenancy includes a reference to a continuous period of occupation under a series of 2 or more tenancies. **[18–31]**

(2) Where the continuous occupation referred to in section 28(1) has been under a series of 2 or more tenancies—

(a) in section 28(2), "the tenancy mentioned in subsection (1)" means the last of those tenancies,

(b) in section 28(2)(a)(i), "the commencement of the tenancy" means the commencement of the first of those tenancies, and

(c) in section 28(3), "the tenancy" means the last of those tenancies,

and section 30 shall be construed accordingly.

Further special case (sub-letting of Part 4 tenancy).

32.—(1) The Schedule to this Act has effect for the purpose of affording protection in relation to a sub-tenancy created out of a Part 4 tenancy or a further Part 4 tenancy. **[18–32]**

(2) The creation of a sub-tenancy in respect of part only of the dwelling, the subject of a Part 4 tenancy or a further Part 4 tenancy, is prohibited.

(3) Any such sub-tenancy purported to be created is void.

Chapter 3

Termination of Part 4 tenancy

Restriction on termination by landlord.

[18–33] 33.—A Part 4 tenancy may not be terminated by the landlord save in accordance with section 34.

Grounds for termination by landlord.

[18–34] 34.—A Part 4 tenancy may be terminated by the landlord—

(a) on one or more of the grounds specified in the Table to this section if—

(i) a notice of termination giving the required period of notice is served by the landlord in respect of the tenancy, and

(ii) that notice of termination cites as the reason for the termination the ground or grounds concerned and, in the case of paragraph 4, 5 or 6 of that Table, contains or is accompanied by the statement referred to in that paragraph,

or

(b) irrespective of whether any of those grounds exist, if—

(i) a notice of termination giving the required period of notice is served by the landlord in respect of the tenancy, and

(ii) that period of notice expires on or after the end of the period of 4 years mentioned in section 28(2)(a) in relation to the tenancy.

TABLE

Grounds for termination

1. The tenant has failed to comply with any of his or her obligations in relation to the tenancy (whether arising under this Act or otherwise) and, unless the failure provides an excepted basis for termination—

(a) the tenant has been notified of the failure by the landlord and that notification states that the landlord is entitled to terminate the tenancy if the failure is not remedied within a reasonable time specified in that notification, and

(b) the tenant does not remedy the failure within that specified time.

2. The dwelling is no longer suitable to the accommodation needs of the tenant and of any persons residing with him or her having regard to the number of bed spaces contained in the dwelling and the size and composition of the occupying household.

3. The landlord intends, within 3 months after the termination of the tenancy under this section, to enter into an enforceable agreement for the transfer to another, for full consideration, of the whole of his or her interest in the dwelling or the property containing the dwelling.

4. The landlord requires the dwelling or the property containing the dwelling for his or her own occupation or for occupation by a member of his or her family and the notice of termination (the "notice") contains or is accompanied, in writing, by a statement—

(a) specifying—

(i) the intended occupant's identity and (if not the landlord) his or her relationship to the landlord, and

(ii) the expected duration of that occupation,

and

(b) that the landlord, by virtue of the notice, is required to offer to the tenant a tenancy of the dwelling if the contact details requirement is complied with and the following conditions are satisfied—

(i) the dwelling is vacated by the person referred to in subparagraph (a) within the period of 6 months from expiry of the period of notice required to be given by the notice or, if a dispute in relation to the validity of the notice was referred to the Board under Part 6 for resolution, the final determination of the dispute, and

(ii) the tenancy to which the notice related had not otherwise been validly terminated by virtue of the citation in the notice of the ground specified in paragraph 1, 2, 3 or 6 of this Table.

5. The landlord intends to substantially refurbish or renovate the dwelling or the property containing the dwelling in a way which requires the dwelling to be vacated for that purpose (and, where planning permission is required for the carrying out of that refurbishment or renovation, that permission has been obtained) and the notice of termination (the "notice") contains or is accompanied, in writing, by a statement—

(a) specifying the nature of the intended works, and

(b) that the landlord, by virtue of the notice, is required to offer to the tenant a tenancy of the dwelling if the contact details requirement is complied with and the following conditions are satisfied—

(i) the dwelling becomes available for reletting, and

(ii) the tenancy to which the notice related had not otherwise been validly terminated by virtue of the citation in the notice of the ground specified in paragraph 1, 2, 3 or 6 of this Table.

6. The landlord intends to change the use of the dwelling or the property containing the dwelling to some other use (and, where planning permission is required for that change of use, that permission has been obtained) and the notice of termination (the "notice") contains or is accompanied, in writing, by a statement—

(a) specifying the nature of the intended use, and

(b) that the landlord, by virtue of the notice, is required to offer to the tenant a tenancy of the dwelling if the contact details requirement is complied with and the following conditions are satisfied—

(i) the dwelling becomes available for reletting within the period of 6 months from expiry of the period of notice required to be given by the notice or, if a dispute in relation to the validity of the notice was referred to the Board under Part 6 for resolution, the final determination of the dispute, and

(ii) the tenancy to which the notice related had not otherwise been validly terminated by virtue of the citation in the notice of the ground specified in paragraph 1, 2 or 3 of this Table.

Note: Paragraph 3 of the Schedule to this Act modifies para (a) and the Table to s 34, and also modifies ss 35 and 39 of this Act when those provisions apply to a sub-tenancy.

Table to section 34 : interpretation and supplemental.

[18–35] 35.—(1) In this section the "Table" means the Table to section 34.

(2) In paragraph 1 of the Table "remedy the failure" means—

(a) in the case of a failure that does not result in financial loss or damage to the landlord or his or her property, to desist from the conduct that constitutes the failure or, if the failure consists of an omission to comply with an obligation, comply with that obligation, and

(b) in the case of a failure that does result in financial loss or damage to the landlord or his or her property—

(i) to pay adequate compensation to the landlord (or, if the failure consists of the non-payment of rent, pay the arrears of rent) or repair the damage fully, and

(ii) unless the failure is not of a continuing nature, to desist from the conduct that constitutes the failure or comply with the obligation concerned, as the case may be.

(3) In paragraph 1 of the Table the reference to a failure that provides an excepted basis for termination is a reference to a failure to comply with section 16(h) where the behaviour in question falls within paragraph (a) or (b) of the definition of "behave in a way that is anti-social" in section 17(1).

(4) In paragraph 4 of the Table the reference to a member of the landlord's family is a reference to any spouse, child, stepchild, foster child, grandchild, parent, grandparent, step parent, parent-in-law, brother, sister, nephew or niece of the landlord or a person adopted by the landlord under the Adoption Acts 1952 to 1998.

(5) In paragraphs 4(b), 5(b) and 6(b) of the Table the reference to the contact details requirement being complied with is a reference to the following requirement being complied with, namely, a requirement (which shall be specified in the statement concerned) that the former tenant notify in writing the landlord—

(a) within 28 days from the service of the notice of termination concerned, or, if a dispute as to the validity of the notice was referred to the Board under Part 6 for resolution, the final determination of the dispute, of the means by which he or she can be contacted by the landlord so that the offer concerned can be made to him or her, and

(b) as soon as practicable after any such change occurs, of any change in the means (as so notified) by which the former tenant can be contacted for that purpose.

(6) If an offer such as is referred to in paragraph 4(b), 5(b) or 6(b) of the Table is accepted (within such reasonable period as shall be specified for that purpose in the offer) by the former tenant concerned (the "accepter")—

(a) the resulting agreement is enforceable by the accepter (as well as by the offeror), and

(b) occupation by the accepter under the tenancy created in favour of him or her on foot of that agreement shall, together with his or her occupation under the former tenancy, be regarded, for the purposes of this Act, as continuous occupation by the accepter under the one tenancy.

Note: Paragraph 3 of the Schedule to this Act modifies para (a) and the Table to s 34, and also modifies ss 35 and 39 of this Act when those provisions apply to a sub-tenancy.

Termination by tenant.

36.—(1) A tenant may terminate a Part 4 tenancy by serving on the landlord in respect of the tenancy a notice of termination giving the required period of notice. [18–36]

(2) This section is without prejudice to Chapter 6.

Deemed termination by tenant.

37.—(1) Subject to subsection (3), a Part 4 tenancy shall be deemed to have been terminated by the tenant on his or her vacating the dwelling if— [18–37]

(a) before or on or about that vacating, he or she serves a notice of termination in respect of the tenancy that does not give the required period of notice, and

(b) before or on that vacating the rent has fallen into arrears.

(2) Subject to subsection (3), a Part 4 tenancy shall also be deemed to have been terminated by the tenant upon any rent owed by him or her being in arrears for a period of 28 days or more if—

(a) whether before or after the end of that period, the tenant has vacated the dwelling, and

(b) no notice of termination has been served by the tenant in respect of the tenancy.

(3) Subsections (1) and (2) do not apply if the Part 4 tenancy has been sub-let or assigned.

(4) Nothing in the preceding subsections affects the liability of the tenant for rent for the period that would have elapsed had a notice of termination giving the required period of notice been served by him or her.

(5) This section is subject to Chapter 6.

Effect of assignment of Part 4 tenancy.

38.—(1) If a Part 4 tenancy is assigned by the tenant with the consent of the landlord then if the assignment is— [18–38]

(a) to a person, other than a sub-tenant of the dwelling concerned, the assignment shall operate to convert the Part 4 tenancy of the dwelling into a periodic tenancy of the dwelling and the protection provided by section 28 for the assignor shall accordingly cease (but without prejudice to that section's fresh application in relation to the assignee should the circumstances mentioned in that section occur),

(b) to a sub-tenant of the dwelling concerned, the protection provided by section 28 for the assignor shall cease (but without prejudice to the Part 4 tenancy's continued subsistence as provided for in subsection (2)).

(2) If the assignment is to a sub-tenant of the dwelling concerned, the Part 4 tenancy shall continue in being (but in favour of that person and not the assignor) for the period that it would have continued in being had the assignment not been made and subject to the provisions of this Chapter; accordingly—

(a) the assignee shall become the tenant of the landlord under the Part 4 tenancy,

(b) the terms of the Part 4 tenancy shall continue to be those under which the assignor held the tenancy immediately before the assignment unless the assignee and the landlord agree to a variation of them, and

(c) the assignee's sub-tenancy of the dwelling shall merge with the Part 4 tenancy.

(3) Subsection (2)(c) does not affect the liabilities (if any) of the assignee to the assignor (or of the assignor to the assignee) that have arisen by virtue of the sub-tenancy concerned.

(4) The assignment of a Part 4 tenancy with respect to only part of the dwelling, the subject of the tenancy, is prohibited.

(5) Any such assignment purported to be made is void.

Termination on tenant's death.

[18–39] 39.—(1) Subject to subsections (2) and (4), a Part 4 tenancy shall terminate on the death of the tenant.

(2) Where the 2 conditions specified in subsection (3) are satisfied—

(a) subsection (1) does not apply, and

(b) the Part 4 tenancy concerned, accordingly, continues in being, subject to the other provisions of this Chapter, for the period for which it would otherwise have continued in being had the tenant concerned not died.

(3) Those conditions are—

(a) the dwelling, at the time of the death of the tenant concerned, was occupied by—

(i) a spouse of the tenant,

(ii) a person who was not a spouse of the tenant but who cohabited with the tenant as husband and wife in the dwelling for a period of at least 6 months ending on the date of the tenant's death,

(iii) a child, stepchild or foster child of the tenant, or a person adopted by the tenant under the Adoption Acts 1952 to 1998, being in each case aged 18 years or more, or

(iv) a parent of the tenant,

and

(b) one or more than one of the foregoing persons elects in writing to become a tenant or tenants of the dwelling.

(4) This section is subject to Chapter 6; without limiting the generality of this subsection, subsections (2) and (3) are not to be read as derogating from the operation of Chapter 6 in circumstances where a person referred to in subsection (3) is a multiple tenant (within the meaning of that Chapter) of the dwelling concerned.

(5) Irrespective of the number of instances of the application to the same dwelling of subsection (2) (by reason of a series of deaths of tenants), the Part 4 tenancy concerned shall not continue in being any longer than it would otherwise have continued in being had the first of those deaths not occurred.

Note: Paragraph 3 of the Schedule to this Act modifies paragraph (a) and the Table to s 34, and also modifies ss 35 and 39 of this Act when those provisions apply to a sub-tenancy.

Chapter 4

Additional statutory right — further Part 4 tenancy

Interpretation (Chapter 4).

40.—(1) In section 41 "4 year period" means, in relation to the Part 4 tenancy concerned, the period mentioned in section 28(2)(a). [18–40]

(2) References in sections 41(4) and 42 to section 34 or Chapter 3 are references to that section or Chapter as applied by section 47.

Further Part 4 tenancy on expiry of 4 year period.

41.—(1) If a Part 4 tenancy continues to the expiry of the 4 year period without a notice of termination under section 34 or 36 having been served in respect of it before that expiry, then a new tenancy shall, by virtue of this section, come into being between the landlord and the tenant on that expiry. [18–41]

(2) Such a tenancy is referred to in this Act as a "further Part 4 tenancy".

(3) The commencement date of a further Part 4 tenancy is the expiry of the 4 year period.

(4) A further Part 4 tenancy shall, subject to Chapter 3, continue in being—

(a) unless paragraph (b) or (c) applies, for the period of 4 years from its commencement,

(b) if a notice of termination is served in accordance with section 42, until the expiry of the period of notice given by that notice, or

(c) if a notice of termination under section 34(b) is served in respect of the tenancy giving a period of notice that expires after the period of 4 years mentioned in paragraph (a), until the expiry of that period of notice.

Termination of additional rights.

42.—(1) Not later than 6 months from its commencement, the landlord may serve a notice of termination in respect of a further Part 4 tenancy. [18–42]

(2) The period of notice given by that notice of termination shall not be less than 112 days.

(3) The means of termination that subsection (1) provides in the period of 6 months mentioned in that subsection is in addition to, and accordingly does not prevent the exercise of, the right of termination under section 34(a) in that period.

Chapter 5

Successive further Part 4 tenancies may arise

Purposes of Chapter.

43.—This Chapter has effect for the purpose of ensuring that the additional rights provided by Chapter 4 are regarded as being of a rolling nature, that is to say, that [18–43] (unless the landlord uses the means under this Part to stop the following happening)—

(a) on the expiry of a further Part 4 tenancy, after it has been in existence for 4 years, another such tenancy comes into being, and

(b) on the expiry of that tenancy, after it has been in existence for 4 years, a further such tenancy comes into being,

and so on.

Construction of certain references.

[18–44] 44.—A reference in section 45 to section 34, Chapter 3 or section 42 is a reference to that section or Chapter as applied by section 47.

Further Part 4 tenancy to arise on expiry of previous tenancy.

[18–45] 45.—(1) If a further Part 4 tenancy continues to the expiry of 4 years from its commencement without a notice of termination under section 34(b) having been served in respect of it before that expiry, then a new tenancy shall, by virtue of this section, come into being between the landlord and the tenant on that expiry.

(2) Such a tenancy is also referred to in this Part as a "further Part 4 tenancy".

(3) The commencement date of a further Part 4 tenancy under this section is the expiry of the further Part 4 tenancy that preceded it.

(4) A further Part 4 tenancy under this section shall, subject to Chapter 3, continue in being—

(a) unless paragraph (b) or (c) applies, for the period of 4 years from its commencement,

(b) if a notice of termination is served in accordance with section 42, until the expiry of the period of notice given by that notice, or

(c) if a notice of termination under section 34(b) is served in respect of the tenancy giving a period of notice that expires after the period of 4 years mentioned in paragraph (a), until the expiry of that period of notice.

Terms of a further Part 4 tenancy.

[18–46] 46.—(1) The terms of a further Part 4 tenancy shall be those of the preceding Part 4 tenancy or, as the case may be, the preceding further Part 4 tenancy.

(2) At any time during the period of a further Part 4 tenancy, the parties may, by agreement, vary its terms.

(3) No term purported to be provided for by a variation under subsection (2) shall be a term of a further Part 4 tenancy if the term is inconsistent with this or any other Part of this Act.

Application of Chapter 3 and section 42 to every further Part 4 tenancy.

[18–47] 47.—(1) Chapter 3 applies to every further Part 4 tenancy as it applies to a Part 4 tenancy.

(2) For that purpose, references in that Chapter to a Part 4 tenancy shall be read as references to a further Part 4 tenancy.

(3) For that purpose the following modifications of sections 33 and 34 (in Chapter 3) also apply.

(4) In section 33 "section 34 or 42" shall be substituted for "section 34", and section 33, as it is to be read and have effect for the purposes of this section, is set out in paragraph 1 of the Table to this section.

(5) In paragraph (b) of section 34 "4 years from the commencement of the tenancy" shall be substituted, in subparagraph (ii), for "4 years mentioned in section 28(2)(a) in relation to the tenancy", and that paragraph (b), as it is to be read and have effect for the purposes of this section, is set out in paragraph 2 of the Table to this section.

(6) Section 42 applies to a further Part 4 tenancy under section 45 as it applies to a further Part 4 tenancy under section 41.

TABLE

1. A further Part 4 tenancy may not be terminated by the landlord save in accordance with section 34 or 42.
2. (b) irrespective of whether any of those grounds exist, if—
   - (i) a notice of termination giving the required period of notice is served by the landlord in respect of the tenancy, and
   - (ii) that period of notice expires on or after the end of the period of 4 years from the commencement of the tenancy.

CHAPTER 6

Rules governing operation of Part in cases of multiple occupants

Interpretation (Chapter 6).

48.—(1) In this Chapter "multiple tenants" means, in relation to a dwelling, 2 or more persons who are tenants of the dwelling (whether as joint tenants, tenants-in-common or under any other form of co ownership) and "multiple tenant" means any onc of thcm. **[18–48]**

(2) References in this Chapter to a Part 4 tenancy coming into existence and cognate references shall be construed as references to the circumstances in which the tenancy referred to in section 28 is continued in being by virtue of that section.

(3) References in subsequent provisions of this Chapter to a Part 4 tenancy include, unless the context does not admit of such construction, references to a further Part 4 tenancy.

General principle in relation to dwellings occupied by more than one person.

49.—(1) Subject to this Chapter, the provisions of this Part apply regardless of the fact that the dwelling concerned is occupied at the particular time by either or both— **[18–49]**

(a) multiple tenants,

(b) one or more persons who are also lawfully in occupation of the dwelling as licensees of the tenant or the multiple tenants, as the case may be.

(2) In particular, the fact that the continuous period of occupation, as respects a particular dwelling, by one or more of the multiple tenants is less than 6 months at a particular time does not prevent a Part 4 tenancy coming into existence at that time in respect of the dwelling if—

(a) another of the multiple tenants has been in continuous occupation of the dwelling for 6 months, and

(b) the condition specified in section 28(3) is satisfied.

Entitlement of multiple occupant to benefit from Part 4 tenancy.

[18–50] 50.—(1) Subsection (2) applies unless the multiple tenant concerned benefits, by virtue of the preceding Chapters of this Part, from the protection of the Part 4 tenancy on its coming into existence.

(2) A multiple tenant who was in occupation of a dwelling immediately before the coming into existence of a Part 4 tenancy in respect of it shall, on his or her having been in occupation of the dwelling for a continuous period of 6 months (and that tenancy still subsists), benefit from the protection of that tenancy; accordingly the rights, restrictions and obligations under this Part shall, on and from the expiry of that period of 6 months, apply in relation to that multiple tenant as they apply in relation to the multiple tenant whose continuous occupation gave rise to the Part 4 tenancy's existence.

(3) Any person who the landlord accepts as a tenant of a dwelling on, or subsequent to, a Part 4 tenancy coming into existence in respect of it, shall, on his or her having been in occupation of the dwelling for a continuous period of 6 months (and that tenancy still subsists), benefit from the protection of that tenancy; accordingly, the rights, restrictions and obligations under this Part shall, on and from the expiry of that period of 6 months, apply in relation to that person as they apply in relation to the multiple tenant whose continuous occupation gave rise to the Part 4 tenancy's existence.

(4) The reference in subsection (3) to a landlord's accepting a person as a tenant is a reference to his or her accepting a person as a tenant—

- (a) whether as a replacement for any of the existing multiple tenants or as an additional tenant to them, and
- (b) whether or not the person was immediately before that acceptance a licensee in occupation of the dwelling.

(5) For the purpose of reckoning the continuous period of occupation referred to in subsections (2) and (3), any period of continuous occupation by the person concerned of the dwelling as a licensee (whether that period begins before, on or after the Part 4 tenancy came into existence) may be counted with any continuous period of occupation by that person of the dwelling as a tenant that follows on immediately from it.

(6) For the purpose of, amongst other things, ensuring that the distinction that exists between licences and tenancies does not operate to frustrate the objectives of this Part in cases to which this Chapter applies, subsections (7) and (8) are enacted.

(7) A person who is lawfully in occupation of the dwelling concerned as a licensee of the tenant or the multiple tenants, as the case may be, during the subsistence of a Part 4 tenancy may request the landlord of the dwelling to allow him or her to become a tenant of the dwelling.

(8) The landlord may not unreasonably refuse to accede to such a request; if the request is acceded to—

- (a) an acknowledgement in writing by the landlord that the requester has become a tenant of the landlord suffices for the purpose,
- (b) the requester shall hold the dwelling—
    - (i) on the same terms, or as appropriately modified, as those on which the existing tenant or multiple tenants hold the dwelling (other than terms comprising the rights, restrictions and obligations which arise

by virtue of a Part 4 tenancy being in existence in respect of the dwelling),

(ii) upon (if such be the case) subsection (3) being satisfied in respect of the requester, subject to the same rights, restrictions and obligations as those subject to which the multiple tenant whose continuous occupation gave rise to the Part 4 tenancy's existence holds the dwelling.

Act of one of multiple tenants cannot prejudice the other's or others' rights.

51.—(1) Without prejudice to subsection (3), no act done by any one or more of the multiple tenants of a dwelling that, apart from this subsection, would have either of the following results, namely— **[18–51]**

(a) the termination of the Part 4 tenancy, or

(b) rendering the Part 4 tenancy liable to be terminated by the landlord,

shall have either such result if another of those tenants provides an explanation or information to the landlord from which a landlord acting reasonably in the circumstances would conclude that that act was done without that person's consent.

(2) For the purposes of subsection (1) a landlord acts reasonably in the circumstances concerned if—

(a) he or she requires the last-mentioned tenant in that subsection to provide such information or assistance as he or she may reasonably need to ascertain with whose consent (if any) and by whom the act concerned was done, and

(b) in case that requirement is not complied with, he or she concludes, on account of that non-compliance, that the act concerned was done with the tenant's consent.

(3) Instead of the result mentioned in paragraph (a) or (b) of subsection (1), an act referred to in that subsection that is shown to have been done without the consent of one or more of the other multiple tenants results in—

(a) the tenant responsible for the act (and any tenant who consented to that act) losing the benefit of the protection, if he or she otherwise has the benefit of it, of the Part 4 tenancy, or

(b) the rendering of the benefit for him or her (and any tenant who consented to that act) of that protection, if he or she otherwise has the benefit of it, liable to be terminated by the landlord in accordance with this Part as adapted by subsection (4),

as the case may be.

(4) For the purposes of subsection (3), any provision of this Part which—

(a) provides for the termination of a Part 4 tenancy,

(b) renders such a tenancy liable to termination by the landlord, or

(c) makes provision incidental to, or consequential on, the foregoing,

shall, in relation to a case to which that subsection applies, be construed and operate as a provision which, as appropriate—

(i) provides for the loss of the benefit of the protection of the Part 4 tenancy for the tenant or tenants concerned,

(ii) renders the benefit for that tenant or those tenants of that protection liable to be terminated by the landlord, or

(iii) makes provision incidental to, or consequential on, the matter referred to in paragraph (i) or (ii).

(5) Without limiting the generality of the foregoing, such adaptation of this Part allows the landlord to obtain a determination under Part 6 requiring the tenant who is in default to vacate possession of the dwelling concerned (without prejudice to the other multiple tenant's or tenants' possession of the dwelling).

(6) For the purpose of subsection (4), Part 5 has effect as if every provision it makes with respect to a notice of termination were a provision with respect to a notice terminating the benefit of the protection of the Part 4 tenancy concerned.

(7) In this section a reference to the doing of an act includes the making of an omission.

Immaterial that tenant whose occupation gave rise to Part 4 tenancy quits or dies.

[18–52] 52.—For the avoidance of doubt, neither—

(a) the vacating of possession of the dwelling concerned by the multiple tenant whose continuous occupation gave rise to the Part 4 tenancy's existence in respect of that dwelling, nor

(b) the death of that tenant,

of itself, deprives the other multiple tenant or tenants of the benefit of that tenancy's protection.

No separate Part 4 tenancy to arise in multiple tenant's favour.

[18–53] 53.—The conferral of the benefit of the protections under this Part on a person referred to in section 50(2) or (3) shall not be read as operating to bring into existence a separate Part 4 tenancy in his or her favour as respects the dwelling concerned.

Chapter 7

Miscellaneous

No contracting out from terms of Part permitted.

[18–54] 54.—(1) No provision of any lease, tenancy agreement, contract or other agreement (whether entered into before, on or after the relevant date) may operate to vary, modify or restrict in any way a provision of this Part.

> **Note:** The "relevant date" is 1st September 2004, being the date Part 4 of this Act commenced — see s 5(1) of this Act and the Residential Tenancies Act 2004 (Commencement) Order 2004 (SI No 505 of 2004).

(2) This section is without prejudice to section 26 (which allows more beneficial rights for a tenant than those accorded by this Part).

Protection under this Part and long occupation equity.

[18–55] 55.—(1) For the avoidance of doubt, occupation under a Part 4 tenancy or a further Part 4 tenancy shall be reckoned for the purposes of section 13(1)(b) of the Landlord and Tenant (Amendment) Act 1980.

(2) Neither—

(a) a termination under section 34 on one or more of the grounds specified in paragraphs 2 to 6 of the Table to that section, nor

(b) a termination under section 42, of a Part 4 tenancy or a further Part 4 tenancy shall be regarded as a termination of that tenancy for the purposes of section 17(1)(a) of the Landlord and Tenant (Amendment) Act 1980.

Note: This section states that occupation under a Part 4 tenancy under this Act qualifies for s 13(1)(b) of the Landlord and Tenant (Amendment) Act 1980.

Damages for abuse of section 34 termination procedure.

56.—(1) This section applies where— **[18–56]**

(a) a tenant under a Part 4 tenancy, or under a further Part 4 tenancy, has vacated possession of the dwelling concerned on foot of a notice of termination served under section 34(a),

(b) that notice of termination cited as the reason for the termination one or more of the grounds specified in paragraphs 3 to 6 of the Table to section 34, and

(c) (i) in case the ground cited is that specified in paragraph 3 of that Table, the thing mentioned in that paragraph is not done within the period specified in that paragraph,

(ii) in case the ground cited is that specified in paragraph 4 of that Table, the occupation by the person concerned does not take place within a reasonable time after the service of the notice of termination or, in circumstances where such a requirement arises, the landlord does not comply with the requirement to make the offer referred to in that paragraph,

(iii) in case the ground cited is that specified in paragraph 5 of that Table, the thing mentioned in that paragraph is not done within a reasonable time after the service of the notice of termination or, in circumstances where such a requirement arises, the landlord does not comply with the requirement to make the offer referred to in that paragraph,

(iv) in case the ground cited is that specified in paragraph 6 of that Table, the thing mentioned in that paragraph is not done within a reasonable time after the service of the notice of termination or, in circumstances where such a requirement arises, the landlord does not comply with the requirement to make the offer referred to in that paragraph.

(2) Where this section applies, the tenant may make a complaint to the Board under Part 6 that, by reason of the matters mentioned in subsection (1), he or she has been unjustly deprived of possession of the dwelling concerned by the landlord.

(3) An adjudicator or the Tribunal, on the hearing of such a complaint, may, if he or she or it considers it proper to do so, make—

(a) a determination comprising a direction that the landlord shall pay to the complainant an amount by way of damages for that deprivation of possession,

(b) subject to section 118, a determination comprising a direction that the complainant be permitted to resume possession of the dwelling concerned, or

(c) subject to section 118, a determination comprising both of the foregoing directions.

(4) Damages may not be directed to be paid to a particular person, in respect of the same deprivation of possession, under both subsection (3) and section 118(1).

(5) If 2 or more of the grounds specified in paragraphs 3 to 6 of the Table to section 34 were cited in the notice of termination concerned, then paragraph (c) of subsection (1) shall be read as meaning that an omission of the kind mentioned in that paragraph must have occurred in relation to each of those grounds.

(6) For the avoidance of doubt—

(a) this section applies even though the tenant vacated possession of the dwelling only after a dispute in relation to the validity of the notice of termination was finally determined under Part 6 (but in such a case subsection (1) has effect as if the paragraph set out in the Table to this section were substituted for paragraph (c) of that subsection), and

(b) this section is without prejudice to the tenant's right to put in issue, in a dispute in relation to the validity of the notice of termination referred to the Board under Part 6, the bona fides of the intention of the landlord to do or, as appropriate, permit to be done the thing or things mentioned in the notice.

TABLE

(c) (i) in case the ground cited is that specified in paragraph 3 of that Table, the thing mentioned in that paragraph is not done within the period of 3 months after the dispute in relation to the validity of the notice of termination is finally determined,

(ii) in case the ground cited is that specified in paragraph 4 of that Table, the occupation by the person concerned does not take place within a reasonable time after the dispute is so determined or, in circumstances where such a requirement arises, the landlord does not comply with the requirement to make the offer referred to in that paragraph,

(iii) in case the ground cited is that specified in paragraph 5 of that Table, the thing mentioned in that paragraph is not done within a reasonable time after the dispute is so determined or, in circumstances where such a requirement arises, the landlord does not comply with the requirement to make the offer referred to in that paragraph,

(iv) in case the ground cited is that specified in paragraph 6 of that Table, the thing mentioned in that paragraph is not done within a reasonable time after the dispute is so determined or, in circumstances where such a requirement arises, the landlord does not comply with the requirement to make the offer referred to in that paragraph.

PART 5 – TENANCY TERMINATIONS — NOTICE PERIODS AND OTHER PROCEDURAL REQUIREMENTS

Chapter 1

Scope of Part and interpretation provisions

Purpose of Part.

[18–57] 57.—The purpose of this Part is to specify the requirements for a valid termination by the landlord or tenant of a tenancy of a dwelling, whether the dwelling is—

(a) one to which this Act applies but to which Part 4 does not apply (by reason of the operation of section 25), or

(b) one to which both this Act and that Part applies (in which case those requirements are in addition to the requirements of that Part with regard to the termination of a Part 4 tenancy or a further Part 4 tenancy).

Termination of tenancies restricted to means provided by this Part.

58.—(1) From the relevant date, a tenancy of a dwelling may not be terminated by the landlord or the tenant by means of a notice of forfeiture, a re-entry or any other process or procedure not provided by this Part. **[18–58]**

Note: The "relevant date" is 1st September 2004, being the date Part 4 of this Act commenced — see s 5(1) of this Act and the Residential Tenancies Act 2004 (Commencement) Order 2004 (SI No 505 of 2004).

(2) Accordingly, the termination by the landlord or the tenant of—

(a) more beneficial rights referred to in section 26 that the tenant enjoys under a tenancy than those created by Part 4, or

(b) a tenancy to which section 25 applies, must be effected by means of a notice of termination that complies with this Part.

(3) Each of the following—

(a) a tenancy referred to in subsection (2)(a) (unless it expressly excludes this means of termination),

(b) a tenancy referred to in subsection (2)(b), and

(c) a tenancy of a dwelling created before or after the relevant date in so far as its operation is not affected by Part 4,

shall be construed as including a term enabling its termination by means of a notice of termination that complies with this Part (but, in the case of a tenancy that is for a fixed period, unless it provides otherwise, only where there has been a failure by the party in relation to whom the notice is served to comply with any obligations of the tenancy).

Note: The "relevant date" is 1st September 2004, being the date Part 4 of this Act commenced — see s 5(1) of this Act and the Residential Tenancies Act 2004 (Commencement) Order 2004 (SI No 505 of 2004).

Exclusion of existing rules and enactments.

59.—Subject to section 60, neither— **[18–59]**

(a) any rule of law, nor

(b) provision of any enactment in force immediately before the commencement of this Part,

which applies in relation to the termination of a tenancy (and, in particular, requires a certain period of notice or a period of notice ending on a particular day to be given) shall apply in relation to the termination of a tenancy of a dwelling.

Greater notice periods not affected.

60.—If, in every case or a particular case or cases in which a right of termination is to be exercised, the lease or tenancy agreement comprising the tenancy requires a **[18–60]** greater period of notice to be given by a notice of termination than that required by this Part, then, subject to section 65(4), that greater period of notice shall be given by that notice in (as appropriate) every such case or such particular case or cases.

Construction of certain references to periods of notice and duration of tenancies.

[18–61] 61.—(1) A reference in this Part to a particular period of notice to be given by the notice of termination concerned is a reference to such a period that begins on the day immediately following the date of service of the notice.

(2) A reference in this Part to the duration of a tenancy is a reference to the period beginning on the day on which the tenancy came into existence or the relevant date, if later, and ending on the date of service of the notice of termination concerned.

Note: The "relevant date" is 1st September 2004, being the date Part 4 of this Act commenced — see s 5(1) of this Act and the Residential Tenancies Act 2004 (Commencement) Order 2004 (SI No 505 of 2004).

CHAPTER 2

What a valid notice of termination must contain

Requirements for a valid notice of termination.

[18–62] 62.—(1) A notice of termination to be valid shall—

(a) be in writing,

(b) be signed by the landlord or his or her authorised agent or, as appropriate, the tenant,

(c) specify the date of service of it,

(d) be in such form (if any) as may be prescribed,

(e) if the duration of the tenancy is a period of more than 6 months, state (where the termination is by the landlord) the reason for the termination,

(f) specify the termination date, that is to say, the day (stating the month and year in which it falls)—

(i) on which the tenancy will terminate, and

(ii) on or before which (in the case of a termination by the landlord) the tenant must vacate possession of the dwelling concerned, (and indicating that the tenant has the whole of the 24 hours of the termination date to vacate possession),

and

(g) state that any issue as to the validity of the notice or the right of the landlord or tenant, as appropriate, to serve it must be referred to the Board under Part 6 within 28 days from the date of receipt of it.

Note: Section 62(1)(g) of this Act does not apply to a notice of termination the date of service of which is earlier than the day on which Part 6 of this Act comes into operation — see the Residential Tenancies Act 2004 (Section 202) Regulations 2004 (SI No 649 of 2004). Part 6 of this Act came into operation on 6 December 2004 — see the Residential Tenancies Act 2004 (Commencement) (No 2) Order 2004 (SI No 750 of 2004).

(2) Subsection (1) is without prejudice to Chapter 4 and section 81(3) (which specify additional requirements in respect of a tenancy that has been sub-let).

Date to be specified for purposes of section 62(1)(f).

63.—For the purposes of section 62(1)(f), the day that is to be specified in a notice of termination is the last day of— [18–63]

(a) the period which, by reason of Chapter 3, is the period of notice to be given by that notice of termination, or

(b) such longer period of notice as the landlord or tenant (as appropriate) chooses, subject to section 65(4), to give by that notice of termination.

Reference to and validity of date of service of notice of termination.

64.—(1) For the avoidance of doubt, the specification in a notice of termination of a date as being its date of service does not comply with section 62(1)(c) if any relevant step in the service of that notice remains untaken on that date. [18–64]

(2) A relevant step in the service of a notice remains untaken for the purposes of subsection (1) if any of the steps that are within the power or control of the landlord or tenant or agent (as appropriate) to take for the purpose of effecting such service remains untaken.

(3) A reference in this Part to the date of service of a notice of termination is a reference to the date the specification of which, in the notice of termination, complies with subsection (1).

Chapter 3

Period of notice to be given

What this Chapter does.

65.—(1) This Chapter states the period of notice to be given by a notice of termination. [18–65]

(2) Nothing in this Chapter is to be read as requiring the period of notice concerned to be actually mentioned in the notice of termination; compliance with section 62(1)(f) (which relates to the termination date) suffices for the purposes of communicating the length of notice being given.

(3) Subject to subsection (4), a greater period of notice than that required by this Chapter may be given if the landlord or tenant (as appropriate) so chooses.

(4) If the duration of the tenancy concerned is less than 6 months, a period of notice of more than 70 days may not be given in respect of it.

Period of notice where section 67 or 68 is inapplicable.

66.—(1) This section applies where the tenancy is being terminated— [18–66]

(a) otherwise than by reason of the landlord's or tenant's failure to comply with any of the obligations of the tenancy, or

(b) by reason of such a failure but a condition in another section of this Chapter is required to be satisfied if the period of notice provided by that section is to apply and that condition is not satisfied.

(2) Where this section applies the period of notice to be given by the notice of termination is—

(a) in the case of a termination by the landlord, the period mentioned in column (2) of Table 1 to this section opposite the mention of the duration of the tenancy concerned in column (1) of that Table, and

(b) in the case of a termination by the tenant, the period mentioned in column (2) of Table 2 to this section opposite the mention of the duration of the tenancy concerned in column (1) of that Table.

(3) This section is subject to section 69.

TABLE 1
Termination by Landlord

Duration of Tenancy (1)	Notice Period (2)
Less than 6 months	28 days
6 or more months but less than 1 year	35 days
1 year or more but less than 2 years	42 days
2 years or more but less than 3 years	56 days
3 years or more but less than 4 years	84 days
4 or more years	112 days

TABLE 2
Termination by Tenant

Duration of Tenancy (1)	Notice Period (2)
Less than 6 months	28 days
6 or more months but less than 1 year	35 days
1 year or more but less than 2 years	42 days
2 or more years	56 days

Period of notice for termination by landlord where tenant in default.

[18–67] 67.—(1) This section applies where the tenancy is being terminated by the landlord by reason of the failure of the tenant to comply with any of the obligations of the tenancy.

(2) Where this section applies the period of notice to be given by the notice of termination is—

(a) 7 days, if the tenancy is being terminated by reason of behaviour of the tenant that is—

(i) behaviour falling within paragraph (a) or (b) of the definition of "behave in a way that is anti-social" in section 17(1), or

(ii) threatening to the fabric of the dwelling or the property containing the dwelling,

or

(b) 28 days, if the tenancy is being terminated—

(i) for any other reason (but not a failure to pay an amount of rent due), or

(ii) for failure to pay an amount of rent due and the condition specified in subsection (3) is satisfied,

regardless of the duration of the tenancy.

(3) The condition mentioned in subsection (2)(b)(ii) is that the tenant has been notified in writing by the landlord that an amount of rent due has not been paid and 14 days elapse from the receipt of that notice without the amount concerned having been paid to the landlord.

(4) This section is subject to section 69.

Period of notice for termination by tenant where landlord in default.

68.—(1) This section applies where— **[18–68]**

(a) the tenancy is being terminated by the tenant by reason of the failure of the landlord to comply with any obligations of the tenancy, and

(b) in a case falling within subsection (2)(b), the condition specified in subsection (3) in relation to a termination in such a case is satisfied.

(2) Where this section applies the period of notice to be given by the notice of termination is—

(a) 7 days, if the tenancy is being terminated by reason of behaviour of the landlord that poses an imminent danger of death or serious injury or imminent danger to the fabric of the dwelling or the property containing the dwelling, or

(b) 28 days, if the tenancy is being terminated for any other reason,

regardless of the duration of the tenancy.

(3) The condition mentioned in subsection (1)(b) is—

(a) the landlord has been notified in writing of the failure concerned by the tenant, and

(b) the landlord does not remedy the failure within a reasonable time after being so notified.

(4) In subsection (3) "remedy the failure" means—

(a) in the case of a failure that does not result in financial loss or damage to the tenant or his or her property, to desist from the conduct that constitutes the failure, or if the failure consists of an omission to comply with an obligation, comply with that obligation, and

(b) in the case of a failure that does result in financial loss or damage to the tenant or his or her property—

(i) to pay adequate compensation to the tenant or repair the damage fully, and

(ii) unless the failure is not of a continuing nature, to desist from the conduct that constitutes the failure or comply with the obligation concerned, as the case may be.

(5) This section is subject to section 69.

Exceptions to requirements of sections 66 to 68.

[18–69] 69.—(1) Subject to subsection (2), the landlord or tenant may agree to a lesser period of notice being given than that required by a preceding provision of this Chapter and such lesser period of notice may be given accordingly.

(2) Such an agreement to a lesser period of notice being given may only be entered into at, or after, the time it is indicated to the tenant or landlord (as appropriate) by the other party that he or she intends to terminate the tenancy.

(3) For the avoidance of doubt, a term of a lease or tenancy agreement cannot constitute such an agreement.

CHAPTER 4

Additional requirements and procedures where tenancy sub-let

Notices of termination in cases of tenancies that are sub-let.

[18–70] 70.—(1) This section applies where—

(a) the tenancy ("the head-tenancy") of the dwelling concerned is the subject of a sub-tenancy ("the sub-tenancy"), and

(b) the landlord under the head-tenancy proposes to terminate the head-tenancy.

(2) Where this section applies, a notice of termination in respect of the head-tenancy must, in addition to its complying with section 62, state whether or not the landlord under the head-tenancy requires the head-tenant to terminate the sub-tenancy.

(3) If a requirement to terminate the sub-tenancy is stated in such a notice, then, in addition to its being served on the head-tenant, a copy of that notice must be served on the tenant of the sub-tenancy ("the sub-tenant").

Procedures on foot of service of notice mentioned in section70 in non-contentious case.

[18–71] 71.—(1) Where—

(a) section 70 applies,

(b) a requirement is stated in the notice of termination of the head-tenancy to terminate the sub-tenancy, and

(c) no dispute in relation to the termination of the head-tenancy is referred under Part 6 to the Board,

the head-tenant must, within 28 days from the receipt of that notice, comply with that requirement, that is to say, serve a notice of termination in respect of the sub-tenancy on the sub-tenant.

(2) "Head-tenancy", "head-tenant", "sub-tenancy" and "sub-tenant" in this section shall be construed in accordance with section 70.

Procedures on foot of service of notice in cases not falling under section 71.

[18–72] 72.—(1) Where—

(a) section 70 applies,

(b) the notice of termination of the head-tenancy does not require the termination of the sub-tenancy, and

(c) no dispute in relation to the termination of the head-tenancy is referred under Part 6 to the Board, the head-tenant must, within 28 days from the receipt of that notice, notify the sub-tenant of the contents of that notice.

(2) Where—

(a) section 70 applies,

(b) the notice of termination of the head-tenancy does not require the termination of the sub-tenancy, and

(c) a dispute in relation to the termination of the head-tenancy is referred under Part 6 to the Board,

the head-tenant must, within 28 days from the receipt of that notice, notify the sub-tenant—

(i) of the contents of that notice, and

(ii) of the fact that that dispute has been referred to the Board.

(3) The particulars of the determination order (if any) made by the Board on foot of that reference must be notified by the head-tenant to the sub-tenant within 14 days from the receipt by the head-tenant of the order.

(4) "Head-tenancy", "head-tenant", "sub-tenancy" and "sub-tenant" in this section shall be construed in accordance with section 70.

CHAPTER 5

Miscellaneous

Notice of termination by multiple tenants.

73.—(1) Subsection (2) applies where a notice of termination is being served in respect of a dwelling by all of the multiple tenants of the dwelling. [18–73]

(2) Where this subsection applies, it suffices, for the purposes of section 62(1)(b), that the notice of termination is signed by one of the multiple tenants if—

(a) the notice states it is signed by that person on behalf of himself or herself and the other tenant or tenants, and

(b) the other tenant or each other tenant is named in the notice.

(3) Any rule of law that a notice of termination served by any of 2 or more multiple tenants under a periodic tenancy of a dwelling without the concurrence of the other or others, or without the knowledge of the other or others, is effective to terminate that tenancy is abolished.

(4) In this section "multiple tenants" has the same meaning as it has in Chapter 6 of Part 4.

Offence to do certain acts on foot of invalid termination.

74.—(1) A person is guilty of an offence if— [18–74]

(a) a notice of termination that is invalid purports to be served by the person (or on his or her behalf) in respect of a tenancy, and

(b) the person does any act, in reliance on the notice, that affects adversely, or is calculated to affect adversely, any interest of the person on whom the notice is served.

(2) In proceedings for an offence under this section, it is a defence to show that the defendant neither knew nor could reasonably be expected to have known of the existence of any fact that gave rise to the invalidity of the notice concerned.

(3) For the purposes of subsection (1), an act is done by a person in reliance on a notice if—

(a) its doing is accompanied or preceded by a statement made by the person (in writing or otherwise and however expressed) that it is being done, or will be done, in reliance on the notice, or

(b) in all the circumstances it is reasonable to infer that it is done in reliance on the notice.

(4) For the avoidance of doubt, references in this section to the doing of an act include references to the making of a statement (whether in writing or otherwise).

PART 6 – DISPUTE RESOLUTION

CHAPTER 1

Referral of matters to Board for resolution

Interpretation (Part 6).

[18–75] 75.—(1) References in this Part to the referral of a matter to the Board for resolution are references to the referral of the matter for the purposes of mediation, a determination by an adjudicator or a determination by the Tribunal under this Part (or more than one of those things) being carried out or made in relation to it.

(2) References in this Part to a dispute include references to a disagreement and, unless the context does not admit of such a construction, a complaint mentioned in section 56(2), 76(4), 77 or 195(4) or paragraph 8(2) of the Schedule to this Act.

(3) For the purposes of subsection (2) "disagreement" shall be deemed to include—

(a) any issue arising between the parties with regard to the compliance by either with his or her obligations as landlord or tenant under the tenancy,

(b) any matter with regard to the legal relations between the parties that either or both of them requires to be determined (for example, whether the tenancy has been validly terminated),

and, without prejudice to the generality of the foregoing, shall be deemed to include a claim by the landlord for arrears of rent to which the tenant has not indicated he or she disputes the landlord's entitlement but which it is alleged the tenant has failed to pay.

(4) References in this Part to a party, without qualification, are references to—

(a) a party to the dispute or disagreement concerned,

(b) in the case of proceedings referred to in section 23 to recover rent or other charges where the landlord or the person alleged to owe the rent or other charges is deceased, the personal representative of the landlord or that other person,

(c) the personal representative of the landlord or the tenant in any other case where, if the matter were a cause of action (within the meaning of the Civil Liability Act 1961), it would have survived for the benefit of, or against, the estate of the landlord or the tenant,

(d) in the case of a complaint mentioned in section 76(4), the licensee and the landlord, and

(e) in the case of a complaint mentioned in section 77—
(i) the complainant, and
(ii) the landlord of the dwelling concerned.

Right of referral by parties to tenancy and certain other persons.

76.—(1) Either or both of the parties to an existing or terminated tenancy of a dwelling may, individually or jointly, as appropriate, refer to the Board for resolution any matter relating to the tenancy in respect of which there is a dispute between them. **[18–76]**

(2) In the case of a tenancy that has been terminated a dispute as to the amount of any rent that had been agreed to or paid by the former tenant may not be referred by him or her to the Board for resolution at any time after the period of 28 days from the termination of the tenancy.

(3) The landlord may refer to the Board for resolution any matter relating to a dwelling in respect of which there is a dispute between the landlord and another, not being the tenant but through whom the other person claims any right or entitlement.

(4) A licensee referred to in section 50(7) may refer to the Board for resolution a complaint by him or her that the landlord referred to in that provision has unreasonably refused to accede to a request of the licensee made under that provision.

Right of referral in respect of breach of duty under section 15.

77.—(1) A person referred to in section 15 may, if the conditions specified in subsection (2) are satisfied, refer to the Board for resolution a complaint by him or her that the landlord of a dwelling has breached the duty owed to him or her under that section. **[18–77]**

(2) The conditions mentioned in subsection (1) are—

(a) the referrer of the complaint is or was directly and adversely affected by the breach of duty alleged in the complaint, and

(b) before making the reference, the referrer, by communicating or attempting to communicate, with the relevant parties or former parties to the tenancy concerned, took all reasonable steps to resolve the matter (but this requirement shall not be read as requiring the institution of legal proceedings or those parties being given to understand that such proceedings might be instituted).

(3) For the purposes of facilitating the person's compliance with subsection (2)(b), the Board may furnish to a person who proposes to make a reference under this section the name and address of the landlord or his or her authorised agent (or the former landlord or his or her authorised agent) of the dwelling concerned if it appears to the Board that the first-mentioned person is a person who may make a reference under this section in relation to the matter concerned.

Particular matters that may be referred (non-exhaustive list).

78.—(1) Without prejudice to the generality of sections 76 and 77, the matters in respect of which disputes and, where appropriate, complaints may be referred to the Board for resolution include— **[18–78]**

(a) the retention or refund of a deposit,

(b) the amount that ought to be initially set (in compliance with section 19) as the amount of rent under a tenancy,

(c) the time at which a review of rent referred to in Part 3 should take place or the amount of rent that should be determined on foot of that review,

(d) an alleged failure by the tenant to comply with any of the obligations applicable to the tenant, including those contained in any lease or tenancy agreement,

(e) an alleged failure by the landlord to comply with any of the obligations applicable to the landlord, including those contained in any lease or tenancy agreement,

(f) an allegation that the landlord has sought to terminate a tenancy other than in accordance with the provisions of Part 4,

(g) an allegation that the ground stated by the landlord for the purposes of terminating a tenancy was not valid or that the notice used to terminate a tenancy did not comply with this Act,

(h) the appropriate period of notice to be given by a notice of termination in respect of a tenancy,

(i) whether a tenancy stands terminated notwithstanding the absence of the service of a notice of termination by the tenant and where the tenant has allegedly vacated the dwelling concerned,

(j) an alleged failure by the tenant or other occupant to offer up, by the specified date, vacant possession of a dwelling on foot of receipt by him or her of a notice of termination validly served by the landlord,

(k) an alleged failure by a sub-tenant to offer up, by the specified date, vacant possession of a dwelling on foot of receipt by him or her of a notice of termination validly served by a head-tenant,

(l) a claim for recovery of costs or damages or both by a landlord or tenant in respect of a failure by either to comply with his or her obligations applicable to the tenancy including those contained in any lease or tenancy agreement,

(m) a claim for costs or damages or both by a landlord or tenant for the purported termination of a tenancy otherwise than in accordance with this Act,

(n) an alleged failure by a person to comply with a determination order made by the Board,

(o) an allegation that a landlord has contravened section 14 (prohibition on penalisation of tenants),

(p) an allegation that an agreement referred to in section 35(6) has not been complied with,

(q) a claim by a landlord for arrears of rent or other charges.

(2) For the avoidance of doubt, a dispute may, subject to the provisions of this Part, be referred by a sub-tenant to the Board for resolution with regard to a notice of termination served in respect of the head-tenancy out of which the sub-tenant's tenancy arises whether or not such a dispute is also so referred by the head-tenant.

(3) On such a reference by the sub-tenant he or she shall have standing to put in issue any matter relating to the notice of termination concerned despite the head-tenant's—

(a) not having taken any issue with the head-landlord in relation to that matter, or

(b) having made any representation to the landlord or done any act that estops him or her from taking any such issue with the head-landlord, or

(c) not putting in issue that matter in any dispute so referred by himself or herself with regard to the notice of termination.

Different matters may be the subject of a single reference.

79.—There may be included in the same reference to the Board under section 76 or 77 disputes and, where appropriate, complaints in respect of 2 or more different matters. [18–79]

Time limit for referring a particular type of dispute.

80.—A dispute relating to the validity of a notice of termination which has been served or purported to be served may not be referred to the Board for resolution at any time after the period of 28 days has elapsed from the date of receipt of that notice. [18–80]

Tenancies and sub-tenancies: referral of disputes concerning their termination.

81.—(1) The purpose of this section is to— [18–81]

(a) limit, in certain circumstances, the right of referral to the Board by a sub-tenant of a dispute concerning the termination of the tenancy out of which his or her sub-tenancy arises, and

(b) require the tenant of such a tenancy (in addition to employing the procedures under Chapter 4 of Part 5) to make a certain inquiry of the sub-tenant before the tenant may himself or herself refer to the Board for resolution a dispute concerning the termination of that tenancy.

(2) If a landlord, in serving a notice of termination on a tenant in respect of a tenancy, requires the tenant to terminate any sub-tenancy arising out of the tenancy, the tenant shall, if the tenant intends to refer to the Board for resolution a dispute concerning the termination of the tenancy, require the sub-tenant to inform him or her, within 10 days from receipt of the notice mentioned in subsection (3), whether or not the sub-tenant intends to refer to the Board for resolution any dispute that the sub-tenant considers thereby arises or exists in the circumstances relating to the termination of the tenancy.

(3) That requirement shall be stated in the notice of termination required by the landlord to be served by the head-tenant on the subtenant.

(4) If a sub-tenant does not comply with the requirement mentioned in subsection (2) within the period specified in that subsection then the sub-tenant may not refer to the Board for resolution any dispute concerning the termination of the tenancy concerned.

(5) If the tenant—

(a) does not comply with the second-mentioned requirement in subsection (2), then the tenant may not refer to the Board for resolution any dispute concerning the termination of the tenancy concerned, or

(b) does comply with that requirement, the tenant may not refer to the Board for resolution such a dispute until 15 days elapse from the date of service of the notice concerned mentioned in subsection (3).

Withdrawal of matter referred to Board.

[18–82] 82.—(1) A party who has referred under this Part any matter to the Board may, at any stage, withdraw the matter.

(2) Subject to subsection (3), a party shall indicate his or her wish to withdraw such a matter by serving a notice in writing on the Board to that effect.

(3) If the matter is being dealt with by a mediator, an adjudicator or the Tribunal, it suffices for the party to indicate, orally to him or her or it, that the party is withdrawing the matter.

(4) Without prejudice to subsection (5), on oral or written notice, as appropriate, being given in respect of the withdrawal, the Board, the mediator, the adjudicator or the Tribunal shall consider the matter concerned withdrawn and, accordingly, shall not deal with it any further.

(5) On such notice being given to it or him or her, the Board, the mediator, the adjudicator or the Tribunal shall ascertain whether the other party to the dispute concerned objects to the withdrawal and, if he or she does so, the Board, mediator, adjudicator or Tribunal may direct that the party withdrawing the matter shall pay to the other party such costs and expenses incurred by that other party as it or he or she determines.

Board not to deal with reference if fee not paid or tenancy not registered.

[18–83] 83.—(1) Subject to subsection (3), the Board shall not—

(a) deal initially with a dispute referred to it under this Part, or

(b) allow any other procedure under this Part to be followed in relation to a dispute referred to it under this Part,

if the fee of the specified amount prescribed by rules under section 109 in relation to that initial dealing or the following of that procedure has not been paid to it.

(2) Subject to subsection (3), the Board shall not deal with a dispute in relation to a tenancy referred to it under this Part by the landlord of the dwelling concerned if the tenancy is not registered under Part 7.

(3) The Board may, in the case of a default in payment of a particular fee or registration under Part 7 of a particular tenancy, notify the person or persons concerned of the default and afford the person or persons concerned a reasonable opportunity to rectify the matter; if the matter is rectified within a reasonable time the Board shall, subject to this Part, deal with the dispute or permit the other procedure to be followed in relation to it, as the case may be.

Further right of Board not to deal with certain references.

[18–84] 84.—(1) If the Board is of opinion that, in relation to a dispute referred to the Board—

(a) the dwelling, the subject of the dispute, is not a dwelling to which this Act applies,

(b) for any other reason, the dispute does not come within the Board's jurisdiction (including by reason of a failure to comply with any condition for its being referred to the Board),

(c) proceedings in any court in respect of the subject matter of the dispute, would, were they to be capable of being instituted at the date of the reference, be statute-barred, or

(d) the matter or matters concerned are trivial or vexatious, then the Board shall serve a notice on the party who referred the matter to it stating that it is of that opinion and, unless the party establishes, in accordance with the following subsections, that the opinion is not well founded, that it will not (subject to subsection (6)) deal with the matter.

(2) For the purposes of subsection (1), the notice referred to in that subsection shall state that the party concerned may, within a period specified in the notice, make submissions to the Board as to why the party considers the opinion of the Board is not well founded.

(3) The Board shall consider any submissions made to it by that party within the period specified in the notice concerned.

(4) Unless the Board decides that any such submissions establish that the opinion of the Board referred to in subsection (1) was not well founded, the Board shall not, subject to subsection (6), deal with the dispute referred to it; the other party or parties to the dispute shall be notified in writing of a decision made by the Board that that opinion was not well founded and shall be furnished by the Board, on request, with a copy of the foregoing submissions (or, if they were not written submissions, a written summary of them prepared by the Board).

(5) The party who referred the dispute concerned to the Board or, as the case may be, any other party to the dispute may appeal to the Circuit Court against a decision of the Board (made in consequence of the procedures under this section having been employed) not to deal with or, as appropriate, to deal with the dispute.

(6) On the hearing of such an appeal the Circuit Court may, as it thinks fit, allow the appeal and direct the Board to deal with or, as appropriate, not to deal with the dispute concerned or dismiss the appeal; an appeal under this section shall be heard by the judge of the Circuit Court for the circuit in which the tenancy or dwelling is or was situated.

(7) For the purpose of subsection (1)(c), proceedings are statute-barred if a defence under the Statute of Limitations 1957 or any other limitation enactment is available in relation to them.

Right of Tribunal or adjudicator not to deal with reference.

85.—(1) The Tribunal or an adjudicator shall, if the Tribunal or adjudicator is of opinion that paragraph (a), (b), (c) or (d) of section 84(1) applies to a dispute with which it or he or she is dealing, not deal any further with the dispute. **[18–85]**

(2) Subsection (1) does not apply if—

(a) previously the Board, in consequence of the procedures under section 84 having been employed by it in relation to the dispute, decided that an opinion formed by it (being a like opinion to that subsequently formed by the Tribunal or adjudicator) in relation to the dispute was not well founded, or

(b) a decision of the Board, in consequence of those procedures having been employed by it, in relation to the dispute (being a decision of a like kind to the opinion subsequently formed by the Tribunal or adjudicator) was the subject of an appeal under section 84(5) and the Circuit Court, on that appeal, directed the Board to deal with the dispute.

Status of certain matters pending determination of dispute.

[18–86] 86.—(1) Subject to subsection (2), pending the determination of a dispute that has been referred to the Board (but subject to that determination when it is made)—

(a) the rent payable under the tenancy concerned and the rent payable under any sub-tenancy arising out of it shall continue to be payable,

(b) if the dispute relates to the amount of rent payable, no increase in the amount of the rent may be made, and

(c) a termination of the tenancy concerned may not be effected.

(2) Subsection (1) does not apply if—

(a) in the case of paragraph (a) of that subsection, the parties concerned agree to payment of the rent being suspended,

(b) in the case of paragraph (b) of that subsection, the parties concerned agree to an increase in the amount of the rent being made,

(c) in the case of paragraph (c) of that subsection (unless the dispute is a dispute specified in subsection (3)), the notice of termination concerned was served—

(i) before the dispute was referred to the Board for resolution, or

(ii) after the dispute was so referred and the required period of notice to be given by the notice of termination is 28 days or less and that period of notice has been given,

or

(d) in any of the cases, the dispute is not dealt with, or ceases to be dealt with, under this Part pursuant to section 82, 83, 84 or 85.

(3) The dispute mentioned in subsection (2)(c) is a dispute relating to the validity of the notice of termination concerned or the right of the landlord or tenant, as appropriate, to serve it.

Remedial action taken by party in certain cases to be disregarded.

[18–87] 87.—If a dispute referred to the Board relates to the termination of a tenancy for failure by the landlord or tenant to fulfil his or her obligations relating to the tenancy, any remedial action taken by the other party subsequent to the receipt of the notice of termination shall not be taken into consideration by the Board, a mediator, an adjudicator or the Tribunal in dealing with the dispute.

Extension of time for referring disputes to Board.

[18–88] 88.—(1) The Board may, on application to it, extend the time limited by any provision of this or any other Part for the referral of a dispute to it for resolution.

(2) The Board shall not extend the time concerned unless the applicant for the extension shows good grounds for why the time should be extended.

(3) The reference in this section to the time limited by any provision of this or any other Part for the referral of a dispute to the Board for resolution includes a reference to the time limited by such a provision for fulfilling any condition precedent that is required by the provision to be fulfilled before a particular dispute may be referred to the Board for resolution.

(4) An appeal shall lie to the Circuit Court (by the applicant for the extension or, as the case may be, any other party to the dispute concerned) against a decision of the Board under this section to, as appropriate—

(a) refuse to extend the time concerned, or

(b) extend the time concerned,

and, on the hearing of such an appeal, the Circuit Court may, as it thinks fit, confirm, vary or cancel the decision of the Board.

(5) An appeal under this section shall be heard by the judge of the Circuit Court for the circuit in which the tenancy or dwelling concerned is or was situated.

CHAPTER 2

Relationship between Part and certain other dispute resolution mechanisms

Dispute subject to discontinued court proceedings may be subject of reference.

89.—For the avoidance of doubt, any dispute that has been the subject of proceedings instituted in any court before the commencement of this Part and which proceedings were discontinued by agreement of the parties after such commencement but before the court made its final determination in the matter may be the subject of a reference to the Board under this Part. **[18–89]**

Arbitration agreement not effective to oust Board's jurisdiction save in certain circumstances.

90.—(1) Notwithstanding any other enactment or any provision of the agreement itself, an arbitration agreement shall not operate to preclude a dispute to which the agreement applies from being referred to the Board for resolution unless the tenant at or after the time the dispute arises consents to the dispute being referred to arbitration. **[18–90]**

(2) In this section "arbitration agreement" has the same meaning as it has in the Arbitration Act 1954.

Dispute may not be referred to Board where alternative remedy is being pursued.

91.—(1) To the extent that an alternative remedy is available in respect of any dispute falling within this Part and a person takes any steps to avail himself or herself of that remedy, that person may not refer the dispute to the Board for resolution. **[18–91]**

(2) If a person, other than the person mentioned in subsection (1), refers a dispute to the Board for resolution, being a dispute—

(a) to which that other person is a party, and

(b) as respects which that other person takes or has taken steps of the kind mentioned in that subsection,

then the Board, a mediator, an adjudicator or the Tribunal may, in dealing with the dispute, take account (with regard to the relief that may be granted and to such extent as it or he or she considers just) of the existence of that alternative remedy.

CHAPTER 3

Preliminary steps by Board (include power to refer matter to Tribunal)

Initial steps that may be taken by Board to resolve matters referred.

[18–92] 92.—(1) As soon as practicable after a dispute is referred to it, the Board may communicate with the parties for the purpose of—

(a) endeavouring to ensure that they are fully aware of the nature of the issue or issues the subject of the reference, and

(b) in cases where it considers the dispute is due to some basic misunderstanding of either or both of them as to the rights or obligations of landlords and tenants, achieving the objective mentioned in subsection (2).

(2) That objective is to have the issue or issues between the parties resolved by agreement between them without recourse being needed to the other procedures in this Part.

(3) Without prejudice to the generality of subsection (1), the communications by the Board under this section with the parties may, where it would be of assistance to the parties, include an indication by the Board, based on appropriate assumptions stated to the parties, of the typical outcome of issues of the kind concerned being determined under this Part.

(4) Any such indication shall be communicated by the Board as fully to one of the parties as the other or others and the Board, in its communications generally with the parties under this section, shall bear in mind the right of the parties to invoke all of the procedures under this Part that are available to them.

Invitation to parties to resolve matter through mediation.

[18–93] 93.—(1) Unless the steps (if any) taken under section 92 have resulted in the parties agreeing a resolution of the matter concerned, the Board shall request each of the parties to state whether he or she consents to the dispute being the subject of mediation under section 95.

(2) If each of the parties states, in response to that request, that he or she consents to the dispute being the subject of such mediation the Board shall arrange for the matter to be the subject of mediation by a person appointed by it from amongst the panel of mediators under section 164(4).

(3) If any of the parties fails to respond to a request under subsection (1) or responds by stating that he or she does not consent to the matter concerned being the subject of mediation under section 95, the Board shall arrange for the matter to be the subject of adjudication under section 97 by a person appointed by it from amongst the panel of adjudicators under section 164(4).

(4) This section is subject to section 94.

Exceptions to section 93: direct reference of matter to Tribunal, etc.

[18–94] 94.—Notwithstanding section 93, the Board shall not be required to arrange for—

(a) mediation of the kind mentioned in that section in relation to a dispute if it has made an application to the Circuit Court under section 189 in relation to the dispute, in which case the Board may, as it thinks appropriate—

(i) arrange for the dispute to be the subject of adjudication under section 97 by a person appointed by it from amongst the panel of adjudicators under section 164(4), or

(ii) refer the dispute to the Tribunal,

or

(b) mediation or adjudication of the kind mentioned in that section in relation to a dispute if, in all the circumstances, it considers it would be more appropriate for it to refer the dispute to the Tribunal and refers it accordingly.

Chapter 4

Mediation and adjudication

Mediation.

95.—(1) The following provisions apply to a mediation which the Board has arranged under section 93 in relation to a dispute. **[18–95]**

(2) The person appointed under section 93(2) to conduct the mediation ("the mediator") shall inquire fully into each relevant aspect of the dispute concerned, provide to, and receive from, each party such information as is appropriate and generally make such suggestions to each party and take such other actions as he or she considers appropriate with a view to achieving the objective mentioned in subsection (3).

(3) That objective is to have the issue or issues between the parties resolved by agreement between them without further recourse to the procedures under this Part being needed.

(4) As soon as practicable after the mediation is completed, the mediator shall prepare a report containing the following—

(a) a statement of what matters, if any, relating to the dispute are agreed by the parties to be fact,

(b) a summary of the matter or matters, if any, whether they go in whole or part to resolving the dispute or not, agreed to by the parties (and this summary shall be contained in a document signed by each of the parties acknowledging that the matter or those matters are agreed to by them), and

(c) relevant particulars in relation to the conduct of the mediation (including particulars in relation to the number and duration of sessions held by the mediator and the persons who attended any such session) and a list of any documents submitted to the mediator (but without disclosing any of their contents).

(5) The mediator shall, after preparing a report under subsection (4), furnish a copy of it to the Director.

(6) There shall then be furnished to the Board by the Director—

(a) if the report contains a document of the kind mentioned in subsection (4)(b), a copy of that document (but not any other part of the report), or

(b) if the report does not contain such a document, a statement that no matters have been agreed to by the parties which resolve in whole or part the dispute (but not any part of the report).

Procedures to be followed on foot of Board's receipt of information under section 95(6).

[18–96] 96.—(1) After the receipt by it of the document or statement referred to in section 95(6), the Board shall serve a copy of the document or statement on each of the parties, together with the following notice.

(2) That notice is a notice requiring the party to inform the Board—

(a) if the information served on the parties indicates that there is agreement between the parties such as to resolve in whole the dispute concerned, whether that agreement still exists,

(b) if the information served does not indicate that to be the case, whether there now exists such an agreement between the parties.

(3) If—

(a) the Board is informed by the parties that an agreement of the kind referred to in subsection (2) exists, or

(b) in the case of paragraph (a) of subsection (2), one or more of the parties fails to indicate whether the agreement referred to in that paragraph still exists,

the Board shall, subject to subsections (4) and (5), follow the procedures under section 121 (which concerns the making of determination orders) in relation to the agreement.

(4) Those procedures shall not be followed—

(a) any sooner than 21 days, nor

(b) any later than 28 days,

from the date of service of the notice mentioned in subsection (2) on each of the parties (or if the date of service of the notice on each of them is not the same whichever of the dates of service is the later or latest).

(5) The Board shall also not follow those procedures, if one or more of the parties, having stated, in the course of being communicated with under the preceding subsections, that agreement of the kind referred to in subsection (2) exists, subsequently, (but not later than 21 days from service of the notice mentioned in subsection (2) on him or her) states to the Board that such agreement no longer exists.

(6) The Board shall, at the request of either or both of the parties, refer the dispute to the Tribunal for its determination if either—

(a) as a result of the steps taken under subsection (1), the Board ascertains that an agreement of the kind referred to in subsection (2) does not exist, or

(b) a statement of the kind referred to in subsection (5) is made to it.

Adjudication.

[18–97] 97.—(1) The following provisions and sections 98 and 99 apply to an adjudication which the Board has arranged under section 93(3) or 94(a) in relation to a dispute.

(2) The person appointed under section 93(3) or 94(a) to conduct the adjudication ("the adjudicator") shall inquire fully into each relevant aspect of the dispute concerned and provide to, and receive from, each party such information as is appropriate.

(3) For that purpose, the adjudicator may require either party to furnish to him or her, within a specified period, such documents or other information as he or she considers appropriate.

(4) The adjudicator shall determine the dispute by either—

(a) reaching a decision himself or herself in the matter, or

(b) subject to section 98, declaring to the parties that he or she has adopted, as his or her determination of the dispute, a decision reached (through the adjudicator's assistance under subsection (5)) by the parties themselves in resolution of the matter,

and the reference in paragraph (a) to the adjudicator's reaching a decision in the matter shall be deemed to include a reference to his or her deciding not to deal with the dispute in accordance with section 85.

(5) Where the adjudicator considers it would be of practical benefit, the adjudicator may provide assistance to the parties with a view to the parties themselves reaching a decision in resolution of the matter concerned; such assistance may include the adjudicator's stating to the parties any provisional conclusion he or she has reached in relation to any of the issues concerned.

(6) Any statement of such a conclusion shall—

(a) not be made in relation to any issue of fact which is in dispute between the parties, unless the parties request the making of such a statement,

(b) not be made before every document submitted to the adjudicator by the parties and any initial oral submissions made by them have been considered by the adjudicator, and

(c) be accompanied by a statement, whether oral or in writing, that the conclusion is of a provisional nature and its making does not absolve the adjudicator of his or her duty to determine the dispute impartially and in accordance with the requirements of procedural fairness

(7) The adjudicator may, in his or her discretion, permit another person to appear on a party's behalf at any hearing before the adjudicator.

"Cooling-off" period for purposes of section 97(4)(b).

98.—(1) A decision reached by the parties themselves in resolution of the matter concerned may not be the subject of a declaration under section 97(4)(b) unless— **[18–98]**

(a) a period of 21 days has elapsed from the date on which the parties first inform the adjudicator that such a decision has been reached by them, and

(b) in that period none of the parties has informed the adjudicator that he or she no longer accepts that decision.

(2) If, in the period mentioned in subsection (1), the adjudicator is informed by any of the parties that he or she no longer accepts the decision mentioned in that subsection, the adjudicator shall, subject to conducting any further hearings in the matter as he or she thinks appropriate, proceed to reach a decision himself or herself in the matter.

(3) The adjudicator shall indicate to the parties the effect of this section upon being first informed by them that a decision has been reached by them in resolution of the matter concerned.

(4) That indication of the adjudicator shall also include an indication that the decision reached is not capable of being appealed to the Tribunal and shall become binding on the parties on a determination order under section 121 being made in relation to it.

Adjudicator's report.

99.—(1) As soon as practicable after an adjudicator has made a determination under section 97 in relation to a dispute, the adjudicator shall prepare a report containing the following— **[18–99]**

(a) a statement of what matters, if any, relating to the dispute are agreed by the parties to be fact,

(b) a summary of the matters (whether they go in whole or part to resolving the dispute or not) agreed to by the parties,

(c) the terms of the determination made by the adjudicator,

(d) in the case of a determination under section 97(4)(a), a summary of the reasons for the determination, and

(e) relevant particulars in relation to the conduct of the adjudication (including particulars in relation to the number and duration of hearings held by the adjudicator, the persons who attended any such hearing and any documents submitted to the adjudicator).

(2) The adjudicator shall, after preparing a report under subsection (1), furnish a copy of it to the Board.

(3) After the receipt by it of a report under subsection (2), the Board shall serve on each of the parties a copy of the report and the following statement.

(4) That statement is one to the effect that the Board will follow the procedures under section 121 (which concerns the making of determination orders) in relation to the determination of the adjudicator unless, in the case of a determination under section 97(4)(a), an appeal is made under, and in accordance with, section 100 against the determination and that appeal is not subsequently abandoned.

Appeal to Tribunal against adjudicator's determination.

[18–100] 100.—(1) One or more of the parties may appeal to the Tribunal against a determination of an adjudicator under section 97(4)(a).

(2) Such an appeal shall be made within 21 days from the date the Board serves on the party the report and statement referred to in section 99(3).

Provisions common to mediators and adjudicators.

[18–101] 101.—(1) In respect of a matter dealt with by him or her under this Chapter, the mediator or adjudicator shall—

(a) declare to the parties at the outset of dealing with the matter any potential conflict of interest of which he or she is aware or ought reasonably be aware,

(b) act at all times in accordance with the highest standards of the professional body, if any, of which he or she is a member,

(c) maintain the confidentiality of the proceedings concerned and shall not disclose any report prepared by him or her under section 95(4) or 99, otherwise than in accordance with those sections.

(2) Where a declaration referred to in subsection (1)(a) is made to the parties then, unless the parties agree to the mediator or the adjudicator continuing to deal with the matter, the Board shall appoint another person from amongst the panel of mediators or adjudicators under section 164(4) to deal with the matter.

(3) References in this Part to the person appointed under section 93(2) or (3) or section 94(a) to conduct the mediation or adjudication concerned shall be construed as including references to the person appointed for that purpose pursuant to subsection (2).

(4) Subject to any rules under section 109, the manner in which a mediation or adjudication is conducted shall be at the discretion of the mediator or adjudicator concerned but it shall be the duty of that person to ensure that the mediation or adjudication is conducted without undue formality.

Chapter 5

Tenancy Tribunal

Tenancy Tribunals and the "Tribunal".

102.—(1) From time to time as occasion requires the Board shall cause to be constituted, for the purposes of this Part, one or more tribunals which or each of which shall be known as a "Tenancy Tribunal". **[18–102]**

(2) A reference in section 103 or any other provision of this Act to the "Tribunal" is a reference to whichever of the tribunals constituted under this section the provision concerned falls to be applied.

Membership of Tribunal, etc.

103.—(1) The number of members of the Tribunal shall be 3. **[18–103]**

(2) Each of the members of the Tribunal shall be a person who is, for the time being, a member of the Dispute Resolution Committee.

(3) The members of the Tribunal shall be appointed by the Board.

(4) One of the members of the Tribunal shall be the chairperson of the Tribunal; subject to subsection (5), the Board shall determine which of the members shall be the chairperson.

(5) If a member of the Board is a member of the Tribunal he or she shall be the chairperson of the Tribunal or, if 2 or more members of the Board are members of the Tribunal, whichever of them the Board determines shall be the chairperson.

(6) The Tribunal shall be independent in the performance of its functions.

(7) A decision of a majority of the members of the Tribunal suffices for any purpose.

Chapter 6

Dispute resolution by Tribunal

Determination of disputes by Tribunal: procedures generally.

104.—(1) This section and the other sections of this Chapter contain the principal provisions regarding the procedures to be adopted by the Tribunal in relation to the determination by it of a dispute, whether that dispute— **[18–104]**

(a) has been referred to it by the Board under section 94 (which provides for the direct reference of a matter without mediation or adjudication taking place in relation to it),

(b) has been referred to it by the Board under section 96(6) (which provides for the reference of a matter after mediation has not resulted in the matter being resolved), or

(c) is the subject of an appeal under section 100 from a determination of an adjudicator of the matter.

(2) The Tribunal shall hold one or more hearings for the purposes of determining the dispute.

(3) The parties to the dispute shall be given by the Tribunal notice (to be of the duration specified in subsection (5)) of the holding of a hearing.

(4) The following information shall be included in such a notice—

(a) the date, time, venue and purpose of the hearing,

(b) an outline of the substance of the matters to be dealt with at the hearing,

(c) an outline of the procedures to be adopted at the hearing,

(d) a reference to the provisions of this Act and any rules made under it that are relevant to the holding of the hearing,

(e) a statement that the Tribunal will, unless substantial grounds arise for its deciding to do otherwise, proceed with the hearing at the date and time concerned notwithstanding that a party does not attend the hearing,

(f) a statement that the Tribunal will determine the dispute notwithstanding that a party does not take part in the proceedings before the Tribunal, and

(g) any other information the Tribunal considers appropriate.

(5) The duration of the notice under subsection (3) shall be—

(a) at least 21 days beginning on the date of the giving of the notice, or

(b) such lesser period as the Board may specify where—

(i) one or more of the parties requests the Board to specify such a period and the other party or parties consent to such a specification, or

(ii) the dispute concerns alleged behaviour by the landlord or the tenant that poses an imminent danger of death or serious injury or imminent danger to the fabric of the dwelling concerned or the property containing that dwelling.

(6) Each of the parties shall be entitled to and be given the opportunity to be heard at the hearing and to be represented and to present evidence and witnesses before the Tribunal.

(7) In the case of an appeal under section 100, the Tribunal may have regard to the report of the adjudicator.

Provisions in relation to evidence, summoning of witnesses, etc.

[18–105] 105.—(1) The Tribunal may require that the evidence of a witness before it be given on oath.

(2) Each witness of a party before the Tribunal (including the party as a witness) may be cross-examined by or on behalf of every other party.

(3) For the purposes of its functions under this Part, the Tribunal may—

(a) summon witnesses to attend before it,

(b) administer an oath, and

(c) require any person to produce to the Tribunal any document in his or her power or control.

(4) A witness before the Tribunal shall be entitled to the same immunities and privileges as if he or she were a witness before the High Court.

(5) Any person who—

(a) on being duly summoned as a witness before the Tribunal and having had tendered to him or her the sum, if any, which has been directed under subsection (6)(a) to be paid in respect of the expenses of his or her attendance makes default in attending,

(b) being in attendance as a witness refuses to take an oath legally required by the Tribunal to be taken, or to produce any document in his or her power or control legally required by the Tribunal to be produced by him or her, or to answer any question to which the Tribunal may legally require an answer, or

(c) does any other thing which, if the Tribunal were a court having power to commit for contempt of court, would be contempt of such court,

is guilty of an offence.

(6) The Tribunal may, out of moneys at the disposal of the Board, direct that the whole or part of the reasonable expenses—

(a) that will be incurred by a person summoned to attend before it in so attending, or

(b) that have been incurred by a person summoned to attend before it in so attending,

shall, as it thinks appropriate, be paid to him or her before he or she so attends or, as the case may be, be re-imbursed to him or her.

Proceedings to be in public.

106.—(1) Proceedings before the Tribunal shall be conducted in public; this is without prejudice to an order that may be made under subsection (2). **[18–106]**

(2) In the particular circumstances of a case, if the Board considers it appropriate to do so, it may make an order directing that the identities of all or one or more of the parties to a dispute over which the Tribunal has jurisdiction shall not be disclosed.

(3) A person who contravenes an order under subsection (2) is guilty of an offence.

Adjournments of hearing.

107.—The Tribunal may adjourn the hearing by it of a matter until a date specified by it. **[18–107]**

Determination by Tribunal of dispute and notification to Board.

108.—(1) Unless it has sooner made a determination of the kind specified in subsection (2), the Tribunal shall, on completion of its hearing in relation to the dispute, make its determination in relation to the dispute and notify the Board of that determination. **[18–108]**

(2) The determination firstly mentioned in subsection (1) is a decision by the Tribunal not to deal with the dispute in accordance with section 85; such a determination shall be notified to the Board by the Tribunal.

Chapter 7

Supplementary procedural matters

Power of Board to make procedural rules.

109.—(1) The procedure to be followed under this Part in relation to a dispute shall, subject to this Part, be such as shall be determined by the Board by rules made by it with the consent of the Minister. **[18–109]**

(2) Without prejudice to the generality of subsection (1), rules under this section may—

(a) specify the forms to be used for referring a dispute to the Board under this Part,

(b) require specified notifications to be given in respect of the referral of a dispute to the Board under this Part,

(c) specify that a fee of specified amount shall be paid to the Board in respect of the Board's initially dealing with a dispute or the following of any other procedure under this Part in relation to it,

(d) specify the period within which—

(i) a mediator or adjudicator must be appointed under section 93(2) or (3) or section 94(a) to deal with or determine a dispute referred to the Board,

(ii) a mediator or adjudicator must furnish his or her report under section 95 or 99 to the Board,

(iii) the Board must serve the documents referred to in subsection (1) of section 96 on each of the parties and ascertain the matters referred to in that section,

(iv) the Board must serve the documents referred to in section 99(3) on each of the parties,

(v) a dispute must be referred under section 94, 96(6) or 100 to the Tribunal,

(vi) the Board must, from the date of receipt by it of a determination of an adjudicator under section 97(4)(a) (contained in a report made to it under section 99), make a determination order on foot of that determination,

(vii) the Tribunal must, from the date of a dispute being referred to it, or a determination in relation to a dispute being appealed to it, arrange a hearing in relation to the dispute,

(viii) the Tribunal must, from the date of completion by it of a hearing or hearings in relation to a dispute, make its determination in relation to the dispute,

(ix) the Board must, from the date of receipt by it of a determination of the Tribunal under section 108 make a determination order on foot of that determination, and

(x) the Board must make an application under section 124 to enforce a determination order on being notified that that order is not being complied with.

(3) In the absence of a specification, by rules under this section, of the period within which a thing referred to in a provision of this Act specified in subsection (2)(d) must be done, the provision shall be construed as requiring the thing to be done as soon as practicable after the doing of the thing that immediately precedes it.

Title to lands or property not to be drawn into question.

[18–110] 110.—The title to any lands or property shall not be drawn into question in any proceedings before a mediator, an adjudicator or the Tribunal under this Part.

Power to enter and inspect dwelling.

[18–111] 111.—(1) Subject to subsection (3), a mediator, an adjudicator or a member of the Tribunal or the Board who is dealing with a dispute under this Part may, for the purposes of his or her functions under this Part, enter and inspect any dwelling to which the dispute relates.

(2) The powers under subsection (1) may be exercised in relation to a dwelling to which a dispute relates even though the dwelling is occupied by a person who takes no part in the proceedings concerned or initially takes part in them but subsequently withdraws from them.

(3) The powers under subsection (1) shall not, without the consent of that person, be exercised in relation to a dwelling occupied by a person referred to in subsection (2) unless, at least 24 hours before the date on which the person concerned intends to exercise those powers, he or she serves on the first mentioned person a notice of that intention.

(4) A person mentioned in subsection (1) may authorise in writing a person who he or she is satisfied has an expertise in any area relevant to the dispute concerned (for example, engineering, valuation or surveying) to exercise the powers under that subsection in relation to the dwelling concerned; a person so authorised shall, if requested, produce to any person concerned his or her authorisation under this subsection before exercising the powers under subsection (1).

(5) A person who obstructs or impedes a person mentioned in subsection (1), or a person authorised under subsection (4), in the exercise of his or her powers under this section is guilty of an offence.

Obligations of confidentiality.

112.—(1) A mediator or adjudicator shall not disclose to any person any statement or information of a confidential nature made or supplied to the mediator or adjudicator in connection with the performance of his or her functions under this Part unless one or more of the conditions specified in subsection (2) is complied with. **[18–112]**

(2) The conditions referred to in subsection (1) are—

(a) the person who makes the statement or supplies the information consents to its disclosure,

(b) the mediator or adjudicator has reasonable grounds for believing that the disclosure is necessary to prevent or reduce the danger of injury to any person or damage to any property,

(c) the disclosure is for the purpose of proceedings for an offence under section 113,

(d) it would not be possible for the mediator or adjudicator to deal with or determine the dispute concerned without disclosing the statement or information.

(3) A statement or information is of a confidential nature for the purposes of subsection (1) if—

(a) it was expressed to be of such a nature by the maker or supplier of it to the mediator or adjudicator, or

(b) from the circumstances in which it was made or supplied to him or her or its subject matter, the mediator or adjudicator ought reasonably to have concluded that it was of such a nature.

(4) A person who contravenes subsection (1) is guilty of an offence.

Offence of providing false information to Board.

113.—A person is guilty of an offence if— **[18–113]**

(a) he or she makes a statement or supplies information to an adjudicator, the Tribunal or the Board in connection with the performance by the adjudicator, Tribunal or Board of his or her or its functions under this Part in relation to a dispute,

(b) that statement or information is false or misleading in a material respect, and

(c) the person knows that that statement or information is so false or misleading.

Certain proceedings and acts privileged.

[18–114] 114.—(1) Any report or other document prepared, or communication made, by the Board, the Tribunal, a mediator or an adjudicator for the purposes of, or in connection with, proceedings under this Part dealt with by it or him or her shall, for the purposes of the law of defamation, enjoy absolute privilege.

(2) Any report or other document prepared, or communication made, by the Board, the Tribunal, a mediator or an adjudicator that does not fall within subsection (1) but which is prepared or made for the purposes of, or in connection with, the performance by it or him or her of functions under this or any other Part of this Act shall, for the purposes of the law of defamation, enjoy qualified privilege.

Chapter 8

Redress that may be granted under this Part

Redress that may be granted on foot of determination.

[18–115] 115.—(1) A power conferred by this Part on an adjudicator or the Tribunal to make a determination in relation to a dispute includes a power to make such declarations or give such directions as the adjudicator or the Tribunal thinks appropriate for the purpose of providing relief to one, or more than one as appropriate, of the parties.

(2) Without prejudice to the generality of subsection (1) and the subsequent provisions of this Chapter, one or more of the following declarations or directions, as appropriate, may be made or given in respect of a dispute—

(a) a direction that a specified amount of rent or other charge shall be paid on, or on and from, or by a specified date,

(b) a declaration as to whether or not an amount of rent set under a tenancy of a dwelling complies with section 19(1) (and if the declaration is that that amount does not so comply, the declaration shall be accompanied by an indication by the adjudicator or the Tribunal as to what amount, in his or her or its opinion, would comply with section 19(1)),

(c) a direction as to the return or payment, in whole or in part, of the amount of a deposit,

(d) a direction that a specified amount of damages or costs or both be paid,

(e) a direction that a dwelling be quitted by a specified date,

(f) a declaration as to the validity or otherwise of a notice of termination of a tenancy,

(g) a declaration with regard to the right to return to, or continue in, occupation of a dwelling (and such a declaration may include provision to the effect that any period of interruption in possession that has occurred is to be disregarded for one or more purposes),

(h) a declaration that a term of a lease or tenancy agreement is void by reason of section 184,

(i) in the special circumstances of a dispute heard under this Part, a direction that the whole or part of the costs or expenses incurred by the adjudicator or the Tribunal in dealing with the dispute shall be paid by one or more of the parties.

(3) The amount (or, as appropriate, the aggregate of the amounts), other than costs or expenses of whatsoever kind, that an adjudicator or the Tribunal may direct to be paid to a party in respect of the matter (or, as appropriate, all of the matters) the subject of a dispute referred to the Board for resolution shall not exceed—

(a) if the amount or amounts consist solely of damages — €20,000,

(b) if the amount or amounts consist solely of an amount or amounts by way of arrears of rent or other charges — €20,000 or an amount equal to twice the annual rent of the dwelling concerned, whichever is the higher (but subject to a maximum under this paragraph of €60,000),

(c) if the amount or amounts consist of both damages and an amount or amounts referred to in paragraph (b)—

(i) in so far as the amount or amounts consist of damages — €20,000,

(ii) in so far as the amount or amounts consist of such other amount or amounts — €20,000 or an amount equal to twice the annual rent of the dwelling concerned, whichever is the higher (but subject to a maximum under this subparagraph of €60,000).

Determination may require sub-tenancy to be quitted in certain cases.

116.—If— **[18–116]**

(a) the determination of an adjudicator or the Tribunal includes a direction that a dwelling, the subject of a tenancy, be quitted by a specified date,

(b) that tenancy is one out of which a sub-tenancy has been created, and

(c) the landlord, when he or she served a notice of termination on the tenant in respect of that tenancy, required the tenant to terminate that sub-tenancy,

then the determination may include a direction requiring the subtenant to quit the dwelling by a specified date.

Redress of an interim nature may be granted.

117.—(1) In addition to the powers conferred by this Part with respect to the determination of disputes, an adjudicator or the Tribunal, in dealing with a dispute, may give such directions as he or she or it thinks appropriate for the purpose of providing relief of an interim nature to one, or more than one as appropriate, of the parties. **[18–117]**

(2) Such a direction shall indicate that the relief it provides for may not necessarily be the relief provided for by the final determination made in the matter.

(3) As soon as such a direction is given, the adjudicator or the Tribunal shall reduce it to writing and forward it immediately to the Board.

(4) This section is without prejudice to section 189 and the power under subsection (1) may not be exercised in a manner which is inconsistent with or would derogate from any interim or interlocutory relief granted by the Circuit Court under that section.

Discretion to refuse direction for possession.

[18–118] 118.—(1) If the inclusion of a direction in a determination that a party ("the first-mentioned person") be permitted to resume possession of a dwelling, the subject of a tenancy, would cause hardship or injustice to a person ("the second-mentioned person") not party to the dispute who is in possession of that dwelling, then the determination may, instead of including such a direction, include—

(a) a declaration that the first-mentioned person was wrongfully deprived of possession of the dwelling, and

(b) a direction that damages of a specified amount be paid by the landlord to that person in respect of that deprivation.

(2) In deciding whether the inclusion in a determination of a direction of the kind firstly mentioned in subsection (1) would cause hardship or injustice to the second-mentioned person, the matters to which regard shall be had shall include—

(a) the length of time the second-mentioned person has been in possession of the dwelling concerned,

(b) any involvement the second-mentioned person may have had in the first-mentioned person being deprived of possession of the dwelling, and

(c) any knowledge the second-mentioned person may have had, before he or she took possession of the dwelling, of the existence of a dispute concerning the right of the first-mentioned person to possession of the dwelling.

(3) The second-mentioned person shall be afforded an opportunity to make submissions with regard to whether a determination should include a direction of the kind firstly mentioned in subsection (1); if necessary, for that purpose, the proceedings concerned shall be adjourned and the second-mentioned person notified of the matter.

Certain directions to be given in the case of arrears of rent.

[18–119] 119.—(1) Any amount of arrears stipulated to be paid by a determination shall be the gross amount of the rent and other charges (if any) concerned which the adjudicator or the Tribunal considers to be in arrears as reduced by—

(a) any relevant debts due, in the opinion of the adjudicator or the Tribunal, by the landlord to the tenant in accordance with section 48 of the Landlord and Tenant Law Amendment Act Ireland 1860,

(b) any set-off for expenditure on repairs the tenant would be entitled to make under section 87 of the Landlord and Tenant (Amendment) Act 1980,

(c) any compensation due by the landlord to the tenant in circumstances where section 61 of the Landlord and Tenant (Amendment) Act 1980 applies,

(d) any other amount which the adjudicator or the Tribunal considers warranted in the circumstances of the case,

and as increased by any amount that the adjudicator or the Tribunal, in all the circumstances of the matter, considers appropriate in respect of—

(i) costs reasonably incurred by the landlord in pursuit of the arrears of rent,

(ii) damages,

(iii) an amount in respect of the cost of any repairs which fell to be carried out by reason of the failure of the tenant to comply with section 16(f).

(2) A determination of an adjudicator or the Tribunal in respect of an amount referred to in subsection (1) shall, if any of paragraphs (a) to (d) or paragraphs (i) to

(iii) of that subsection have had to be applied in calculating the amount, indicate how the amount was calculated by reason of the application of the paragraph or paragraphs concerned.

Circumstances of landlord or tenant not to be taken account of in certain cases.

120.—(1) If the dispute being dealt with by a mediator, adjudicator or the Tribunal relates to the amount of the rent that ought to be set under a tenancy at a particular time or as to when a review of such rent ought to take place, the circumstances, financial or otherwise, of the landlord or tenant may not be taken into consideration— **[18–120]**

(a) by the mediator in taking any of the steps mentioned in section 95, or

(b) by the adjudicator or the Tribunal in determining the dispute.

(2) The reference in subsection (1) to the setting of the rent under a tenancy shall be construed in accordance with section 19(2).

CHAPTER 9

Determination orders and enforcement generally

Determination orders.

121.—(1) Each of the following— **[18–121]**

(a) an agreement mentioned in a report of a mediator under section 95(4),

(b) a determination mentioned in a report of an adjudicator under section 99,

(c) a determination of the Tribunal notified to the Board under section 108,

(d) a direction given by an adjudicator or the Tribunal under section 82(5) or 117,

shall be the subject of a written record (in this Act referred to as a "determination order") prepared by the Board and issued by it to the parties concerned.

(2) A determination order shall contain the terms of the agreement, determination or direction concerned; those terms may be expressed in the order in a manner different from the manner in which they are expressed in the agreement, determination or direction if the Board considers it appropriate to do so for the purpose mentioned in subsection (3).

(3) That purpose is to remove any ambiguity that the Board considers exists in the terms of the agreement, determination or direction or to clarify, generally, those terms in a manner that it considers will be of benefit to the parties or will facilitate compliance with the agreement, determination or direction.

(4) In considering whether it is appropriate to exercise the power under subsection (2) with respect to the terms of a particular agreement or determination referred to in paragraph (a) or (b) of subsection (1), the Board shall have regard to—

(a) in the case of such an agreement, the relevant document furnished to it under section 95(6),

(b) in the case of such a determination, the relevant report of the adjudicator furnished to it under section 99(2).

(5) In the case of doubt as to whether it is appropriate to exercise that power the Board may also consult with, as appropriate, the mediator, the adjudicator or the Tribunal and with the parties themselves.

(6) The seal of the Board shall be affixed to a determination order.

(7) Subsection (1) is, in the case of an agreement to which paragraph (a) of that subsection applies, subject to subsections (4) and (5) of section 96.

(8) The reference in subsection (1)(b) to a determination mentioned in a report of an adjudicator under section 99 does not include a reference to such a determination against which an appeal has been made under, and in accordance with, section 100 unless that appeal has been subsequently abandoned.

Provision to ensure consistency between determinations.

[18–122] 122.—(1) If, on consideration of a determination of the Tribunal, the Board is of opinion that the determination is not consistent with previous determinations of the Tribunal in relation to disputes of a similar nature to the dispute concerned then the Board may exercise the powers under subsection (2).

(2) Those powers are—

(a) to notify the members of the Tribunal who made the determination concerned of that opinion and request each of them to submit any views he or she has in relation to the matter to the Board,

(b) having had regard to the views, if any, submitted by those members to it, pursuant to that request, to notify the parties to the dispute concerned of that opinion and request each of them to indicate whether he or she consents to a fresh determination being made pursuant to paragraph (c) by the Tribunal in relation to the dispute or wishes to make representations to the Board in relation to the matter,

(c) if the parties consent to such a fresh determination being made or the Board, having had regard to the representations, if any, made to it by one or more of them pursuant to the request under paragraph (b), considers it appropriate to direct the Tribunal to do so, to direct the Tribunal to make a fresh determination in relation to the dispute.

(3) The making of any such fresh determination shall be preceded by a re-hearing of the matter by the Tribunal and the provisions of Chapters 5 to 7 shall apply accordingly.

(4) For the purposes of subsection (1), one dispute is of a similar nature to another dispute if the issues involved in each of them are the same and the facts that gave rise to each of them, as appearing from any record kept by the Tribunal in relation to its proceedings or any other record available to the Board, are the same in all material respects.

Binding nature of determination orders.

[18–123] 123.—(1) A determination order embodying the terms of an agreement mentioned in a mediator's report under section 95(4) or the determination of an adjudicator under section 97 shall become binding on the parties concerned on the order being issued to them.

(2) A determination order embodying the terms of a determination of the Tribunal shall, on the expiry of the relevant period, become binding on the parties concerned unless, before that expiry, an appeal in relation to the determination is made under subsection (3).

(3) Any of the parties concerned may appeal to the High Court, within the relevant period, from a determination of the Tribunal (as embodied in a determination order) on a point of law.

(4) The determination of the High Court on such an appeal in relation to the point of law concerned shall be final and conclusive.

(5) The High Court may, as a consequence of the determination it so makes, direct the Board to cancel the determination order concerned or to vary it in such manner as the Court specifies and the Board shall cancel or vary the order accordingly; if the cancellation or variation directed to be made relates to a determination of the Tribunal not to deal with the dispute in accordance with section 85, the Board shall, in addition, refer all or part, as appropriate, of the dispute to the Tribunal for determination by the Tribunal and the provisions of this Part shall, with any necessary modifications, apply to that determination.

(6) References in section 124 to a determination order shall, where that order embodies the terms of a determination of the Tribunal, be construed as references to—

- (a) such an order as respects which an appeal against the determination embodied in it has not been made under this section within the relevant period or, if such appeal has been brought, it has been abandoned, or
- (b) if such an appeal has been brought (and the result of the appeal does not require the Board to cancel the order under subsection (5)), as the case may be—
  - (i) such an order in the terms as it was originally made, or
  - (ii) such an order in the terms as it stands following the variation of it by the Board under subsection (5).

(7) The Board may publish, in such manner as it thinks fit—

- (a) a determination order issued by it (including such an order as it stands varied by it under subsection (5)),
- (b) notice of the cancellation of such an order under subsection (5) or section 125.

(8) In this section "relevant period" means the period of 21 days beginning on the date that the determination order concerned is issued to the parties.

Enforcement of determination orders.

124.—(1) If the Board or a party mentioned in a determination order is satisfied that another party has failed to comply with one or more terms of that order, the Board or the first-mentioned party may make an application under this section to the Circuit Court for an order under subsection (2). **[18–124]**

(2) On such an application and subject to section 125, the Circuit Court shall make an order directing the party concerned (the "respondent") to comply with the term or terms concerned if it is satisfied that the respondent has failed to comply with that term or those terms, unless—

- (a) it considers there are substantial reasons (related to one or more of the matters mentioned in subsection (3)) for not making an order under this subsection, or
- (b) the respondent shows to the satisfaction of the court that one of the matters specified in subsection (3) applies in relation to the determination order.

(3) The matters mentioned in subsection (2) are—

- (a) a requirement of procedural fairness was not complied with in the relevant proceedings under this Part,

(b) a material consideration was not taken account of in those proceedings or account was taken in those proceedings of a consideration that was not material,

(c) a manifestly erroneous decision in relation to a legal issue was made in those proceedings,

(d) the determination made by the adjudicator or the Tribunal, as the case may be, on the evidence before the adjudicator or Tribunal, was manifestly erroneous.

(4) If, on the hearing of an application under this section, it appears by credible testimony that there is reason to believe the respondent will be unable to pay the costs of the applicant of so much of the hearing as relates to the determination of whether any of the matters specified in subsection (3) have been established by the respondent (in the event that none of them is established) the court may require sufficient security to be given for those costs.

(5) If the determination order, the subject of an application under this section, is one requiring a dwelling to be vacated and—

(a) the basis for that requirement is that the tenancy concerned was validly terminated by service of a notice of termination, and

(b) that notice was served by reason of the tenant's failure to pay an amount of rent due,

the court may, before hearing any arguments or receiving any evidence in relation to whether any of the matters specified in subsection (3) have been established, require the respondent to lodge in court or pay to the applicant, as it thinks appropriate, that amount of rent together with such amount as it specifies in respect of the dwelling's continued occupation by the respondent after the service of that notice.

(6) If the applicant under this section is not the Board, the respondent shall give notice to the Board that he or she proposes to oppose the application and the Board shall be entitled to appear and be heard at the hearing of the application.

(7) The court may make such ancillary or other orders as it considers just on the hearing of an application under this section.

(8) The Board may furnish to the registrar of the court such information derived from the register as, in its opinion, is likely to assist in the execution of an order made by the court under subsection (2) (including, if the court gives a direction authorising the Board to give that number to the registrar, the personal public service number of any party concerned).

(9) An application under this section to the Circuit Court shall be made to the judge of the Circuit Court for the circuit in which the tenancy or dwelling concerned is or was situated.

Cancellation of determination orders in cases of non-appearance.

[18–125] 125.—(1) A person who establishes to the satisfaction of—

(a) the Board, or

(b) if the determination order is the subject of an application under section 124, the Circuit Court, on the hearing of that application,

that, in relation to a determination order embodying the terms of a determination of the Tribunal or an adjudicator, there are good and substantial reasons for his or her having failed to appear at the relevant hearing conducted by the Tribunal or the adjudicator, the Board or the Circuit Court may, subject to subsection (3), exercise the powers referred to in subsection (2).

(2) The powers mentioned in subsection (1) are to cancel the determination order and direct that a fresh determination of the matter shall be made by the adjudicator or the Tribunal as appropriate (and the making of any such fresh determination shall be preceded by a re-hearing of the matter by the adjudicator or the Tribunal and the provisions of Chapters 4 to 7 shall apply accordingly).

(3) The Board or the Circuit Court, as the case may be, may direct that that cancellation shall not have effect unless specified conditions are, within a specified period, complied with by the person referred to in subsection (1) (being conditions analogous to the terms the High Court may impose under the Rules of the Superior Courts (SI No. 15 of 1986) for setting aside a judgment obtained in circumstances where one of the parties did not appear at the trial concerned).

(4) Without prejudice to subsection (3), if it is sought to oppose an application under section 124 on the grounds that the determination order ought to be cancelled under this section, subsections (4) and (5) of section 124 shall apply as if references to the determination of, or evidence in relation to, whether any of the matters specified in subsection (3) of that section have been established include references to the determination of, or evidence in relation to, the issue as to whether the grounds for the court's exercising its powers under this section have been established.

(5) The Board, before deciding whether to exercise the powers under this section, shall afford the other party or parties concerned an opportunity to be heard.

(6) The reference in subsection (3) to the Rules of the Superior Courts is a reference to those Rules as amended for the time being; if those Rules should be revoked then the reference to them in that subsection shall be read as a reference to such rules corresponding to those Rules as may be for the time being in force.

Offence for failure to comply with determination order.

126.—(1) A person who fails to comply with one or more terms of a determination order is guilty of an offence. **[18–126]**

(2) Subsection (1) has effect notwithstanding the means provided under section 124 for enforcement of a determination order.

(3) A person convicted of an offence under this section shall not be sentenced to any term of imprisonment in respect of that offence if he or she shows that the failure to comply with the term or terms concerned was due to his or her limited financial means.

PART 7 – REGISTRATION OF TENANCIES

Chapter 1

Private residential tenancies register

Establishment of register.

127.—(1) The Board shall, as soon as practicable after the establishment day, establish and maintain a register which shall be known as the "private residential tenancies register" and is in this Act referred to as the "register". **[18–127]**

Note: The establishment day for the purposes of Part 8 of this Act is 1 September 2004 —see the Residential Tenancies Act 2004 (Establishment Day) Order 2004 (SI No 525 of 2004) and see s149 of this Act.

(2) There shall be registered in the register each tenancy of a dwelling in the State the subject of an application for registration made under, and in accordance with, this Part.

(3) The form of the register, the types of information to be contained in it, the format of any aspect of that information and any other matters relevant to the maintenance of the register shall be such as the Board determines from time to time.

(4) Save under and in accordance with this Act and subject to subsection (5), no information contained in the register shall be disclosed to any person.

(5) Subsection (4) does not apply to a disclosure of information contained in the register by—

(a) a member of the Board,

(b) a member of a committee of the Board,

(c) a member of staff of the Board,

(d) a mediator or adjudicator, or

(e) a person whose services are provided to the Board under section 167,

in the performance of any of his or her functions under this Act, being a disclosure the making of which is necessary for the performance by him or her of any such function.

Published register.

[18–128] 128.—(1) The Board shall, as soon as practicable after the establishment of the register, prepare a document (in this Act referred to as the "published register").

(2) Subject to subsections (3) and (4), the published register shall consist of an extract of the information contained in the register.

(3) The extent of that extract shall be such as the Board determines is likely to make the published register useful to members of the public.

(4) The published register shall not contain any information, as respects a particular dwelling, that discloses or could reasonably lead to the disclosure of—

(a) the identity of the landlord or the tenant or tenants of the dwelling,

(b) the amount of the rent payable under a tenancy of the dwelling.

(5) The form of the published register, the format of any aspect of the information contained in it and any other matters relevant to its maintenance shall be such as the Board determines from time to time.

Inspection of published register.

[18–129] 129.—(1) The published register shall be kept at an office that is designated, for the time being, by the Board for that purpose.

(2) The published register shall be made available for inspection, at all reasonable times, at that office and by such other means, if any, as the Board may determine.

(3) A fee of such amount as the Board determines to be reasonable may be charged in respect of the inspection of the published register.

Register and published register may be kept in electronic form.

[18–130] 130.—The register and the published register may each be prepared and maintained otherwise than in a legible form but only if that form allows the particular register to be converted into a legible form and any entry in it to be copied or reproduced in a legible form.

Publication of aggregated details derived from register.

131.—(1) Without prejudice to section 128, the Board may publish details concerning the private rented sector derived from the register, being details of an aggregated nature. [18–131]

(2) In this section—

"details of an aggregated nature" means details of such a nature as could not reasonably lead to a disclosure of the kind mentioned in section 128(4) occurring;

"private rented sector" has the same meaning as it has in section 151.

Furnishing of entries in registers, etc.

132.—(1) On application by the landlord or tenant of a dwelling, the Board shall, on being supplied by the landlord or tenant with such information as it may require for the purpose of confirming the identity of the applicant concerned, provide to him or her a copy of the entry in respect of that dwelling in the register. [18–132]

(2) On application by a person who is not the landlord or tenant of a particular dwelling, the Board shall provide to him or her a copy of the entry in respect of that dwelling in the published register (but not the entry in the register).

(3) A fee of such amount as the Board determines to be reasonable may be charged in respect of the provision of a copy of an entry under subsection (1) or (2).

(4) A copy of an entry in the register or the published register purporting to be certified by an officer of the Board as being a true copy of that entry shall, without proof of that person's authority to so certify the copy, of any signature of the person appearing on the copy or that he or she is or was an officer of the Board, be received in evidence in any proceedings and shall be presumed to be such a copy unless the contrary is shown.

(5) Evidence that any particular matter in respect of a dwelling stood registered in the register on a particular date may be given by the production of a copy of the entry in respect of that dwelling under subsection (4) and which copy bears that date beside, or as part of, the certification mentioned in that subsection.

Confirmation to parties to tenancy as to particulars specified in an application under section 134.

133.—(1) Either party to a tenancy of a dwelling may request the Board to confirm to him or her what are the particulars specified in an application made under section 134 to register the tenancy. [18–133]

(2) The Board shall comply with such a request if it is satisfied, having been supplied by the person making the request with such information as it may require, that the person is a party to the tenancy.

CHAPTER 2

Procedure for registration

Obligation to apply to register tenancy.

134.—(1) The landlord of a dwelling shall apply to the Board to register the tenancy of the dwelling under this Part. [18–134]

(2) An application under this section shall be made—

(a) in the case of a tenancy that commences on a date that falls 3 or more months from the commencement of this Part — within 1 month from the commencement of the tenancy,

(b) in the case of a tenancy that has commenced on a date falling before or after the commencement of this Part (other than one to which paragraph (a) applies but including one that commenced before the passing of this Act)—

(i) in case it commenced before the passing of this Act — within 3 months from the commencement of this Part,

(ii) in any other case — within whichever of the following periods expires the later—

(I) the period of 3 months from the commencement of this Part, or

(II) the period of 1 month from the commencement of the tenancy.

(3) An application under this section shall be in the prescribed form and, subject to subsection (4), be accompanied by the fee specified in section 137.

(4) The foregoing requirement with respect to the application being accompanied by a fee does not apply in relation to an application (the "relevant application") by a person (the "applicant") in respect of a particular dwelling (the "relevant dwelling") if the application is made within the period specified in subsection (2)(a) or (b) and one of the following conditions is satisfied.

(5) Those conditions are that, in the 12 months preceding the relevant application—

(a) 2 applications, each accompanied by the fee specified in section 137, have been made under this section by the applicant in respect of the relevant dwelling (and each within the period specified in subsection (2)(a) or (b)),

(b) the applicant has paid, in respect of several applications falling within subsection (3) of section 137, the single fee referred to in subsection (2) of that section and the dwellings to which those several applications related included the relevant dwelling,

(c) an application, under the Housing (Registration of Rented Houses) Regulations 1996 and accompanied by the fee specified in those Regulations, to register a tenancy in respect of the relevant dwelling has been made by the applicant.

(6) An application under this section may not relate to more than one tenancy of a dwelling; accordingly separate applications under this section are required for separate tenancies.

Section 134: supplemental provisions.

[18–135] 135.—(1) For the avoidance of doubt—

(a) a fresh application must be made under section 134 in respect of each new tenancy that is created in respect of a dwelling,

(b) the fact that a tenancy is continued in being as a Part 4 tenancy does not give rise to any requirement under section 134 to apply to register the Part 4 tenancy, and

(c) the coming into being of a further Part 4 tenancy in respect of a dwelling does, however, give rise to a requirement under section 134 to apply to register that further Part 4 tenancy.

(2) The form used for making an application under section 134 shall—

(a) be signed by the landlord of the dwelling concerned or his or her authorised agent and bear the date on which it is so signed, and

(b) be signed by the tenant or each of the tenants, as the case may be, of the dwelling concerned and bear the date or dates on which it is signed by the tenant or tenants.

(3) The Board shall assign a unique number to each application made under section 134 to register a tenancy and that number shall be used by the Board as the reference number for the tenancy when it is registered.

(4) An acknowledgement, in such form as the Board considers appropriate, shall be given to an applicant under section 134 of the receipt by the Board of his or her application and the fee mentioned in subsection (3) of that section.

(5) When an application under section 134 is received by the Board that is incomplete or is not accompanied by the fee mentioned in subsection (3) of that section, the Board shall notify the applicant of the omission concerned and afford him or her a reasonable opportunity to rectify the matter.

Particulars to be specified in application under section 134.

136.—An application under section 134 shall contain the following particulars— **[18–136]**

(a) the address of the dwelling,

(b) the name, address for correspondence and personal public service number (if any) of the landlord and, where the application is made by his or her authorised agent, the name, address for correspondence and personal public service number (if any) of the agent,

(c) if the landlord is a company, the registered number and registered office of that company,

(d) if (where the application is made by the landlord's authorised agent) the authorised agent is a company, the registered number and registered office of that company,

(e) the number of occupants of the dwelling,

(f) the name and, unless it cannot be ascertained by reasonable inquiry, personal public service number of the tenant, or (as the case may be) of each of the tenants, of the dwelling,

(g) the name of the housing authority in whose functional area the dwelling is situated,

(h) if the dwelling is one of a number of dwellings comprising an apartment complex, the name of the management company (if any) of the complex and the registered number and registered office of that company,

(i) a description of the dwelling, indicating—

(i) the estimated floor area,

(ii) the number of bed spaces,

(iii) a statement as to which of the following categories it belongs namely, a whole or part of a house, a maisonette, an apartment, a flat or a bedsitter and, in case it falls within the category of a house or maisonette, an indication as to whether the house or maisonette is detached, semi-detached or terraced, and

(iv) the number of bedrooms,

(j) the date the tenancy of the dwelling commenced,

(k) the amount of the rent payable under that tenancy, the frequency with which it is required to be paid and any taxes or other charges required to be paid by the tenant,

(l) if the tenancy is for a fixed term, the period of that term,

(m) if the tenancy consists of a sub-letting, an indication to that effect,

(n) the number assigned under section 135(3) in respect of a previous tenancy that was registered under this Part in respect of the dwelling (but only if the particulars provided under paragraph (f) in respect of that tenancy were the same as those that are being provided, under that paragraph, in respect of the immediate tenancy), and

(o) such other matters as may be prescribed.

Fee to accompany application under section 134.

[18–137] 137.—(1) The fee to accompany an application under section 134 shall, subject to subsections (2) and (6), be—

(a) if the application is made in the period of 12 months beginning on the commencement of section 134, a fee of the amount of €70, or

(b) if the application is made in any subsequent period of 12 months—

(i) unless subparagraph (ii) applies, a fee of that amount, or

(ii) such fee of a greater or lesser amount as may stand declared for the time being under section 138(1) for the purposes of this paragraph.

(2) The requirement under section 134(3) for a fee specified in this section to accompany an application under section 134 shall be regarded as satisfied, as respects the applications mentioned in subsection (3), if the applicant mentioned in that subsection opts to pay to the Board a single fee of the amount specified in subsection (4) in respect of those applications.

(3) The applications referred to in subsection (2) are applications made by the same person at the same time in respect of tenancies of dwellings comprised in the same property.

(4) The amount of the single fee referred to in subsection (2) is—

(a) if the applications concerned are made in the period of 12 months beginning on the commencement of section 134, €300, or

(b) if the applications concerned are made in any subsequent period of 12 months—

(i) unless subparagraph (ii) applies, €300, or

(ii) such greater or lesser amount as may stand declared for the time being under section 138(1) for the purposes of this paragraph.

(5) The option of paying the single fee referred to in subsection (2) is not available to the person mentioned in subsection (3) if the applications concerned are not made within the period specified in section 134(2)(a) or (b).

(6) If an application under section 134 is not made within the period specified in subsection (2)(a) or (b) of that section then the fee to accompany that application shall be a fee of an amount that is double the amount referred to in paragraph (a) or (b)(i) or, as the case may be, paragraph (b)(ii) of subsection (1).

Variation of fee in line with changes in value of money.

138.—(1) If the Board is satisfied that, having regard to changes in the value of money generally in the State that have occurred in— [18–138]

(a) any period ending on or before the date that falls 12 months after the commencement of section 134, or

(b) any period subsequent to that date,

it is appropriate for it to declare a fee of a greater or lesser amount than—

(i) in the case of section 137(1)(b)—

(I) €70, or

(II) the amount that was last previously declared (in exercise of the power under this section) for the purposes of that provision,

or

(ii) in the case of section 137(4)(b)—

(I) €300, or

(II) the amount that was last previously declared (in exercise of the power under this section) for the purposes of that provision,

it may, subject to subsection (2), declare in writing, for the purposes of subsection (1)(b) or (4)(b) of section 137, a fee of such a greater or lesser amount.

(2) The amount (expressed as a percentage) by which the amount of a fee declared under this section is greater or lesser than the amount of the relevant fee mentioned in subsection (1) shall be such as, in the opinion of the Board, approximates to the percentage increase or decrease in the value of money generally in the State that has occurred in—

(a) unless paragraph (b) applies, the period beginning on the commencement of section 134 and ending on the making of the declaration, or

(b) if the power under this section has previously been exercised for the purpose of subsection (1)(b) or (4)(b) of section 137, as the case may be, the period beginning on the date that that power was last exercised and ending on the making of the declaration.

CHAPTER 3

Updating of register and enforcement of requirement to register

Updating of particulars entered in the register.

139.—(1) Within 1 month from an alteration of the rent payable under a tenancy registered in the register taking effect, the landlord under the tenancy shall furnish to the Board the information mentioned in subsection (2) in the prescribed form. [18–139]

(2) That information is—

(a) the amount of that rent as it stands altered and the date from which that alteration took effect, and

(b) so far as any of the other matters in respect of which particulars were entered in the register in respect of the tenancy have changed in any material respect since, as appropriate—

(i) the tenancy was registered in the register, or

(ii) information in respect of them was last previously furnished to the Board under subsection (1),

particulars in respect of those other matters as they stand at the date of this furnishing of information under subsection (1).

(3) No fee shall be payable in respect of the furnishing to the Board of the information mentioned in this section.

(4) The Board, as soon as may be after receipt of the information mentioned in this section, shall amend the relevant particulars in the register with respect to the tenancy concerned.

Amendment of register by Board of its own volition.

[18–140] 140.—(1) If the Board becomes aware that any particular entered in the register is incorrect it shall amend the register to correct the matter.

(2) For the purpose of complying with subsection (1) and, in particular, for the purpose of determining what needs to be stated in the register by way of correction of the matter, the Board may make such inquiries as it thinks fit (whether of the landlord or tenant under the tenancy concerned or any other person).

Deletion from register of a tenancy.

[18–141] 141.—(1) Where, in the opinion of the landlord of the dwelling, a dwelling in respect of which a tenancy has been registered in the register has ceased to be a dwelling to which this Act applies, the landlord shall notify in writing the Board of that opinion and the grounds for it.

(2) That notification shall be made within 1 month from the date that, in the opinion of the landlord, the cessation concerned occurred.

(3) Having considered the grounds stated in a notification made to it under subsection (1), the Board shall—

(a) if it is satisfied that the dwelling concerned is no longer a dwelling to which this Act applies, delete the entry in the register in respect of the dwelling and notify the landlord of that deletion, or

(b) if it is not satisfied that the dwelling is no longer a dwelling to which this Act applies, notify the landlord that it is not so satisfied.

(4) For the avoidance of doubt, no refund of the whole or part of the fee charged under section 134 in respect of the registration under this Part of the dwelling concerned may be made to the landlord in a case to which subsection (3)(a) applies.

(5) Despite the deletion, under subsection (3)(a), of the entry in the register in respect of a tenancy of a dwelling, the Board may, if it considers it appropriate to do so for the purpose of its functions under section 151, keep a record of all or any of the particulars in respect of that tenancy that were contained in the entry.

Presumption in relation to date of commencement of tenancy.

[18–142] 142.—In any proceedings under Part 6, it shall be presumed until the contrary is shown that the date stated in the register as the date on which the tenancy, the subject of the proceedings, commenced is the date on which that tenancy commenced.

Offence for furnishing false or misleading information.

[18–143] 143.—A person who, in purported compliance with section 134 or 139, furnishes information to the Board which is false or misleading in a material respect knowing it to be so false or misleading or being reckless as to whether it is so false or misleading is guilty of an offence.

Provision in aid of enforcement of registration requirements.

144.—(1) If it appears to the Board that a particular tenancy that ought to be registered in the register has not been the subject of an application for registration under section 134, it shall serve the notice referred to in subsection (2) on the person whom it considers to be the landlord under that tenancy. **[18–144]**

(2) That notice is a notice—

(a) stating the Board's opinion that the tenancy mentioned in the notice is required to be registered in the register and, accordingly, that an application for registration of the tenancy under section 134 must be made by the addressee of the notice, and

(b) requesting the addressee of the notice to furnish to the Board, within a period specified in the notice, the reasons why the addressee considers (if such be the case) that the opinion is not well founded.

(3) If the addressee of the notice referred to in subsection (2)—

(a) does not furnish to the Board, in accordance with the notice, the reasons requested, or

(b) furnishes, in accordance with the notice, reasons to the Board which do not result in its altering the opinion stated in that notice,

the Board shall (unless an application has by then been made under section 134 to register the tenancy) serve a further notice on the addressee stating that he or she is required to apply to the Board under section 134 to register the tenancy in the register and that, if he or she fails to do so within 14 days from the receipt by him or her of the notice, he or she is guilty of an offence.

(4) A person who fails to comply with a notice under subsection (3) within the period of 14 days from the receipt by him or her of the notice is guilty of an offence.

(5) For the purpose of a person's complying with the requirement in a notice under subsection (2) or (3) to register a tenancy under section 134, that section shall apply as if subsection (2) were omitted from it (but for that purpose only and not so as to affect the application of section 137(6) (fee of double the ordinary amount to be paid on late application)).

(6) Proceedings for an offence under subsection (4) may not be brought if more than a year has elapsed between the date of service of the notice under subsection (2) and of the notice under subsection (3) in relation to the matter concerned.

(7) The reference in subsection (1) to a particular tenancy that ought to be registered shall be deemed to include a reference to a tenancy which, in the opinion of the Board, exists in respect of a dwelling and, accordingly, ought to be registered; where the Board is of that opinion in respect of a dwelling then the notice referred to in subsection (2) concerning that dwelling shall expressly state that as part of the opinion stated by the Board in the notice.

Further provisions in aid of enforcement of registration requirements.

145.—(1) A person authorised in writing by the Board for the purposes of this section as respects the particular dwelling may, at all reasonable times, enter into and inspect a dwelling for the purposes of determining the correctness of any particular **[18–145]** specified in an application made under section 134 in respect of a tenancy of that dwelling.

(2) A person shall not be authorised under subsection (1) unless the Board has reasonable grounds for believing that a particular specified in the application mentioned in that subsection is false or misleading in a material respect.

(3) A person who obstructs or impedes a person authorised under subsection (1) in the exercise by that person of his or her powers under that subsection is guilty of an offence.

(4) If it appears to the Board that a particular tenancy that ought to be registered in the register has not been the subject of an application for registration under section 134 it may, by service of a notice on the tenant under the tenancy, require the tenant to supply to it, within a period specified in the notice, the name and address of the landlord under the tenancy or, if those particulars are not known to the tenant, any information in the possession of the tenant that could reasonably lead to the Board's ascertaining the identity of the landlord or his or her address

(5) A person who fails to comply with a notice under subsection (4) or supplies information to the Board in purported compliance with the notice which is false or misleading in a material respect knowing it to be so false or misleading or being reckless as to whether it is so false or misleading is guilty of an offence.

Chapter 4

Data exchange — private residential tenancies

Data exchange — private residential tenancies.

[18–146] 146.—(1) A local authority shall, at such intervals as are specified by the Board, supply to the Board such information in its possession as falls within any class of information specified by the Board for the purpose of this subsection, being a class of information the supply of which to the Board is reasonably necessary for the performance by the Board of its functions.

(2) The Minister for Social and Family Affairs shall, at such intervals as are specified by the Board, supply to the Board such information in his or her possession as falls within any class of information specified by the Board for the purpose of this subsection, being a class of information the supply of which to the Board is reasonably necessary for the performance by the Board of its functions.

(3) The Board shall, at such intervals as are specified by a local authority, supply to the local authority such information in the possession of the Board as falls within any class of information specified by the local authority for the purpose of this subsection, being a class of information the supply of which to the authority is reasonably necessary for the performance by the authority of its functions relating to houses, dwellings or other structures (either generally or those which have been provided by it).

(4) The Board shall, at such intervals as are specified by the Minister for Social and Family Affairs, supply to that Minister of the Government such information in the possession of the Board as is reasonably necessary for the performance by that Minister of his or her functions under Chapter 11 of Part III of the Social Welfare (Consolidation) Act 1993.

Exchange of public service data.

147.—(1) A local authority shall, at such intervals as are specified by the Minister for Social and Family Affairs, supply to that Minister of the Government such information in its possession as falls within any class of information specified by that Minister for the purpose of this subsection, being a class of information the supply of which to that Minister is reasonably necessary for the performance by that Minister of his or her functions under Chapter 11 of Part III of the Social Welfare (Consolidation) Act 1993. [18–147]

(2) The Minister for Social and Family Affairs shall, at such intervals as are specified by a local authority, supply to the local authority such information in his or her possession as falls within any class of information specified by the local authority for the purpose of this subsection, being a class of information the supply of which to the authority is reasonably necessary for the performance by the authority of its functions relating to houses, dwellings or other structures (either generally or those which have been provided by it).

Provision of details of tenancy to Revenue Commissioners.

148.—(1) In this section "identification number" means— [18–148]

(a) in the case of an individual, the individual's personal public service number, and

(b) in the case of a company, the registered number of the company.

(2) On the request of—

(a) a landlord of a dwelling, on his or her furnishing—

(i) his or her identification number, or

(ii) his or her name and the identification number of his or her authorised agent,

or

(b) the Revenue Commissioners, on their furnishing

(i) the identification number of a landlord of a dwelling, or

(ii) the name of a landlord of a dwelling and the identification number of his or her authorised agent,

the Board shall, at such time or times as are reasonably specified in the request, furnish to the Revenue Commissioners—

(I) confirmation as to whether the landlord has registered a tenancy in respect of a dwelling, and

(II) in the event of there being one or more than one tenancy so registered, such of the particulars registered in respect of it or them as the Revenue Commissioners may require.

PART 8 – PRIVATE RESIDENTIAL TENANCIES BOARD

Chapter 1

Establishment and principal functions of Board

Establishment day.

[18–149] 149.—The Minister shall by order appoint a day to be the establishment day for the purposes of this Part.

> **Note:** The establishment day for the purposes of Part 8 of this Act is 1st September 2004 — see the Residential Tenancies Act 2004 (Establishment Day) Order 2004 (SI No 525 of 2004).

Establishment of Board.

[18–150] 150.—(1) On the establishment day there shall stand established a board to be known as An Bord um Thionóntachtaí Cónaithe Príobháideacha or, in the English language, the Private Residential Tenancies Board (in this Act referred to as "the Board") to perform the functions conferred on it by this Act.

(2) The Board shall be a body corporate with perpetual succession and an official seal and power to sue and be sued in its corporate name and, with the consent of the Minister, to acquire, hold and dispose of land, or an interest in land and to acquire, hold and dispose of any other property.

(3) The Board shall, subject to the provisions of this Act, be independent in the performance of its functions.

(4) The Board shall have all such powers as are necessary or expedient for or incidental to the performance of its functions under this Act.

Functions of Board.

[18–151] 151.—(1) The principal functions of the Board shall be—

(a) the resolution of disputes between tenants and landlords in accordance with the provisions of Part 6,

(b) the registration of particulars in respect of tenancies in accordance with the provisions of Part 7,

(c) the provision to the Minister of advice concerning policy in relation to the private rented sector,

(d) the development and publication of guidelines for good practice by those involved in the private rented sector,

(e) the collection and provision of information relating to the private rented sector, including information concerning prevailing rent levels,

(f) where the Board considers it appropriate, the conducting of research into the private rented sector and monitoring the operation of various aspects of the private rented sector or arranging for such research and monitoring to be done,

(g) the review of the operation of this Act (and, in particular, Part 3) and any related enactments and the making of recommendations to the Minister for the amendment of this Act or those enactments,

(h) the performance of any additional functions conferred on the Board under subsection (3).

(2) The Board shall provide information to the Minister on such matters related to its functions and the private rented sector as may be requested by the Minister from time to time.

(3) The Minister may, if he or she so thinks fit or if so requested by another Minister of the Government, after consultation with—

(a) the Board,

(b) that other Minister of the Government, and

(c) the Minister for Finance,

by order—

(i) confer on the Board such additional functions connected with the functions for the time being of the Board or activities that the Board is authorised for the time being to undertake as he or she considers appropriate,

(ii) make such provision as he or she considers necessary or expedient in relation to matters ancillary to or arising out of the conferral on the Board of functions under this subsection or the performance by the Board of functions so conferred.

(4) In this section "private rented sector" means the sector of commercial activity in the State consisting of the letting of dwellings.

Model lease.

152.—(1) Guidelines published under section 151(1)(d) may include a precedent for a model lease of a dwelling. **[18–152]**

(2) Such a precedent shall—

(a) contain all of the provisions necessary to make the lease of the dwelling concerned an instrument which is consistent with this Act and any other relevant enactments,

(b) be worded, so far as is practicable, in plain language, and

(c) to the extent necessary having regard to the requirements of paragraph (a), contain provisions best calculated to ensure harmonious relations between the parties to the lease as regards their conduct towards one and another in their capacity as such parties.

CHAPTER 2

Composition of Board

Membership of Board.

153.—(1) The members of the Board shall be such number, not less than 9 and not more than 15, as the Minister considers appropriate from time to time. **[18–153]**

(2) The members of the Board shall be appointed by the Minister as soon as may be after the establishment day and shall be persons who, in the Minister's opinion, have experience in a field of expertise relevant to the Board's functions.

(3) Except as provided for by subsection (2), the members of the Board shall be appointed from time to time as occasion requires by the Minister.

(4) The Minister shall, in so far as is practicable, ensure an equitable balance between the numbers of members of the Board who are women and the number of them who are men.

(5) The Minister when appointing a member shall fix such member's period of membership which shall not exceed 5 years and, subject to this section, membership shall be on such terms as the Minister may determine.

(6) The members of the Board (including the chairperson) may be paid such remuneration as the Minister, with the consent of the Minister for Finance, may determine.

Supplemental provisions as to membership of Board.

[18–154] 154.—(1) A member of the Board may at any time resign his or her membership by letter addressed to the Minister and the resignation shall take effect from the date specified in the letter or upon receipt of the letter by the Minister, whichever is the later.

(2) A member of the Board may, at any time, be removed from membership of the Board by the Minister if, in the Minister's opinion, the member has become incapable through ill-health of performing his or her functions, or has committed stated misbehaviour, or his or her removal appears to the Minister to be necessary for the effective performance by the Board of its functions.

(3) A person shall cease to be, and shall be disqualified from being, a member of the Board where he or she—

(a) is adjudicated bankrupt,

(b) makes a composition or arrangement with creditors,

(c) is sentenced by a court of competent jurisdiction to a term of imprisonment, or

(d) is disqualified or restricted from being a director of any company.

(4) If a member of the Board dies, resigns, becomes disqualified or is removed from membership, the Minister may appoint a person to be a member of the Board and fill the casual vacancy so caused.

(5) A member of the Board whose term of membership of the Board expires shall be eligible for re-appointment as a member of the Board.

Chairperson of Board.

[18–155] 155.—(1) The Minister shall appoint a person, from among the members of the Board, as chairperson of the Board.

(2) Where the chairperson of the Board ceases to be a member of the Board he or she shall also thereupon cease to be chairperson of the Board.

(3) The chairperson of the Board may at any time resign his or her office as chairperson of the Board while continuing to serve as a member of the Board and the resignation, unless previously withdrawn, shall take effect at the commencement of the meeting of the Board held after the Board has been informed by the Minister of the resignation.

(4) The chairperson of the Board shall, unless he or she sooner dies or otherwise ceases to be chairperson by virtue of subsection (2), hold office until the expiry of his or her period of membership of the Board and, if re-appointed as a member of the Board, shall be eligible for re-appointment as chairperson of the Board.

Chapter 3

Meetings and committees

Meetings of Board.

156.—(1) The Board shall hold such and so many meetings as may be necessary for the performance of its functions. **[18–156]**

(2) The Minister shall fix the date, time and place of the first meeting of the Board and the Board shall fix the date, time and place of subsequent meetings.

(3) The quorum for a meeting of the Board shall be 5.

(4) At a meeting of the Board the chairperson of the Board shall, if present, chair the meeting and if not present, or if the office of chairperson is vacant, the members of the Board present at the meeting shall choose one of their number to chair the meeting.

(5) At a meeting of the Board each person present, including the chairperson, shall have a vote and any question on which a vote is required so as to establish the Board's position on a matter shall be determined by a majority of the votes of the members present and voting on the question and, in the case of an equal division of the votes, the chairperson of the meeting shall have a second and casting vote.

(6) The Board may act notwithstanding one or more vacancies among its members (but this subsection is without prejudice to subsection (3)).

(7) Subject to the provisions of this Act, the Board may regulate its own procedures and business.

Committees of Board.

157.—(1) The Board may establish committees consisting in whole or in part of persons who are members of the Board— **[18–157]**

(a) to assist and advise the Board on matters relating to any of its functions or on such matters as the Board may from time to time determine, or

(b) to perform such functions of the Board as may be delegated by it from time to time.

(2) Without prejudice to the generality of subsection (1), the Board shall establish a committee which shall be known and is in this Act referred to as the "Dispute Resolution Committee".

(3) The Board, when appointing a member of a committee, shall—

(a) have regard to the range of qualifications and experience necessary for the proper and effective discharge of the functions of the committee,

(b) have regard to the desirability of such balance between the numbers of each sex on the committee as is appropriate and determined from time to time,

(c) fix the member's period of membership (which, in the case of a member of the Dispute Resolution Committee, shall not be less than a period of 3 years),

(d) fix the terms of his or her membership.

(4) The members of a committee may be paid by the Board such fees as the Board may determine, subject to the consent of the Minister and the Minister for Finance.

Supplemental provisions as to committees of Board.

[18–158] 158.—(1) In this section "committee" means a committee established under section 157.

(2) A member of a committee may be removed by the Board at any time for stated reasons.

(3) The acts of a committee and the performance by a committee of functions delegated to it under section 157 shall be subject to confirmation by the Board, unless the Board otherwise determines.

(4) The Board may, subject to this Act, determine the terms of reference and regulate, by standing orders or otherwise, the procedures and business of a committee including the filling of casual vacancies but, subject to any such regulation, a committee may regulate its own procedures.

(5) A committee shall appoint, from time to time, a chairperson from among its members.

(6) The Board may at any time dissolve a committee.

(7) A committee shall provide the Board with such information as the Board may from time to time require, in respect of its activities and operation, for the purposes of the performance of the functions of the Board.

(8) Subsections (4) to (6) do not apply to the Dispute Resolution Committee.

Dispute Resolution Committee.

[18–159] 159.—(1) There shall be delegated to the Dispute Resolution Committee by the Board such of the functions of the Board under Part 6 (except those under sections 109, 121 and 124) as the Board determines; functions under that Part may not be delegated to any other committee established under section 157.

(2) The Dispute Resolution Committee shall consist of not more than 40 members, of which at least 4 must be members of the Board (including the member of the Board appointed as chairperson of the Dispute Resolution Committee).

(3) A member of the Board shall not be eligible for appointment as a member of the Dispute Resolution Committee unless the unexpired period of his or her term of office as a member of the Board is 3 or more years at the date of his or her appointment as a member of the Committee.

(4) The members of the Dispute Resolution Committee shall be appointed by the Board after consultation with the Minister.

(5) The Board, after consultation with the Minister, shall appoint a member of the Dispute Resolution Committee as chairperson of the Committee; that member must be a person who is also a member of the Board.

(6) The Dispute Resolution Committee shall adopt, subject to the approval of the Board and the Minister, rules and procedures for the conduct of its meetings and the performance of its functions generally.

(7) A member of staff of the Board shall act as secretary to the Dispute Resolution Committee.

Chapter 4

Management of Board

Director of Board.

160.—(1) There shall be a chief officer of the Board who shall be known and is referred to in this Act as the "Director". [18–160]

(2) The Director shall be appointed by the Board in accordance with procedures that have been determined by the Board with the consent of the Minister.

(3) The first appointment by the Board of a person to be the Director shall be made within 3 years from the establishment day.

(4) The Director may, at any time, for stated reasons be removed from office by the Board with the consent of the Minister.

(5) The Director shall carry on, manage and control generally the administration and business of the Board and perform such other functions as may be determined by the Board.

(6) The Director shall hold office for such period and upon and subject to such terms and conditions (including terms and conditions relating to remuneration) as may be determined from time to time by the Minister, after consultation with the Board and with the consent of the Minister for Finance.

Supplemental provisions in relation to Director.

161.—(1) The Director shall perform his or her functions subject to such policies as may be determined from time to time by the Board and shall be answerable to the Board for the efficient and effective management of the Board and for the due performance of his or her functions. [18–161]

(2) The Director may delegate any of his or her functions to a member of staff of the Board (other than functions that have been delegated to the Director subject to a condition that they are not to be sub-delegated), and the member of staff shall be accountable to the Director for the performance of the functions so delegated.

(3) Notwithstanding subsection (2), the Director shall at all times remain accountable to the Board for the performance of functions delegated by him or her.

(4) The Director may make proposals to the Board on any matter relating to the activities of the Board.

(5) The Director shall not be a member of the Board or of any committee of the Board, but he or she may, in accordance with procedures established by the Board or a committee, as the case may be, attend meetings of the Board or the committee or both and shall be entitled to speak at and advise such meetings.

Chapter 5

Staff of Board and superannuation matters

Staff of Board.

162.—(1) In addition to the Director, the Board may, from time to time, appoint such and such number of persons to be members of the staff of the Board as it may determine with the consent of the Minister and the Minister for Finance. [18–162]

(2) The grades of the staff of the Board, the numbers of staff in each grade and the appropriate level of remuneration for each grade shall be determined by the Board with the consent of the Minister and the Minister for Finance.

(3) Subject to such conditions as it thinks fit, the Board may delegate to the Director any of the functions of the Board in relation to the employment of staff and the determination of selection procedures.

(4) The staff of the Board shall—

(a) be paid out of moneys available to the Board,

(b) perform such functions as determined from time to time by the Director, and

(c) hold office or employment for such period and upon and subject to such terms and conditions as may be determined from time to time by the Director, with the consent of the Minister and the Minister for Finance.

(5) Every member of the staff of the Minister designated by order made by the Minister for the purposes of this section shall, on being so designated, be transferred to and become a member of the staff of the Board.

(6) The Minister may make an order for the purposes of subsection (5) at any time but shall not do so without first having—

(a) notified in writing any recognised trade union or staff association concerned of the Minister's intention to do so, and

(b) considered, within such time as may be specified in the notification, any representations made by such trade unions or staff associations in relation to the matter.

(7) Except in accordance with a collective agreement negotiated with any recognised trade unions or staff associations concerned, a person referred to in subsection (5) shall not, while in the service of the Board, receive a lesser scale of pay or be made subject to less beneficial terms and conditions of service than the scale of pay to which he or she was entitled and the terms and conditions of service to which he or she was subject immediately before his or her transfer into such service.

Superannuation.

[18–163] 163.—(1) As soon as practicable after the establishment day, the Board shall prepare and submit to the Minister a scheme or schemes for the granting of superannuation benefits to or in respect of such members of the staff of the Board as it may think fit.

(2) Every such scheme shall fix the time and conditions of retirement for all persons to or in respect of whom superannuation benefits are payable under the scheme, and different times and conditions may be fixed in respect of different classes of persons.

(3) Every such scheme may be amended or revoked by a subsequent scheme prepared, submitted and approved under this section.

(4) A scheme submitted by the Board under this section shall, if approved by the Minister, with the consent of the Minister for Finance, be carried out by the Board in accordance with its terms.

(5) Superannuation benefits granted under schemes under this section to persons, who immediately before their being designated by an order under section 162, were members of the staff of the Minister, and the terms and conditions relating to those

benefits, shall not be less favourable to those persons than those to which they were entitled immediately before such designation.

(6) No superannuation benefit shall be granted by the Board nor shall any other arrangements be entered into by the Board for the provision of such a benefit to or in respect of a member of the staff of the Board otherwise than in accordance with a scheme under this section or, if the Minister, with the consent of the Minister for Finance, sanctions the granting of such a benefit, in accordance with that sanction.

(7) If any dispute arises as to the claim of any person to, or the amount of, any superannuation benefit payable in pursuance of a scheme or schemes under this section, such dispute shall be submitted to the Minister who shall refer it to the Minister for Finance, whose decision shall be final.

(8) A scheme under this section shall be laid before each House of the Oireachtas as soon as may be after it is made and, if a resolution annulling the scheme is passed by either such House within the next 21 days on which that House has sat after the scheme is laid before it, the scheme shall be annulled accordingly, but without prejudice to the validity of anything previously done thereunder.

Chapter 6

Appointment or engagement of certain persons

Mediators and adjudicators.

164.—(1) The Board may from time to time appoint such and so many persons who shall be known and are in this Act referred to as "mediators" to carry out the functions assigned to them by the Board in accordance with Part 6. **[18–164]**

(2) The Board may from time to time appoint such and so many persons who shall be known and are in this Act referred to as "adjudicators" to carry out the functions assigned to them by the Board in accordance with Part 6.

(3) The Board may appoint a person as both a mediator and an adjudicator.

(4) The Board shall form 2 panels, one comprising the names of the persons who stand appointed as mediators and the other comprising the names of the persons who stand appointed as adjudicators.

(5) Mediators and adjudicators shall each be appointed for such period (not being less than 3 years) as the Board may determine and shall be paid such fees and expenses as the Board, with the consent of the Minister and of the Minister for Finance, may determine from time to time; the other terms and conditions on which each of them shall stand appointed shall be such as the Board may determine from time to time.

(6) Those other terms and conditions shall, in relation to adjudicators, include such terms and conditions as are likely, in the opinion of the Board, to secure the independence and impartiality of the adjudicators.

(7) A mediator or adjudicator may at any time resign from his or her appointment as mediator or adjudicator.

(8) Neither the Civil Service Commissioners Act 1956 (or any enactment that replaces in whole or in part that Act) nor the Civil Service Regulation Acts 1956 to 1996 shall apply to a mediator or an adjudicator.

Removal of an adjudicator from the panel.

165.—(1) The Board may, in accordance with this section, remove an adjudicator from the panel formed under section 164(4) ("the panel"). **[18–165]**

(2) If it appears to the Board that an adjudicator has been guilty of misconduct in his or her capacity as an adjudicator, it may apply to the District Court for an order under subsection (3) authorising the removal of the adjudicator from the panel.

(3) On the hearing of an application under this section and having considered the evidence adduced by the Board in the matter and any evidence adduced by or on behalf of the adjudicator, the District Court shall, if it finds that the adjudicator has been guilty of misconduct in his or her capacity as an adjudicator, make an order authorising the Board to remove the adjudicator from the panel.

(4) On the making of such an order (or, if the order is appealed to the Circuit Court and the Circuit Court confirms the order, on the order being so confirmed), the Board shall remove the adjudicator from the panel.

(5) Save where the period of his or her appointment has expired or a failure (not amounting to misconduct) by him or her to comply with the terms and conditions upon which he or she was appointed occurs, an adjudicator shall not be removed from the panel otherwise than in accordance with this section or with his or her consent.

(6) In this section "misconduct" means any conduct likely to bring the procedures for determinations by adjudicators under Part 6 into disrepute and includes—

(a) any demonstration by an adjudicator of bias towards the interests of a party before him or her,

(b) gross discourtesy by an adjudicator to one or more of the parties before him or her, and

(c) wilful failure by an adjudicator to attend to his or her duties as an adjudicator.

Consultants and advisers.

[18–166] 166.—(1) Subject to such conditions (if any) as may for the time being stand specified by the Minister for the purposes of this section, the Board may from time to time engage such consultants or advisers as it may consider necessary for the performance of its functions and any fees due to a consultant or adviser engaged pursuant to this section shall be paid by the Board out of moneys at its disposal.

(2) Any person who wishes to be engaged by the Board as a consultant or adviser pursuant to this section may notify the Board in writing of this fact and any notification for that purpose shall include particulars of the person's qualifications and experience.

(3) The Board shall maintain a list of the persons who notify the Board pursuant to subsection (2).

(4) The Board shall, in engaging a consultant or adviser under this section, have regard to the list maintained under subsection (3), but nothing in this subsection shall be construed as precluding the Board from engaging as a consultant or adviser a person whose name is not on that list.

(5) The Board shall include in its annual report under section 180 a statement of the names of the persons (if any) engaged pursuant to this section during the year to which the report relates.

Provision of services to Board.

[18–167] 167.—(1) For the purposes of enabling the Board to perform its functions as and from the establishment day, the Minister may, for such period as he or she thinks appropriate, supply to the Board any services, including services of staff, required by the Board and the Board may avail itself of such services for which arrangements are made under this section.

(2) The supply of services of staff under subsection (1) may include the supply of services of a person to perform the functions of the Director under this Part and Part 6.

(3) For so long as the services of a person are provided for the purpose mentioned in subsection (2)—

(a) the functions mentioned in that subsection shall be performable by that person, and

(b) sections 160(6) and 161 shall apply to that person.

Chapter 7

Supplemental provisions with regard to Board's administration and management

Indemnification of certain persons.

168.—(1) Where the Board is satisfied that a person to whom this section applies has discharged the functions appropriate to that person in relation to the functions of the Board in good faith, it shall indemnify that person against all actions or claims however they arise in respect of the discharge by that person of those functions. **[18–168]**

(2) This section applies to—

(a) a member of the Board,

(b) a member of a committee of the Board,

(c) a member of staff of the Board,

(d) a mediator or adjudicator,

(e) an adviser or consultant to the Board engaged under section 166, and

(f) a person whose services are provided to the Board under section 167.

Membership of either House of the Oireachtas, etc.

169.—(1) Where a member of the Board or the Dispute Resolution Committee or a member of the staff of the Board— **[18–169]**

(a) accepts nomination as a member of Seanad Éireann,

(b) is elected to either House of the Oireachtas or to the European Parliament,

(c) is regarded, pursuant to Part XIII of the Second Schedule to the European Parliament Elections Act 1997, as having been elected to that Parliament, or

(d) becomes a member of a local authority,

he or she shall thereupon—

(i) in the case of a member of the Board or the Dispute Resolution Committee, cease to be a member of the Board or that Committee,

(ii) in the case of a member of the staff of the Board, stand seconded from employment by the Board for the period specified in subsection (2).

(2) A person who stands seconded under subsection (1)(ii) shall not be paid by, or be entitled to receive from, the Board any remuneration in respect of the period commencing on such nomination or election or his or her membership of the local authority or the date on which he or she is so regarded as having been elected, as the case may be, and ending on the date on which he or she ceases to be a member of either such House or such Parliament or such local authority.

(3) Without prejudice to the generality of subsection (2), that subsection shall be construed as prohibiting, among other things, the reckoning of a period mentioned in that subsection as service with the Board for the purposes of any superannuation benefits.

(4) A person who is for the time being entitled under the Standing Orders of either House of the Oireachtas to sit therein or who is a representative in the European Parliament or a member of a local authority shall, while he or she is so entitled or is such a representative or member, be disqualified from becoming a member of the Board or the Dispute Resolution Committee or a member of the staff of the Board.

Disclosure of interests.

[18–170] 170.—(1) Where a member of the Board, a member of a committee of the Board, a member of the staff of the Board or a consultant or adviser engaged under section 166 has a pecuniary interest or other beneficial interest in, or material to, any matter which falls to be considered by the Board or a committee, he or she shall comply with the following requirements:

(a) he or she shall disclose to the Board the fact of such interest and the nature of the interest in advance of any consideration of the matter;

(b) he or she shall neither influence nor seek to influence a decision in relation to the matter;

(c) he or she shall take no part in any consideration of the matter;

(d) if he or she is a member of the Board or a committee or both or a member of the staff of the Board, he or she shall withdraw from any meeting concerned for so long as the matter is being discussed or considered and shall not vote or otherwise act as such Board or committee member or member of staff in relation to the matter.

(2) For the purposes of this section, but without prejudice to the generality of subsection (1), a person shall be regarded as having a beneficial interest in, or material to, a matter referred to in that subsection if—

(a) the person or any member of his or her household, or any nominee of him or her or of his or her household, is a member of a company or any other body which has a beneficial interest in, or material to, such a matter,

(b) the person or any member of his or her household is in partnership with or is in the employment of a person who has a beneficial interest in, or material to, such a matter,

(c) the person or any member of his or her household is a party to any arrangement or agreement (whether or not enforceable) concerning property to which such a matter relates, or

(d) any member of his or her household has a beneficial interest in, or material to, such a matter.

(3) A person shall not be regarded as having a beneficial interest in, or material to, any matter by reason only of an interest of the person or of any company or of any other body or person mentioned in subsection (2) which is so remote or insignificant that it cannot reasonably be regarded as likely to influence a person in considering, discussing or voting on any question with respect to the matter, or in performing any function in relation to that matter.

Section 170: supplemental provisions.

171.—(1) Where at a meeting or proceeding of the Board or a committee of the Board a question arises as to whether or not a course of conduct, if pursued by a person, would constitute a failure by the person to comply with the requirements of section 170, then, if the meeting or proceeding is of a committee, it shall be adjourned until the question has been referred to and determined by the Board, and if the meeting is of the Board, the question shall be determined by the Board, whose decision in all cases shall be final, and particulars of the determination shall be recorded in the minutes of the Board's meeting. [18–171]

(2) Where a disclosure is made under section 170, the disclosure shall be recorded in the minutes of the meeting concerned and, for so long as the matter to which the disclosure relates is being considered or discussed by the meeting, the person by whom the disclosure is made, where he or she is a member of the Board, shall not be counted in the quorum for the meeting unless the Board otherwise determines.

(3) A person who contravenes section 170 is guilty of an offence.

(4) In any proceedings for an offence under subsection (3), it shall be a defence for the defendant to prove that at the time of the alleged offence he or she did not know and had no reason to believe that a matter in which, or in relation to which, he or she had a beneficial interest had fallen to be considered by him or her, by the Board or by a committee of the Board or that the beneficial interest to which the alleged offence relates was one in relation to which a requirement of section 170 applied.

(5) A member of the Board, or of a committee of the Board, if convicted of an offence under subsection (3) shall, on such conviction, cease to be and be disqualified from being such a member.

Disclosure of information.

172.—(1) Save as otherwise provided by law and subject to subsection (3), a person shall not, other than with the consent of the Board, disclose confidential information obtained by him or her while performing (or as a result of having performed) functions as— [18–172]

(a) a member of the Board,

(b) a member of the staff of the Board,

(c) a member of a committee of the Board,

(d) an adviser or consultant to the Board engaged under section 166.

(2) A person who contravenes subsection (1) is guilty of an offence.

(3) Nothing in subsection (1) shall prohibit the disclosure of information by means of a report made to the Board or made by, or on behalf of, the Board to the Minister.

(4) In this section "confidential information" includes—

(a) information that is expressed by the Board or a committee of the Board, as the case may be, to be confidential either as regards particular information or as regards information of a particular class or description,

(b) proposals of a commercial nature or tenders submitted to the Board by contractors, consultants or any other person,

(c) information the disclosure of which is prohibited by virtue of section 128(4).

(5) A member of the Board or of a committee of the Board, if convicted of an offence under subsection (2) shall, on such conviction, cease to be and be disqualified from being such a member.

Seal of Board.

[18–173] 173.—(1) The Board shall, as soon as may be after its establishment, provide itself with a seal.

(2) The seal of the Board shall be authenticated by the signature of—

(a) the chairperson of the Board or another member of the Board authorised by the Board to act in that behalf, and

(b) the Director or a member of the staff of the Board authorised by the Board to act in that behalf.

(3) Judicial notice shall be taken of the seal of the Board and every document purporting to be an instrument made by the Board and to be sealed with the seal of the Board (purporting to be authenticated in accordance with subsection (2)) shall be received in evidence and be deemed to be such instrument without proof unless the contrary is shown.

Chapter 8

Financial and accountability provisions

Grants to Board.

[18–174] 174.—The Minister may, in each financial year, after consultation with the Board in relation to its proposed work programme and projected expenditure for that year, make to the Board a grant of such amount, as may be sanctioned by the Minister for Finance, out of moneys provided by the Oireachtas for the purposes of expenditure by the Board in the performance of its functions.

Borrowings by Board.

[18–175] 175.—(1) The Board may, for the purpose of providing for current or capital expenditure, from time to time, borrow money (whether on the security of the assets of the Board or otherwise).

(2) The exercise of this power is subject to the consent of the Minister and the Minister for Finance and to such conditions as they may specify.

Fees.

[18–176] 176.—(1) The Board may charge, receive and recover such fees as the Board may from time to time determine, subject to the consent of the Minister, in relation to the performance by the Board of its functions, the provision by it of services (other than a service consisting of the provision of information or advice to the Minister) and the carrying on by it of activities.

(2) Subsection (1) does not apply in respect of any fee provision for the charging for, or payment of, which is made by any other provision of this Act.

(3) Without prejudice to the generality of subsection (1), the Board may charge fees in respect of all or any of the following:

(a) access to records of determination orders made under section 121,

(b) provision of a sealed and certified copy of a determination order made under section 121,

(c) copies of publications produced by the Board,

(d) the provision of details of an aggregated nature under section 131.

(4) The Board may recover, as a simple contract debt in any court of competent jurisdiction, from the person by whom it is payable, any amount due and owing to it under this or any other provision of this Act.

(5) Fees received by the Board under this Act shall be paid into or disposed of for the benefit of the Exchequer in such manner as the Minister may direct.

(6) The Public Offices Fees Act 1879 shall not apply to any fees payable under this Act.

Accounts.

177.—(1) The Director shall submit estimates of income and expenditure of the Board to the Minister in such form, in respect of such periods, and at such times as may be required by the Minister and shall furnish to the Minister any information which the Minister may require in relation to such estimates, including proposals and future plans relating to the discharge by the Board of its functions over a period of years, as required. **[18–177]**

(2) The Director shall consult with the Board in performing the functions under subsection (1) and may submit to the Minister any estimates, information, proposals or other matters under that subsection only after obtaining the Board's consent to do so.

(3) The Director, under the direction of the Board, shall cause to be kept on a continuous basis and in a legible or a machine readable form or both all proper books and records of account of all income and expenditure of the Board, and of the sources of such income and the subject matter of such expenditure, and of the property, assets and liabilities of the Board; the Director shall also keep and shall account to the Board for all such special accounts as the Minister or the Board, with the consent of the Minister, may from time to time direct should be kept.

(4) The financial year of the Board shall be the period of 12 months ending on 31 December in any year and, for the purposes of section 174, this section and section 178, the period commencing on the establishment day and ending on the following 31 December shall be deemed to be a financial year.

Further provisions with respect to accounts (including their audit).

178.—(1) The Board, the Director and any relevant member of the staff of the Board shall, whenever so requested by the Minister, permit any person appointed by the Minister to examine the books or other records of account of the Board in respect of any financial year or other period and shall facilitate any such examination, and the Board shall pay such fee therefor as may be fixed by the Minister. **[18–178]**

(2) In subsection (1) "relevant member of the staff of the Board" means a member of the staff of the Board to whom there has been duly assigned functions relating to the books or other records of account referred to in that subsection.

(3) The accounts of the Board for each financial year shall be prepared in such a form and manner as may be specified by the Minister and be prepared by the Director and approved by the Board as soon as practicable but not later than three months after the end of the financial year to which they relate for submission, as soon as practicable, to the Comptroller and Auditor General for audit.

(4) A copy of such of the accounts referred to in subsection (3) as the Minister directs and the report of the Comptroller and Auditor General thereon shall be presented to the members of the Board and to the Minister, as soon as practicable

after the audit of them is completed, and the Minister shall cause a copy of those documents to be laid before each House of the Oireachtas.

Accountability of Director to Oireachtas Committees.

[18–179] 179.—(1) The Director shall, whenever he or she is so required by a Committee of Dáil Éireann established under the Standing Orders of Dáil Éireann to examine and report to Dáil Éireann on the appropriation accounts and reports of the Comptroller and Auditor General, give evidence to that Committee on—

(a) the regularity and propriety of the transactions recorded or required to be recorded in any account subject to audit by the Comptroller and Auditor General which the Director or the Board is required by or under statute to prepare,

(b) the economy and efficiency of the Board in the use of its resources,

(c) the systems, procedures and practices employed by the Board for the purpose of evaluating the effectiveness of its operations, and

(d) any matter affecting the Board referred to in a special report of the Comptroller and Auditor General under section 11(2) of the Comptroller and Auditor General (Amendment) Act 1993 or in any other report of the Comptroller and Auditor General (in so far as it relates to a matter specified in paragraph (a), (b) or (c)) that is laid before Dáil Éireann.

(2) The Director shall, at the request in writing of any other Oireachtas Committee, attend before it and give evidence to it on any matter related to the functions of the Board.

(3) In subsection (2), "other Oireachtas Committee" means a committee appointed by either House of the Oireachtas or jointly by both Houses of the Oireachtas (other than the committee referred to in subsection (1)) or a subcommittee of such a committee.

Reports and information to Minister.

[18–180] 180.—(1) The Board shall, not later than 30 June in each year subsequent to the year in which the establishment day falls, make a report to the Minister (in this section referred to as the "annual report") in such form as the Minister may approve, on the performance of its functions and activities during the preceding year and the Minister shall cause copies of each annual report to be laid before each House of the Oireachtas.

(2) Each annual report shall include information in such form and regarding such matters as the Minister may direct.

(3) The Board may, from time to time, make such other reports to the Minister relating to its functions as it thinks fit and shall, whenever so requested by the Minister, supply to the Minister such information, in addition to that provided in its annual report, regarding the performance of its functions as the Minister may from time to time require.

(4) The Board may publish such other reports on matters related to its activities and functions as it may from time to time consider relevant and appropriate.

Reports to Board.

[18–181] 181.—(1) The Board may, on its request, be furnished with reports on any matter which, in the Board's opinion, concerns the private rented sector by the appropriate

Minister of the Government or local authority who or which has responsibility for the area to which the matter pertains.

(2) The Board may make a report furnished to the Board under this section available to the Minister.

(3) In this section "private rented sector" has the same meaning as it has in section 151.

PART 9 – MISCELLANEOUS

Limitation on certain disputes being the subject of court proceedings.

182.—(1) On and from the commencement of Part 6, proceedings may not be instituted in any court in respect of a dispute that may be referred to the Board for resolution under that Part unless one or more of the following reliefs is being claimed in the proceedings— [18–182]

(a) damages of an amount of more than €20,000,

(b) recovery of arrears of rent or other charges, or both, due under a tenancy of an amount, or an aggregate amount, of more than €60,000 or such lesser amount as would be applicable in the circumstances concerned by virtue of section 115(3)(b) or (c)(ii).

(2) In this section "dispute" has the same meaning as it has in Part 6.

Guidelines to Board.

183.—(1) The Minister may, from time to time, issue to the Board such guidelines in relation to the performance of its functions under this Act (other than functions under Part 6) as he or she considers appropriate and the Board shall have regard to such guidelines in the performance of those functions. [18–183]

(2) The Minister may amend or revoke guidelines issued under this section.

Voidance of provisions designed to facilitate terminations.

184.—(1) A provision of a lease or tenancy agreement in relation to a dwelling that imposes an obligation on a party (the "first party") to do or refrain from doing any thing is void if, from all the circumstances (including any of the matters specified in subsection (3)), it is a reasonable inference that the sole or main purpose for the provision being included is that mentioned in subsection (2). [18–184]

(2) That purpose is to allow the other party (the "second party") to serve a notice of termination in respect of the tenancy concerned (for a failure to comply with the provision) for any reason that suits the interests of that party at the particular time rather than because the failure to comply has occurred.

(3) The matters mentioned in subsection (1) are—

(a) the provision concerned cannot, in its ordinary operation, be reasonably regarded as conferring any practical benefit on the second party or in respect of his or her interest in the dwelling,

(b) compliance with the provision concerned by the first party is likely to be impracticable,

(c) the terms in which the provision concerned is framed are such that the situations in which the provision must be complied with and those in which it need not be complied with are arbitrary.

(4) Any tenancy or sub-tenancy of a dwelling (the "first-mentioned tenancy") purported to be created is void if, from all the circumstances, it is a reasonable inference that it is a transaction not of a bona fide nature effected at arm's length but effected solely or mainly for the purpose of facilitating the termination (through collusion between some or all of the parties to that transaction) of any sub-tenancy created out of the first-mentioned tenancy.

(5) If the first-mentioned tenancy in subsection (4) is void by reason of that subsection any sub-tenancy created out of it that is not so void shall be deemed to be a tenancy held by the person in whose favour the sub-tenancy was granted from the person who purported to create the first-mentioned tenancy (but of no greater term than the term of the sub-tenancy).

Obligation to inform prospective sub-tenant of nature of tenancy.

[18–185] 185.—(1) A tenant of a dwelling who proposes to create in favour of any person a sub-tenancy out of the tenancy shall, before he or she—

(a) creates the sub-tenancy, or

(b) if its creation is preceded by the entering into of an agreement to create (whether the word "create" or any other word is used) such a tenancy, enters into that agreement,

inform the person of the fact that it is a sub-tenancy that will be created in the person's favour.

(2) A person who fails to comply with subsection (1) is guilty of an offence.

(3) If, in respect of the entering into of an agreement referred to in paragraph (b) of subsection (1), a failure to comply with that subsection occurs, the agreement shall not be enforceable by the tenant referred to in that subsection.

Tenant may terminate where consent to assignment or sub-letting withheld.

[18–186] 186.—(1) This section has effect—

(a) despite the fact that the tenancy concerned is one for a fixed period, and

(b) despite anything to the contrary in the lease or tenancy agreement concerned.

(2) If a landlord of a dwelling refuses his or her consent to an assignment or sub-letting of the tenancy concerned by the tenant, the tenant may serve a notice of termination in respect of the tenancy and terminate it accordingly.

(3) The period of notice to be given by that notice of termination is—

(a) that specified in section 66, or

(b) such lesser period of notice as may be agreed between the landlord and the tenant in accordance with section 69,

even if the lease or tenancy agreement provides for a greater period of notice to be given.

Duty of management companies in relation to certain complaints.

[18–187] 187.—(1) This section applies where a tenant of a dwelling which is one of a number of dwellings comprising an apartment complex makes a complaint of the kind referred to in section 12(1)(h) to the landlord of the dwelling and that complaint (the "relevant complaint") is forwarded to the management company of the complex (the "relevant company").

(2) Where this section applies the relevant company, in performing any of its functions in relation to the apartment complex concerned, shall have regard to the relevant complaint and shall furnish to the landlord mentioned in subsection (1) (for the purpose of its being forwarded to the tenant concerned) a statement in writing as to the steps, if any, it has taken to deal with the matter or matters to which the complaint relates.

Provision of information in relation to service charges by management companies.

188.—(1) A tenant of a dwelling which is one of a number of dwellings comprising an apartment complex may request the management company (if any) of the complex ("the company") to furnish to him or her particulars in writing of the service charges made by the company in respect of the dwelling in a specified period and how those charges have been calculated. **[18–188]**

(2) Subject to subsection (3), it shall be the duty of the company to comply with such a request.

(3) If the owner of the dwelling were to make a request of the company to furnish to him or her the particulars mentioned in subsection (1) and the company would not be obliged to furnish all of those particulars to him or her then the duty of the company under subsection (2) shall be read as extending only to the particulars that the company would be obliged to furnish to the owner were such a request to be made.

(4) In this section "service charges" means charges made by the company in respect of the performance of functions by it in relation to the apartment complex concerned.

Jurisdiction in aid of Part 6 resolution procedure.

189.—(1) In this section "dispute" means a dispute falling within the jurisdiction of the Board under Part 6. **[18–189]**

(2) The following provisions have effect if the circumstances giving rise to or involving the dispute are such that, were proceedings in the Circuit Court to be brought in relation to the dispute, it would be appropriate to apply to that court for interim or interlocutory relief in the matter.

(3) On being requested by the person (the "referrer") who has referred or is referring a dispute to it to do so, the Board may apply, on the referrer's behalf, to the Circuit Court for such interim or interlocutory relief in the matter as the Board considers appropriate.

(4) In deciding whether to accede to such a request the Board may have regard to—

(a) the merits, as they appear to it, of the referrer's contentions that will be dealt with by an adjudicator or the Tribunal,

(b) the amount of damages the Board is likely to have to pay to the respondent to the application (on foot of an undertaking required of it by the court to pay such damages) in the event such damages have to be paid, but the Board's opinion—

(i) that those contentions of the referrer are unlikely to be accepted by an adjudicator or the Tribunal, or

(ii) that the amount of those damages is likely to be substantial,

shall, in neither case, and without prejudice to subsection (5) be conclusive in favour of the Board's refusing to accede to the request if, in all the circumstances, the Board considers that it ought to accede to it.

(5) The fact of the Board's being of the opinion referred to in subsection (4)(ii) shall not be taken into account by it in deciding whether to accede to a request under subsection (3) if the referrer undertakes to defray in whole the amount of damages the Board may become liable to pay in the circumstances mentioned in subsection (4) and the Board is satisfied the referrer has the means to be able to comply with that undertaking.

(6) On application to the Circuit Court by the Board under this section, the Circuit Court may grant such interim or interlocutory relief in the matter as it thinks appropriate.

Section 189: supplemental provisions.

[18–190] 190.—(1) For the purpose of section 189 there is, by virtue of this section, vested in the Circuit Court, with the modifications specified in subsection (2), the jurisdiction vested in that court with respect to the grant, variation and discharge of interim or interlocutory relief in proceedings brought in that court in respect of any matter.

(2) The modifications mentioned in subsection (1) are that the rules of law (including those of equity) and enactments relating to the foregoing jurisdiction shall be construed and operate so as to enable the Circuit Court to—

(a) provide that any interlocutory relief granted by it, on foot of an application under section 189, may have effect until the final determination of the dispute concerned under Part 6,

(b) if it considers it appropriate so to provide, authorise an adjudicator or the Tribunal, as the case may be, to include in his or her or its determination under section 97 or 108 in relation to a dispute an award of costs with respect to the application or applications under section 189 in the matter.

(3) Costs the subject of such an award may be taxed in the same manner as costs the subject of an award made by the Circuit Court.

Long occupation equity (ability to renounce entitlement to it).

[18–191] 191.—(1) In this section the "Act of 1980" means the Landlord and Tenant (Amendment) Act 1980.

(2) *Omitted. Amends s 17(1)(a) of the Landlord and Tenant (Amendment) Act 1980.*

(3) *Omitted. Amends s 85 of the Landlord and Tenant (Amendment) Act 1980.*

Note: The "relevant date" is 1 September 2004, being the date Part 4 of this Act commenced—see s 5(1) of this Act and the Residential Tenancies Act 2004 (Commencement) Order 2004 (SI No 505 of 2004).

Long occupation equity (prospective abolition of entitlement to it.)

[18–192] 192.—(1) In this section "Act of 1980" has the same meaning as it has in section 191.

(2) Subject to subsection (3), on and from the fifth anniversary of the relevant date, Part II of the Act of 1980 shall not apply to a dwelling to which this Act applies.

(3) Subsection (2) does not have effect in relation to a dwelling in respect of which the tenant has served a notice of intention to claim relief under and in accordance with section 20 of the Act of 1980 before the fifth anniversary mentioned in that subsection.

(4) Subsection (3) is without prejudice to the generality of section 21 of the Interpretation Act 1937.

> **Note:** The "relevant date" is 1st September 2004, being the date Part 4 of this Act commenced — see s 5(1) of this Act and the Residential Tenancies Act 2004 (Commencement) Order 2004 (SI No 505 of 2004).

Non-application of certain enactments.

193.—None of the following enactments applies to a dwelling to which this Act applies— **[18–193]**

(a) section 42 of the Landlord and Tenant Law Amendment Act Ireland 1860,

(b) section 14 of the Conveyancing Act 1881,

(c) sections 2, 3 and 4 of the Conveyancing and Law of Property Act 1892,

(d) sections 66, 67 and 68 of the Landlord and Tenant (Amendment) Act 1980, and

(e) section 16 of the Housing (Miscellaneous Provisions) Act 1992.

Deemed termination of tenancy to which Part 4 does not apply.

194.—Subsections (1) to (4) of section 37 apply to a tenancy of a dwelling in so far as its operation is not affected by Part 4 or to which that Part does not apply as those subsections apply to a Part 4 tenancy. **[18–194]**

Proposed overholding under a fixed term tenancy.

195.—(1) In this section "relevant dwelling" means a dwelling, the subject of a tenancy that is for a fixed period of at least 6 months. **[18–195]**

(2) The tenant of a relevant dwelling, if he or she intends to remain (on whatever basis, if any, that is open to him or her to do so) in occupation of the dwelling after the expiry of the period of the tenancy concerned, shall notify the landlord of that intention.

(3) That notification shall not be made to the landlord—

(a) any later than 1 month before, nor

(b) any sooner than 3 months before, the expiry of the period of that tenancy.

(4) If a tenant fails to comply with subsection (2) and the landlord suffers loss or damage in consequence of that failure the landlord may make a complaint to the Board under Part 6 that he or she has suffered such loss or damage.

(5) An adjudicator or the Tribunal, on the hearing of such a complaint, may make a determination, if the adjudicator or the Tribunal considers it proper to do so, that the tenant shall pay to the complainant an amount by way of damages for that loss or damage.

Equal Status Act 2000 not prejudiced.

196.—Nothing in this Act— **[18–196]**

(a) authorises conduct prohibited by section 6 of the Equal Status Act 2000, or

(b) operates to prejudice the powers under Part III of that Act to award redress in the case of such conduct.

Amendment of the Housing (Miscellaneous Provisions) Act 1997.

197.—*Omitted. Amends ss 1, 3, 3A, 4, 9, and 14 of the Housing (Miscellaneous Provisions) Act 1997.* **[18–197]**

Amendment of the Housing Act 1966.

[18–198] 198.—*Omitted. Amends s 79(1) and the Third Schedule to the Housing Act 1966.*

Amendment of sections 58 and 60 of Landlord and Tenant (Amendment) Act 1980.

[18–199] 199.—*Omitted. Amends ss 58(13)(1) and 60(1) of the Landlord and Tenant (Amendment) Act 1980.*

Amendment of sections 3 and 20 of Housing (Miscellaneous Provisions) Act 1992.

[18–200] 200.—*Omitted. Amends ss 3(8)(b) and 20(8) of the Housing (Miscellaneous Provisions) Act 1992.*

Amendment of section 34 of the Housing (Miscessaneous Provisions) Act 1992.

[18–201] 201.—*Omitted. Amends s 34(1) of the Housing (Miscellaneous Provisions) Act 1992.*

> **Note:** The fairly obvious typographical error in the spelling of "Miscellaneous" in the marginal note appears in the Act as published.

Regulations to remove difficulties.

[18–202] 202.—If in any respect any difficulty arises during the period of 3 years after the commencement of this section in bringing any provision of this Act into operation or in relation to the operation of any such provision, the Minister may by regulations do anything that appears to the Minister to be necessary or expedient for the purposes of bringing that provision into operation or securing or facilitating its operation.

> **Note:** Such Regulations have been made — see the Residential Tenancies Act 2004 (Section 202) Regulations 2004 (SI No 649 of 2004) which relate to problems encountered with the application of s 62(1)(g) of this Act. See further s 62(1)(g) of this Act.

SCHEDULE

Protection for Sub-Tenancies Created out of Part 4 Tenancies

1. In this Schedule—

"head-landlord" means the landlord under the Part 4 tenancy concerned;

"head-tenant" means the tenant under the Part 4 tenancy concerned;

"sub-tenant" means the person in whose favour the sub-tenancy concerned has been created;

"sub-tenancy" means the sub-tenancy referred to in paragraph 2;

"Part 4 tenancy" includes a further Part 4 tenancy and references to a Part 4 tenancy continuing in being shall be construed as including references to—

(a) if it occurs, the circumstance in which a further Part 4 tenancy comes into being (in respect of the dwelling concerned) after that Part 4 tenancy and continues in being, and

(b) if it occurs, the circumstance in which a further Part 4 tenancy comes into being (in respect of that dwelling) after the further Part 4 tenancy mentioned in subparagraph (a) and continues in being, and

(c) if it occurs, each further circumstance of the kind mentioned in subparagraph (b).

2. (1) If a sub-tenancy is created out of a Part 4 tenancy with the written consent of the landlord then the following protection applies for the benefit of the sub-tenant.

(2) Without prejudice to paragraphs 5 and 6, that protection is that that sub-tenancy shall (if it would not or might not do so otherwise) continue in being for so long as the Part 4 tenancy continues in being unless it is sooner terminated under the provisions of Part 4 as adapted by this Schedule.

3. Paragraph (a) of, and the Table to, section 34 and sections 35 to 39 apply in relation to the sub-tenancy as they apply in relation to a Part 4 tenancy with the following modifications—

(a) for references in them to a Part 4 tenancy or a tenancy there shall be substituted references to the sub-tenancy,

(b) for references in them to the landlord there shall be substituted references to the head-tenant,

(c) for references in them to the tenant there shall be substituted references to the sub-tenant, and

(d) in paragraph (a) of section 34 for "on one or more of the grounds specified in the Table to this section" there shall be substituted "on one or more of the grounds specified in paragraphs 1, 2 and 4 of the Table to this section".

4. (1) For so long as the sub-tenancy continues in being the following obligations of the head-landlord shall be owed to the subtenant, namely the obligations under paragraphs (a) and (b) of section 12(1) and, for the purpose of this paragraph—

(a) the reference in that paragraph (a) to the tenant shall, for so long as the sub-tenancy continues in being, be construed as a reference to the sub-tenant, and

(b) a dispute between the head-landlord and the sub-tenant with respect to compliance by the head-landlord with either or both of those obligations may be referred under Part 6 to the Board for resolution.

(2) For so long as the sub-tenancy continues in being the following obligations of the sub-tenant shall be owed to the head-landlord, namely the obligations under paragraphs (f) and (g) of section 16 and, for the purpose of this paragraph—

(a) references in those paragraphs to the tenancy shall, for so long as the sub-tenancy continues in being, be construed as references to the sub-tenancy,

(b) references in those paragraphs to the landlord shall, for so long as the sub-tenancy continues in being, be construed as references to the head-landlord, and

(c) a dispute between the sub-tenant and the head-landlord with respect to compliance by the sub-tenant with either or both of those obligations may be referred under Part 6 to the Board for resolution.

(3) Save to the extent provided by the foregoing subparagraphs, nothing in this paragraph affects the obligations owed—

(a) by the head-landlord to the head-tenant (or the head-tenant to the head-landlord), or

(b) by the head-tenant to the sub-tenant (or the sub-tenant to the head-tenant),

under the Part 4 tenancy or the sub-tenancy, as appropriate.

5. In addition to the protection provided by paragraph 2, where the head-landlord serves a notice of termination in respect of the Part 4 tenancy out of which the sub-tenancy has been created and does not include in that notice of termination a requirement to terminate the sub-tenancy, then — if the notice of termination is effective to terminate the Part 4 tenancy — on that termination—

(a) the sub-tenant shall become the tenant of that landlord and the sub-tenancy under which he or she held the dwelling concerned shall be deemed to be converted into that Part 4 tenancy (without prejudice to the notice's effect as against the former head-tenant),

(b) the terms of that Part 4 tenancy under which he or she holds the dwelling concerned shall be those on which he or she held it under the sub-tenancy (subject to their not being inconsistent with this Act) unless he or she and that landlord agree to a variation of them,

(c) the period of that Part 4 tenancy's duration shall, subject to Chapter 3 of Part 4, be the same as that which would have been its period of duration if the notice of termination mentioned in this paragraph had not been served.

6. Subparagraphs (a), (b) and (c) of paragraph 5 also apply if the Part 4 tenancy is validly terminated by the head-tenant and, for this purpose, the relevant references in that paragraph which precede those subparagraphs shall be read accordingly.

7. Paragraphs 5 and 6 do not affect the liabilities (if any) of the sub-tenant to the head-tenant (or of the head-tenant to the subtenant) that have arisen by virtue of the sub-tenancy.

8. (1) This paragraph applies where—

(a) the sub-tenant has vacated possession of the dwelling concerned on foot of a notice of termination served under section 34(a) (as adapted by this Schedule),

(b) that notice of termination cited as the reason for the termination the ground specified in paragraph 4 of the Table to section 34 (as so adapted), and

(c) the occupation by the person concerned mentioned in that paragraph does not take place within a reasonable time after the service of the notice or, in circumstances where such a requirement arises, the head-tenant does not comply with the requirement to make the offer referred to in that paragraph.

(2) Where this paragraph applies, the sub-tenant may make a complaint to the Board under Part 6 that, by reason of the matters mentioned in subparagraph (1), he or she has been unjustly deprived of possession of the dwelling concerned by the head-tenant.

(3) An adjudicator or the Tribunal, on the hearing of such a complaint, may make a determination, if the adjudicator or the Tribunal considers it proper to do so, that the head-tenant shall pay to the complainant an amount by way of damages for that deprivation of possession.

(4) For the avoidance of doubt—

(a) this paragraph applies even though the sub-tenant vacated possession of the dwelling only after a dispute in relation to the validity of the notice of termination was finally determined under Part 6 (but in such a case subparagraph (1) has effect as if the clause set out in the Table to this paragraph were substituted for clause (c) of that subparagraph), and

(b) this paragraph is without prejudice to the sub-tenant's right to put in issue, in a dispute in relation to the validity of the notice of termination referred to the Board under Part 6, the bona fides of the intention of the head-tenant to do or, as appropriate, permit to be done the thing mentioned in the notice.

TABLE

(c) the occupation by the person concerned mentioned in that paragraph does not take place within a reasonable time after the dispute in relation to the validity of the notice is finally determined under Part 6 or, in circumstances where such a requirement arises, the head-tenant does not comply with the requirement to make the offer referred to in that paragraph.

Chapter 19

LANDLORD AND TENANT (GROUND RENTS) ACT, 2005

(2005 No. 7)

ARRANGEMENT OF SECTIONS

ACTS REFERRED TO

Landlord and Tenant (Ground Rents) Act 1967 1967, No. 3
Landlord and Tenant (Ground Rents) (No. 2) Act 1978 1978, No. 16

AN ACT TO AMEND SECTION 4 OF THE LANDLORD AND TENANT (GROUND RENTS) (NO. 2) ACT 1978 AND TO PROVIDE FOR RELATED MATTERS.

[19TH MAY 2005]

BE IT ENACTED BY THE OIREACHTAS AS FOLLOWS:

Definitions.

1.—In this Act— **[19–01]**

"Act of 1967" means the Landlord and Tenant (Ground Rents) Act 1967;

"Act of 1978" means the Landlord and Tenant (Ground Rents) (No. 2) Act 1978

Amendment of section 4 of Act of 1978.

2.—*Omitted. Substitutes s 4 of the 1978 (No. 2) Act.* **[19–02]**

Saver.

3.—The amendment of section 4 of the Act of 1978 effected by section 2 of this Act shall not apply to— **[19–03]**

(a) an application to the Registrar of Titles under Part III of the Act of 1978 made before the passing of this Act,

(b) a notice of intention to acquire a fee simple under section 4 of the Act of 1967 served before the passing of this Act,

(c) an application to a county registrar under section 17 of the Act of 1967, or an arbitration under that Act, relating to a notice to which paragraph (b) of this section applies,

(d) an arbitration under the said Part III relating to an application to which paragraph (a) of this section applies,

(e) an appeal to the Circuit Court from a decision of a county registrar under the Act of 1967 relating to a notice to which paragraph (b) of this section applies, or

(f) an appeal to the Circuit Court from a decision of the Registrar of Titles under the said Part III relating to an application to which paragraph (a) of this section applies.

Short title and collective citation.

[19–04] 4.—(1) This Act may be cited as the Landlord and Tenant (Ground Rents) Act 2005.

(2) The Landlord and Tenant Acts 1967 to 1994 and this Act may be cited together as the Landlord and Tenant Acts 1967 to 2005.

Note: As this Act has no commencement provision it commences as and from the end of the day before the date of its passing. The Act was passed on 19th May 2005 — see s 8(3) of the Interpretation Act 1937.

INDEX